THE RESEARCH AND REPORT HANDBOOK

For Business,
Industry,
and Government

Student Edition

Ruth Moyer
Eleanour Stevens
Ralph Switzer

JOHN WILEY & SONS, INC.
New York   Chichester   Brisbane   Toronto

In appreciation for their patience and understanding, we dedicate this book to Goldie, Lois, Sam, and Julie.

Editorial and Production Services by Cobb/Dunlop Publisher Services, Inc.

Copyright © 1981, by John Wiley & Sons, Inc.

Library of Congress Cataloging in Publication Data

Moyer, Ruth, 1924-
   The research and report handbook.

   Bibliography: p.
   Includes index.
   1. Business report writing. I. Stevens, Eleanour V., joint author. II. Switzer, Ralph, joint author.
III. Title.
HF5719.M69   808'.066651021   80-18922
ISBN 0-471-04257-9
ISBN 0-471-04258-7 (pbk.)

Printed in the United States of America

10 9 8 7 6 5 4 3 2

Preface

The Research and Report Handbook has been specifically designed to meet the needs of students, managers, administrators, and others who perform research and write reports on topics pertinent to any area of business. The content, organization, and illustrations make this book a useful reference for business applications or a valuable supplement to a textbook in any business course where reports are prepared.

This book contains seven parts:

Part I—Business Reports Explains the purpose, characteristics, writer's function, organization, and format of long reports and short reports (letter and memorandum reports). Illustrates complete short reports and preliminary, body, and supplementary pages in long reports.

Part II—Special Reporting Situations Discusses and illustrates five reporting situations: legal brief, minutes, policy statements, procedures, and proposals.

Part III—Preparing the Report Explains these tasks: defining the problem, outlining the information, performing the research, preparing graphic aids, and presenting the final report.

Part IV—Documentation Gives general and legal requirements for documentation. Contains illustrations of various types of reference notes; shows examples of first and second notes and bibliographical entries for books, periodicals, and miscellaneous sources of business information.

Part V—Selected Government References Provides descriptions, illustrations, and reference notes for various sources published by all levels of government as well as the United Nations.

Part VI—Selected Sources of Business Information Provides a comprehensive annotated listing of 17 indexes to books, periodicals, and articles; 6 directories; 8 dictionaries; 58 services and newsletters; 24 handbooks; 74 general references for publications in business, industry, and government; 20 compiled sources of legal information and 19 of tax information. Also includes an explanation and list of computerized sources of information in business and economics.

Part VII—Style Guide Gives rules and examples of abbreviated forms, capitalization, number usage, and punctuation, based on student needs as indicated by a survey of human relations, tax research, labor relations, and report writing classes.

Following Part VII is a list of sources consulted during the development of this book.

We sincerely thank these persons for their contribution to this handbook: Ms. Elizabeth Young who attended our organizational meetings and typed and edited the manuscript and Mrs. Floye Johnson, Management Department secretary, who typed our correspondence and reproduced numerous copies of the manuscript.

Dr. Ruth Moyer
Dr. Eleanour Stevens
Dr. Ralph Switzer

Acknowledgments

We thank the following individuals for their helpful reviews:

Professor J. Douglas Andrews
University of Southern California

Dr. William Anthony
College of Business
Florida State University

Ms. Martha Ashmon
Graduate School of Business
Stanford University

Mr. M. Balachandran
University of Illinois

Professor Marian C. Crawford
University of Arkansas at Little Rock

Ms. Ellen Castellan Dotterer
Business Librarian
Rohm and Haas Company

Ms. Lynn Freedman
American Can Company

Dr. James Harper
San Jose State University

Dr. Martha Lightwood
Lippincott Library of the Wharton School
University of Pennsylvania

Mr. C. J. Martindale, Jr.
California State University
Golden Gate University, San Francisco

Dr. Bette Ann Stead
University of Houston

Dr. Eleanor H. Tedesco
Plymouth State College

Professor James Watt
Texas Tech University

Dr. Patricia Wells
School of Business
Oregon State University

Professor Charlotte Williams
Florida State University

ACKNOWLEDGMENTS

Contents

PART ONE

Business Reports

Reports contain factual information about an organization's activities and operations. They are written in business, industry, government agencies at all levels, educational institutions, and in many other types of organizations.

CHAPTER ONE

Introduction to Business Reports

The purpose and characteristics of long reports, letter reports, and memorandum reports determine the writer's function. In addition to describing these features, Part One gives examples of reporting situations, explains the organization of various reports, and shows the suggested format for each report.

1.1 PURPOSE

The purposes of a long report and a letter or memorandum report are (1) to transmit factual information to the person(s) who need(s) it, (2) to provide a basis for decision making, and (3) to serve as a record.

1.2 CHARACTERISTICS

Some characteristics of business reports are relative and open to interpretation, and others may overlap. The difficulty in classifying these diverse characteristics is explained in the following paragraphs.

LENGTH

"Long" and "short" are relative terms. Some writers consider a report long when it contains preliminary pages (for example, title page, table of contents, and summary) and supplementary pages (reference pages and appendix). Such writers would consider a report short if the preliminary pages and supplementary pages were omitted (as in most memorandum and letter reports). On the other hand, some writers may consider a 10-page report that includes some preliminary pages a long report, and others may consider it a short report.

FORMALITY

Some writers consider a report formal when it is written without the use of first and second person pronouns ("I" and "you") and informal if these pronouns are used. Other writers may not make this distinction.

Another element in determining the formality of a report is the degree to which it is "dressed up." In other words, the more preliminary and supplementary pages a report has, the more "formal" it may be considered.

TIME

A report may be prepared on a periodic basis (weekly sales report), on a one-time basis (feasibility study), or when needed (information report).

ORIGIN AND READERSHIP

A report may be prepared by a person at some level of middle management, at the supervisory level, or at the top management level. Many reports are directed upward in the organization; some are directed to subordinates; and still others may be directed to a person on the same organizational level.

Two or more persons may prepare parts of a report (annual report) that are coordinated by still another person. Some reports are assigned, some are originated, and some are inherent in an employee's job.

A report may be read only by the person who assigned it, or the report (or a summary) may be routed to others who have an interest in the topic. Most reports are directed to one person within the organization, but some are directed to one or more outside readers, such as stockholders.

A business report may cover a complex topic that requires considerable primary and/or secondary research with comparable in-depth analysis and many graphic aids. On the other hand, a report may be written on daily operations and require little or no research and analysis. On some occasions a comprehensive report may be prepared, but only a memorandum or a summary is presented to others. The complete report then substantiates the memorandum and becomes a record of the complete activity.

Obviously, classifying reports by characteristics can only be done arbitrarily. In this chapter, reports are presented according to length and defined as follows: (1) long reports—those having preliminary and supplementary pages and (2) memorandum and letter reports—those not having preliminary and supplementary pages.

1.3 WRITER'S FUNCTION

The writer must consider the purpose for which a report is written; the topic being presented; and the requirements, needs, and organizational level (or location) of the reader(s). In all circumstances, the writer must prepare a clear, concise report that is correct in content and mechanics and tells the reader what he or she needs to know.

Each type of report problem may require a slightly different approach because of variations in the topics covered. The following steps, however, are commonly accepted as the appropriate procedure for solving most problems upon which long and short reports are based:

1. Define the problem.
2. Gather the facts.
3. Organize the facts.
4. Analyze and interpret the facts.
5. Draw conclusions and determine recommendations, if requested.
6. Write the report.

1.4 EXAMPLES OF REPORTING SITUATIONS

Reporting situations are as diverse as the organizations that prepare reports. Chapters Two and Three give examples of topics that represent problems typical of those treated in long and short reports.

1.5 ORGANIZATION

A report should be organized in a manner compatible with the topic and acceptable to the reader. The order (or omission) of certain preliminary pages and the omission (or inclusion) of certain content parts may depend upon (1) organizational policy, (2) the reader's desire, or (3) the writer's decision. The longer a report, the more important it is that headings and subheadings are used to name and divide the topics and subtopics, providing a roadmap for the reader. A well-organized report follows a logical train of thought from the beginning to the end.

1.6 FORMAT

The format of a report determines its appearance and often its acceptability. Format includes the location of margins, page numbers, and headings, as well as the amount and consistency of vertical and horizontal spacing. The report format may be established by an organization's style manual, by the reader, by the writer, or by a published manual. No two style manuals are likely to show exactly the same format; therefore, the writer should follow one style manual consistently.

CHAPTER TWO

Long Reports

Reports with preliminary and supplementary pages are classified here as long reports. Any type of report may include such pages; typical examples are comprehensive analytical, examination, and information reports, and feasibility studies.

2.1 PURPOSE

The purpose of including preliminary and supplementary pages in a report is (1) to show the writer's approach to the problem, (2) to provide references for support or further research, (3) to substantiate qualitative and quantitative data, and (4) to recognize the formality of the reporting occasion.

Each page added before or after the body should serve to clarify the problem and to facilitate the reading and understanding of the report.

2.2 CHARACTERISTICS

A long report is intended to cover a complex, comprehensive problem and usually requires a considerable amount of secondary and/ or primary research. It often includes numerous graphic aids and references to clarify and identify the data.

A superior usually assigns this type of report to a subordinate (or group of subordinates) who has the professional qualifications, the interest, and the research and writing ability to pursue the project.

The superior's level in the organization, the company's policy, the nature of the problem, and the writer's understanding of the problem influence the characteristics of the report. These factors help to determine the needed preliminary and supplementary pages, the degree of formality, the readership, and the complexity.

2.3 WRITER'S FUNCTION

The writer's function depends upon the nature of the problem that is the basis for the report.

In an analytical report or a feasibility study, the writer presents, analyzes, and interprets the facts and draws conclusions. If requested, the writer makes a recommendation. In an examination report, the writer presents, analyzes, and interprets the facts; the reader draws conclusions on the basis of these facts. In an information report, the writer merely presents the facts. This report expands a reader's knowledge and may become the basis for a decision or for further research.

The writer must define the problem and establish a schedule to complete the report.

The problem is defined and the problem statement is prepared after (1) thoughtful consideration of the written or oral authorization, (2) preliminary research on the topic, and (3) discussion with the person(s) who assigned the report.

When the problem has been defined, the writer should be able to (1) understand the background of the problem, (2) determine valid, logical assumptions, (3) define the scope of the problem, (4) select the appropriate research methods, and (5) realize the limitations (time, money, and other resources) that may affect the quality of the report.

After the problem is defined and the problem statement is written and, if necessary, approved, the writer needs to schedule each phase of the problem-solving effort. The amount of time devoted to gathering, organizing, analyzing, and interpreting the data and writing the report depends upon the writer's familiarity with the topic and skill in carrying out each phase. In addition, the writer must work within any time constraints that may have been set by the person who assigned the report.

2.4 REPORTING SITUATIONS

The report topic is expressed in a written statement which represents the scope of the problem and establishes the purpose for which the report is being written. Also, the nature of the statement may guide the writer in selecting research methods and organizing the report. This statement may be expressed in the form of a declarative sentence, a question, or an infinitive phrase.

ANALYTICAL REPORT

An analytical report is often based on a problem that requires making a comparison of alternatives and evaluating criteria to determine the better (or best) alternative.

> The top management of a manufacturing company wants to select a site for an assembly plant. The report writer might prepare this statement:
>
> The purpose of this report is to compare Seoul, Korea; Taipei, Taiwan; and Mexico City, Mexico, to determine which is the best location for an assembly plant. The solution will be based on labor supply, transportation facilities, legal restrictions, and total costs.
>
> The alternatives (subjects) are the three locations, and the criteria are the bases upon which each alternative is evaluated to arrive at a decision.

FEASIBILITY STUDY

In reality, the feasibility study is an analytical report. However, instead of comparing two or more alternatives, the writer determines the feasibility or practicality of (1) retaining the present system or initiating a proposed system, (2) initiating one of two proposed systems, or (3) selecting one type of system over another. Although the study is often considered an inherent part of system analysis, it can be used for any situation in which the writer must determine the feasibility of adopting one system, operation, usage, and so on, over another.

> A plant manager may request a study of inventory procedures; the writer might prepare this statement:
>
> The purpose of this study is to determine the feasibility of computerizing the raw materials inventory.

EXAMINATION REPORT

In this type of report, the data is presented, analyzed, and interpreted to the degree requested by the person who assigned the report. The examination may take the form of qualitative or quantitative analysis, or both.

A financial vice president may need information about a company before making a decision regarding a merger; the report writer might prepare this statement:

To examine the financial condition of World-Wide Heavy Equipment Company and evaluate its potential in a merger.

Some problems are examined by the use of hypotheses, statements that are suppositions of the reason for the problem. The writer establishes a hypothesis, gathers relevant data, tests its validity empirically and/or statistically, and accepts or rejects it.

The vice president of administration may need to solve this problem: Why have the costs of preparing internal communications increased?

Hypotheses:

1. The equipment used to process these communications is inefficient.

2. Employees who process these communications are inadequately trained.

3. Originators are unable or unwilling to use the technology available to them.

INFORMATION REPORT

For this report, the writer presents the factual information obtained through research.

The marketing manager of a pipe manufacturing company may want to know about pipelines as a channel of distribution; the writer might prepare this statement:

How is the underground pipeline used as a channel of distribution for various products?

2.5 ORGANIZATION

A complete formal report may contain all the parts listed below. However, those parts designated by an asterisk are rarely used.

Preliminary Pages

*Title fly

Title page

*Letter (or memo) of authorization

*Letter (or memo) of acceptance

Letter (or memo) of transmittal

Table of contents

Table of illustrations

*Preface

*Acknowledgments

Synopsis

Body

Introduction
Text
Conclusions
Recommendations

Supplementary Pages

Appendix
Bibliography

PRELIMINARY PAGES

Preliminary pages are those between the cover and the first page of the report body.

1. Title Fly (Fig. 2.1, p. 12). This page contains only the title of the report. The reader may wish to use this page for comments to the writer.

The title of a long report is descriptive, but brief. It is as complete as necessary considering the content of the report and the background of the reader. Some titles show the decision the writer has reached after completing the research:

> "Why Seoul, Korea, Should Be Selected as a Site for the New Assembly Plant"

Others (again considering the content and readership) show a condensed problem statement as the title:

> "Evaluation of Seoul, Korea; Taipei, Taiwan; and Mexico City, Mexico, as Sites for an Assembly Plant"

2. Title Page (Fig. 2.2, p. 13). The title page contains five parts: (1) title, (2) identification of recipient, (3) identification of writer, (4) location where report was prepared, and (5) date of submission.

The title contains the same words in the same order as shown on the title fly (if used).

Parts (2) and (3) show names, titles, and departments (or organizational units). The words "Prepared for" and "Prepared by" may be replaced by synonyms of the writer's choice.

Most reports show the writer's location (city and state). Any further identification of the location that clarifies the relationship between the reader and writer should be added.

WHY SEOUL, KOREA, SHOULD BE SELECTED AS

THE SITE FOR THE NEW ASSEMBLY PLANT

33

1½"   1"

Suggested Format:

1. Center the title vertically on the upper half of the page.
2. Type the title in capital letters (with or without underscores)
    and center it between the margins.
3. If the title requires two or more lines, arrange the lines in
    reverse pyramid form and center each line.
4. Double-space between the lines in the title.

(vertical spaces) → 66

FIGURE 2.1

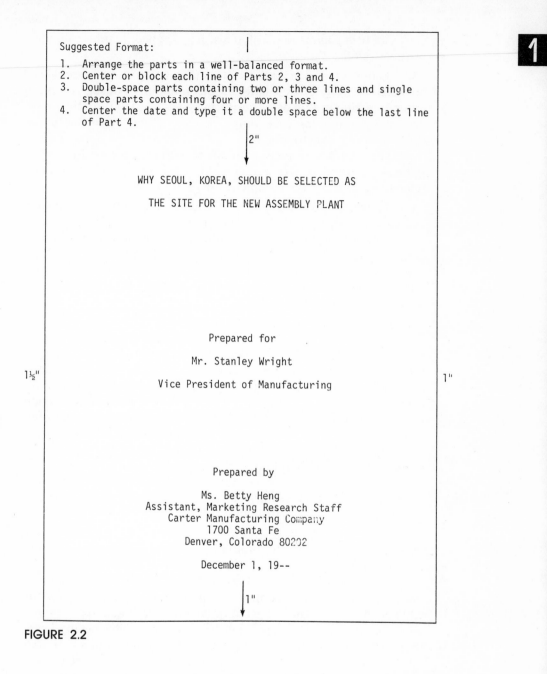

Suggested Format:

1. Arrange the parts in a well-balanced format.
2. Center or block each line of Parts 2, 3 and 4.
3. Double-space parts containing two or three lines and single space parts containing four or more lines.
4. Center the date and type it a double space below the last line of Part 4.

2"

WHY SEOUL, KOREA, SHOULD BE SELECTED AS

THE SITE FOR THE NEW ASSEMBLY PLANT

Prepared for

Mr. Stanley Wright

Vice President of Manufacturing

1½" 1"

Prepared by

Ms. Betty Heng
Assistant, Marketing Research Staff
Carter Manufacturing Company
1700 Santa Fe
Denver, Colorado 80202

December 1, 19--

1"

FIGURE 2.2

The title page is one of the last pages typed. It shows the date of submission.

3. *Letter (Memo) of Authorization (Fig. 2.3, p. 15). A report may be assigned orally or by a letter or memorandum request. A written letter or memorandum of authorization gives the details of the report project, including the background, scope, methods of research, and time or money constraints.

When a letter or memorandum of authorization is directed to the report writer, it is included in the final report and serves as a reference regarding the completeness of the report.

4. *Letter of Acceptance (Fig. 2.4, p. 16). A written response is not usually expected if the project is authorized orally. However, this communication may be a requirement of the organization to show that a contractual agreement exists, particularly when an outside consultant accepts a project. If a letter of authorization is directed to the writer, then the writer responds with a letter, as opposed to a memorandum.

5. Letter (or Memorandum) of Transmittal (Fig. 2.5, p. 17). The first paragraph of the letter (or memorandum) of transmittal transmits the report. The next paragraph(s) may tell the recommendations, give highlights of the findings, or include a brief synopsis of the findings (particularly if a synopsis is not among the preliminary pages). In the last paragraph, the writer may express appreciation for the opportunity to have undertaken the project and may offer further assistance, if necessary and appropriate. If a foreword or an acknowledgments page is not used in the report, the writer may include the information that would normally be on those pages.

Some readers prefer to read the letter of transmittal first. Under these circumstances, it may be attached in front of the cover or preceding the first page (title fly or title page).

6. Table of Contents (Fig. 2.6, pp. 19–20). This page shows the headings that identify the preliminary pages, report sections, and supplementary pages.

The report section headings are derived from the writing outline and condensed to conform to an acceptable structure for the table of contents. Major division (roman numeral) headings are parallel. To provide for parallel construction, the writer begins headings with the same part of speech: adjective, noun, and so on. Parallel headings are also shown in the same type of construction: sentence, phrase, or caption (meaningful thoughts representing the topic).

Usually a table of contents shows no heading after those iden-

AUTOMOTIVE PARTS SUPPLY, INC.
1211 Wabash Avenue
Chicago, Illinois 60652

January 20, 19--

Ms. Arlene Gray, Manager
Resources Information Management Department
Automotive Parts Supply, Inc.
1800 Michigan Avenue
Chicago, Illinois 60784

Dear Ms. Gray:

In a recent survey, we found that 480 of our 600 dealers nationwide
are dissatisfied with the physical construction and revision methods
of the parts catalog. You are authorized to investigate the feasibility of placing the information in the parts catalog on microfilm.

I will send you the dealer surveys and comments. Please consider
them in your overall investigation. I would like to supply the
dealers with the same information that is currently in the parts
1½"   catalog, but in an easy-to-use form. Price changes on some items   1"
are issued weekly, and on other items, they are issued whenever
necessary. The nomenclature on some parts is lengthy, and on some,
it consists of only a word or two. These are just a few of the
problems you will encounter in devising an appropriate microfilm
system.

In addition, please determine the feasibility of in-house filming and
processing as opposed to using a service bureau for these jobs.

After a thorough analysis of the present system, you may want to
consult vendors, inspect various types of equipment, contact other
companies with similar problems, and even use some equipment on a
trial basis. The allowance for the proposed system is $80,000 for the
first year of operation.

The target date for the submission of your report on this project is
May 20, 19--. Please inform me within ten days whether you can fit
this project into your schedule.

Sincerely,

John Bellamy
Administrative Vice President

FIGURE 2.3

AUTOMOTIVE PARTS SUPPLY, INC.
1800 Michigan Avenue
Chicago, Illinois 60784

January 25, 19--

Mr. John Bellamy
Administrative Vice President
Automotive Parts Supply, Inc.
1211 Wabash Avenue
Chicago, Illinois 60652

Dear Mr. Bellamy:

1½" I shall be pleased to undertake the feasibility study to determine   1"
if the parts catalog can be placed on microfilm and whether in-house
or service bureau filming and processing is appropriate.

At present, Barry Gore, senior systems analyst, is reviewing sources
in the technical library and in professional journals to obtain
background information for us. My first step will be to analyze the
procedures, costs, and efficiency of the current system.

I expect to have a work schedule set up by February 5. May I
discuss it with you at that time?

Sincerely,

Arlene Gray, Manager
Resources Information Management Department

AG/bh

FIGURE 2.4

SECURITY INSURANCE COMPANY
801 Brake Street
Sacramento, California 95666

TO: A. J. Sherman, Vice President of Finance

FROM: Doris Kashe, Financial Analyst

SUBJECT: Financial Report on Common Stock of Solaradd and
           Sunray Corporations

DATE: March 10, 19--

Here is the report you requested on February 10, evaluating the
common stock of Solaradd and Sunray Corporations.

The evaluation shows the common stock of Sunray Corporation would
be a more conservative long-term investment because the company
has a better growth potential, provides a better opportunity for
long-term gain, and has a better future outlook. Mention of this
purchase in the next annual report would represent the conservative attitude of Security Insurance Company's management and
impress the stockholders favorably.

I appreciate the opportunity to make this evaluation. If you need
additional data or more comprehensive analyses on these stocks, I
would be glad to provide them.

DK/ts

1½"   1"

FIGURE 2.5

tified with a capital letter. Each heading must contain the same words in the same order as used in the report body.

7. List of Tables (Fig. 2.7, p. 21). The title of this page should reflect the nature of the items listed below it: List of Illustrations, List of Tables and Charts, List of Figures, and so on.

The listing may begin on the table of contents page or the next page. When two or more kinds of graphic aids are used, each is shown by a subheading.

8. Foreword (or Preface) (Fig. 2.8, p. 22). This page may contain (1) the writer's philosophy underlying the presentation of the topic, (2) the topic's contribution to knowledge in a discipline or specific area, and (3) a brief comment as to how the report content can be used to benefit the reader(s).

If an acknowledgments page is not included in the report, the writer may acknowledge assistance in the foreword (or in the letter or memorandum of transmittal).

This page may appear after the table of contents, the title page, or elsewhere among the preliminary pages.

9. Acknowledgments (Fig. 2.9, p. 23). This page may be included to acknowledge (give credit to) the persons or groups who assisted the writer in various ways: giving advice; providing materials; permitting the use of records, premises, or staff; and typing or editing the report.

Even though this page is included, the writer also credits specific contributions by using appropriate documentation methods in the report itself.

If this page is not included, the letter of transmittal may contain comments regarding the contributions.

10. Synopsis (Fig. 2.10, pp. 25–26). The synopsis (also called summary, abstract, or epitome) is an organized condensation of the entire report, prepared after the report has been written. Most writers recommend that the synopsis be no longer than one or two pages, or in a 10:1 ratio with the report.

The first paragraph may contain the purpose of the report, conclusions and recommendations, and the names of the writer and the person for whom the report was prepared. If the recommendations are negative or would be unpleasant to the reader, they may be more easily accepted when placed at the end of the synopsis, after all the supporting facts have been presented to the reader.

Each paragraph gives a summary of the findings from a major division of the report, in the same order shown in the report.

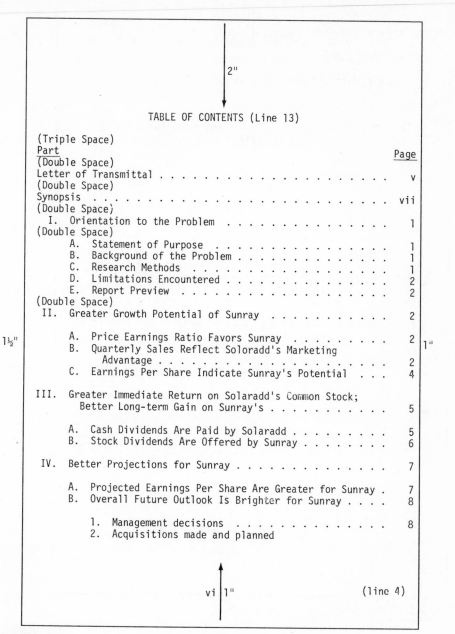

2"

TABLE OF CONTENTS (Line 13)

(Triple Space)
Part   Page
(Double Space)
Letter of Transmittal   v
(Double Space)
Synopsis vii
(Double Space)
  I. Orientation to the Problem   1
(Double Space)
       A. Statement of Purpose   1
       B. Background of the Problem   1
       C. Research Methods   1
       D. Limitations Encountered   2
       E. Report Preview   2
(Double Space)
 II. Greater Growth Potential of Sunray   2

       A. Price Earnings Ratio Favors Sunray   2
       B. Quarterly Sales Reflect Soloradd's Marketing
           Advantage   2
       C. Earnings Per Share Indicate Sunray's Potential . . .   4

III. Greater Immediate Return on Solaradd's Common Stock;
      Better Long-term Gain on Sunray's   5

       A. Cash Dividends Are Paid by Solaradd   5
       B. Stock Dividends Are Offered by Sunray   6

 IV. Better Projections for Sunray   7

       A. Projected Earnings Per Share Are Greater for Sunray .   7
       B. Overall Future Outlook Is Brighter for Sunray   8

          1. Management decisions   8
          2. Acquisitions made and planned

vi 1"   (line 4)

FIGURE 2.6

1"

NOTE:

1. In main and first subdivisions, capitalize the first letter of each word except short prepositions (three or fewer letters), conjunctions, and articles (<u>a</u>, <u>an</u>, and <u>the</u>).

1½"   2. The last line of type should be no lower than line 7 from the   1"
    bottom of the page.
3. Start the second page of the Table of Contents one inch from the top of the paper (line 7).
4. Carry over only a full division (with its subdivisions).

vii

FIGURE 2.6 (Continued)

↓

2" margin

LIST OF TABLES AND CHARTS (Line 13)

(Triple Space)
Table   Page
(Double Space)
   I.   Quarterly Sales (in Millions) of Solaradd and Sunray . . .   3
(Double Space)
  II.   Earnings Per Share for Solaradd and Sunray   5

 III.   Value of Cash and Stock Dividends   6

(Triple Space)
Chart

  1.   Comparative Monthly Earnings Per Share for a Three-year
       Period   7

  2.   Estimated Increase in Spending for Energy Facilities
       through 1985   8

1½"   1"

NOTE:

    Use the same format for headings, capitalization, margins, and
    spacing as on the table of contents page.

viii

FIGURE 2.7

1

2"

FOREWORD
(Triple Space)

Because Swedish Modern Interiors, Inc., has no retail outlets in the medium-size cities of Region VI, this report will supplement previous analyses in that location. With this information available, management will be able to capitalize on it immediately when expansion in Region VI is deemed appropriate.

Government statistics and independent research reports indicate a continuing growth rate and stable employment picture through the late 1980s. Analysts will be able to update these forecasts on short notice and with minimum effort.

1½"   1"

The Production and Financial Planning Departments, as well as the Marketing Department, will benefit by an awareness of the predicted trends, and the Executive Committee can select the optimal point for expansion.

NOTE:

If the lines are single-spaced, a double space is used after the title and between each paragraph.

ix

FIGURE 2.8

2"

ACKNOWLEDGMENTS
(Triple Space)

The completeness of this report was made possible by the courte-
sies extended by many persons and organizations.

Unpublished reports containing recent financial data were
obtained from these marketing directors: Sally Pierce, Desert State
Bank of Albuquerque; John Alder, Broadmoor State Bank, Colorado
Springs; and Jamie Rekuma, First National Bank of Phoenix. These
reports provided the basis for analyzing current sales, per capita
income, demand deposits, installment loans, and construction starts.

1½"   Alan Gore, Swedish Modern's head technical librarian, used the
services of two area universities to make a computerized product/   1"
competitor search. Having this data in hand saved many, many hours
of intensive library research.

The final draft, as well as three preceding drafts of this
report, was prepared in the Word Processing Center under the direction
of Myron Taylor, center supervisor. I am grateful for his patience
and appreciate the time spent by Center personnel to edit and process
this report.

NOTE:

If the lines are single-spaced, a double space is used after the
title and between each paragraph.

x

FIGURE 2.9

The body consists of the introduction, text, conclusions, and recommendations.

1. Introduction (Fig. 2.11, p. 27). The first major division (called Introduction, Orientation to the Problem, or some other title that represents the content) functions to bring the reader to the writer's level of understanding. It may also assist in conducting a follow-up study. The subdivision titles depend upon the content the writer believes is necessary for the reader to know. The subdivisions listed here are often included in the introduction.

a. Statement of Purpose (Fig. 2.11, p. 27). The purpose or objective tells why the report is needed. It should require no more than two sentences. However, if no specific section is devoted to the background, additional sentences may be included to explain the problem and its importance to the organization.

b. Background of the Problem (Fig. 2.11, p. 27). This subdivision includes a history of the problem, the current situation, and the reasons for the problem (if known). Problems are created (e.g., expansion) or develop (e.g., decreasing sales). The problem is described as it is perceived at a specific time. This subdivision serves as a reminder to the reader or as further explanation of the problem.

Any assumptions the writer makes may be included here or in a separate subdivision. These assumptions are ideas that the writer had in mind when preparing the report and which the reader needs to know to evaluate the report.

An especially long background section may be presented as the next major division or may be included in the appendix. This arrangement helps to keep the introduction brief.

c. Research Methods (Fig. 2.11, p. 28). This subdivision includes a brief explanation of the primary and secondary research methods and sources. With this information, the reader can evaluate the completeness and validity of the findings.

Typical examples of the information included in this section are:

1. Number and type of people interviewed.

2. Number of questionnaires sent, number and percentage returned, and categories of respondents.

3. Nature of research: experiments, observation, type of statistical computations, for example.

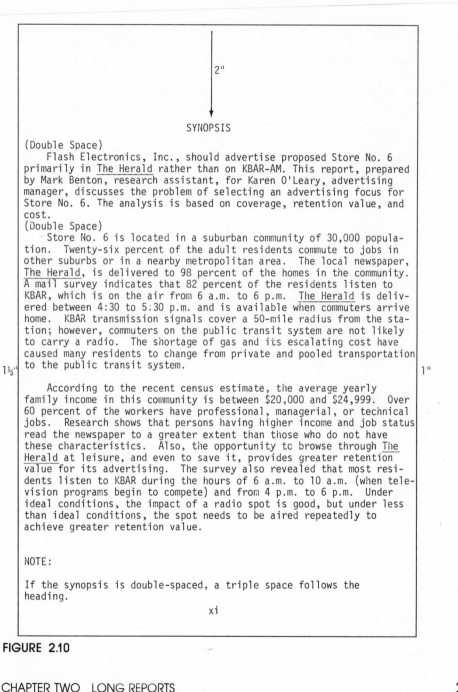

2"

SYNOPSIS

(Double Space)

Flash Electronics, Inc., should advertise proposed Store No. 6 primarily in The Herald rather than on KBAR-AM. This report, prepared by Mark Benton, research assistant, for Karen O'Leary, advertising manager, discusses the problem of selecting an advertising focus for Store No. 6. The analysis is based on coverage, retention value, and cost.

(Double Space)

Store No. 6 is located in a suburban community of 30,000 population. Twenty-six percent of the adult residents commute to jobs in other suburbs or in a nearby metropolitan area. The local newspaper, The Herald, is delivered to 98 percent of the homes in the community. A mail survey indicates that 82 percent of the residents listen to KBAR, which is on the air from 6 a.m. to 6 p.m. The Herald is delivered between 4:30 to 5:30 p.m. and is available when commuters arrive home. KBAR transmission signals cover a 50-mile radius from the station; however, commuters on the public transit system are not likely to carry a radio. The shortage of gas and its escalating cost have caused many residents to change from private and pooled transportation to the public transit system.

According to the recent census estimate, the average yearly family income in this community is between $20,000 and $24,999. Over 60 percent of the workers have professional, managerial, or technical jobs. Research shows that persons having higher income and job status read the newspaper to a greater extent than those who do not have these characteristics. Also, the opportunity to browse through The Herald at leisure, and even to save it, provides greater retention value for its advertising. The survey also revealed that most residents listen to KBAR during the hours of 6 a.m. to 10 a.m. (when television programs begin to compete) and from 4 p.m. to 6 p.m. Under ideal conditions, the impact of a radio spot is good, but under less than ideal conditions, the spot needs to be aired repeatedly to achieve greater retention value.

NOTE:

If the synopsis is double-spaced, a triple space follows the heading.

xi

1½"   1"

FIGURE 2.10

Based on rate sheets from The Herald and KBAR, a comparable advertising plan for the opening, sales, and continuing operations is 15 percent less with the former. In addition, greater coverage and retention value can be gained from Herald advertising. An advertising mix with 70 percent of the budget devoted to Herald and 30 percent to KBAR advertising will meet the needs of Store No. C.

1½"   1"

Note: The second page begins on line 7 from the top of the page.

xii   (line 4)

FIGURE 2.10   (Continued)

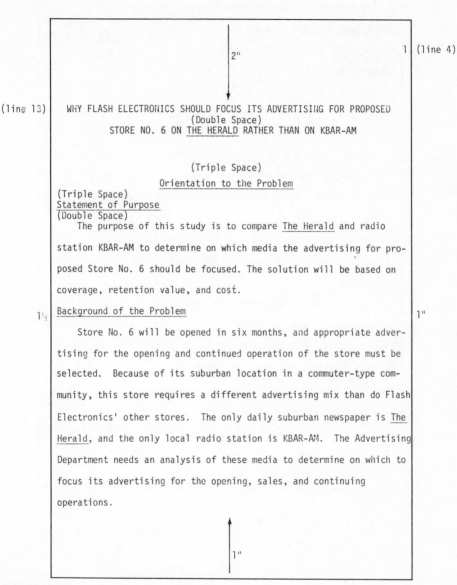

(line 4)   1

(line 13)   WHY FLASH ELECTRONICS SHOULD FOCUS ITS ADVERTISING FOR PROPOSED
(Double Space)
STORE NO. 6 ON THE HERALD RATHER THAN ON KBAR-AM

(Triple Space)
Orientation to the Problem
(Triple Space)
Statement of Purpose
(Double Space)
The purpose of this study is to compare The Herald and radio
station KBAR-AM to determine on which media the advertising for pro-
posed Store No. 6 should be focused. The solution will be based on
coverage, retention value, and cost.

Background of the Problem

Store No. 6 will be opened in six months, and appropriate advertising for the opening and continued operation of the store must be
selected. Because of its suburban location in a commuter-type community, this store requires a different advertising mix than do Flash
Electronics' other stores. The only daily suburban newspaper is The
Herald, and the only local radio station is KBAR-AM. The Advertising
Department needs an analysis of these media to determine on which to
focus its advertising for the opening, sales, and continuing
operations.

2"

1½   1"

1"

FIGURE 2.11

(line 7)   One can assume that the demographics of the community will

remain very much the same and that the study will remain valid in

the foreseeable future.
(Double Space)
Research Methods

Data on retention value and coverage were obtained from

Standard Rate and Data Services, Ayer Directory of Publications, and

similar sources. In addition to the demographic data from the 1970

census and later state census estimates, a recent study by the local

First National Bank was used. To determine listening and reading

habits, a random sample of the residents was obtained by mail

questionnaire.

Costs for radio and newspaper advertising were computed by using

the most recent advertising rate schedules from The Herald and KBAR.
(Double Space)
Limitations

Figures from the 1970 census and those from the state's 1976

estimated census are the only official ones available. However, the

First National Bank's recent community profile analysis and the mail

survey supplemented the official census reports.
(Double Space)
Report Preview

The criteria are presented in this order: coverage, retention

value, and cost. The cost factor is discussed last because the value

received from the expenditure is dependent upon the coverage and

retention value of the media.

NOTE:

The text may begin a triple space below the last line of the
Introduction or on the next page. When the text begins on a new page,
the page number may be centered at the bottom of the page (see Page
Numbers, page 34).

FIGURE 2.11 (Continued)

4. Identification and explanation of canned, constructed, or adjusted computer programs.

5. Categories and location of secondary research.

The reader might have reason to believe that the purpose and background of the problem require greater (or different) coverage than the writer plans. To clarify the coverage, the writer can define the scope (depth and breadth) more specifically in this subdivision or in a separate one.

d. Limitations (Fig. 2.11, p. 28). This subdivision is included only when the writer needs to explain circumstances (e.g., lack of funds, data, or time) that cause the report to be of lesser quality than the reader has a right to expect. Failure to provide good reasons gives the impression that a less-than-adequate report is due to poor planning.

e. Report Preview (Fig. 2.11, p. 28). The reader needs a roadmap to the report text. This subdivision gives the order in which the topics will be discussed. In addition, the writer may present a reason for the chosen order.

2. Text (Fig. 2.12, p. 30). The report text contains an explanation of the findings for each major division. In an especially long report, the writer may elect to show a numerical or alphabetic designation preceding each heading.

Each major division contains (1) a lead-in statement that introduces the topic(s) covered, (2) the text of the topics, (3) a summary of the topics, and (4) transition to the next major division. The summary and transition may be (1) in the same sentence (or paragraph) or (2) in separate sentences (or paragraphs). Because the summary is derived from the preceding paragraphs but is not a part of the findings, it is not attached to the end of the last paragraph explaining the topic.

3. Conclusions (Fig. 2.13, p. 32). The conclusions are developed from the facts presented in the text. The conclusion section is concise, but complete. As each major division contributes to the conclusions, failure to mention the contribution of any major division leads the reader to question the reliability of the report.

The conclusions are often preceded by a lead-in statement. They may be presented in paragraph form, or each conclusion may be itemized or set off by mechanical devices (dashes, tabulation, asterisks, and so on).

4. Recommendations (Fig. 2.13, p. 32). The recommendations are based on the conclusions. If recommendations are shown separate from conclusions, a lead-in statement usually precedes them, or a

3

Report Preview

The criteria are presented in this order: coverage, retention value, and cost. The cost factor is discussed last because the value received from the expenditure is dependent upon the coverage and rentention value of the media.
(Triple Space)

Greater Coverage by <u>The Herald</u>

(Double Space)
The reach and selectivity of radio and newspaper coverage for a specific area are analyzed to determine the extent to which each contributes to the total advertising strategy. (lead-in)

(Following this lead-in are subdivisions giving the findings concerning the coverage of newspaper and radio advertising in the community where the proposed store will be located.)

1½   (Summary) The number of residents who read <u>The Herald</u> exceeds   1"
the number who listen to KBAR. Radio coverage is restricted by transmission hours and penetration distance.

(Transition) The unique characteristics of this commuter-type suburban area have an influence on the <u>retention value</u> as well as the coverage of these media.

NOTE:
Each major division heading in the text (e.g., II and III) may begin a triple space after the last line of the preceding major division (Figure 2.11) or on a separate page. Consistency in the format of headings helps the reader to follow the writer's approach.

FIGURE 2.12

topic sentence sets the stage. When recommendations and conclusions are presented in the same major division, each must be clearly distinguishable.

The research may result in one overall recommendation or more than one recommendation. One or more of the recommendations may be contingent on circumstances developing in the future.

Recommendations may be justified in this section or in another report to management. Justification requires that the writer present the specific advantages that will accrue from following the recommendations.

SUPPLEMENTARY PAGES

The supplementary pages consist of the appendix and a reference section.

1. Appendix (Fig. 2.14, p. 33). The appendix follows the body and precedes the reference section. The appendix contains information that supports the text but is not essential to its understanding, such as:

Tabulated questionnaire

Addresses to which questionnaires were sent

Letters (or copies) sent and received

Graphic aids (charts, tables, maps, photographs) from which data were abstracted for the text or that clarify the text

Formulas and statistical calculations

A long history or background section

Printouts

When more than one appendix is used, each is identified by a letter (A, B, C) or an arabic number (1, 2, 3). Each type of information (e.g., tabulated questionnaire and letters) is placed in a separate appendix. Preceding each appendix is a page identifying it and naming the information it contains.

The first time an item in the appendix is mentioned in the report body, the appendix identification is given in a parenthetical or subordinate construction (see Parentheses, p. 293).

2. Reference Pages. The bibliography is usually the last part of a report. (See Part Four for illustration and explanation.)

NOTE:

As other major divisions, this one may begin 2 inches (line 13)   9
from the top of the page or a triple space below the last line of
the previous major division.

<u>Conclusions and Recommendations</u>

(Double Space)
 This report recommends that Energy Kit Manufacturing Company

(EKMC) should change from the average cost method of valuing its

inventory to the FIFO rather than the LIFO method, based on these

conclusions:

Requirements   . . . Because of its increased business and

           rapid inventory turnover, EKMC is more in

           need of a method which will represent

           the physical flow of goods than one that

           matches the current costs with current

           revenues.

Replacement Costs . . . Under the FIFO method, the cost of goods

           sold and ending inventory figures will

1½"   provide a better estimate of the replace- 1"

           ment costs than under the LIFO method.

Financial Statements . . . The FIFO method will result in a higher

           tax expense than the LIFO method and, as

           a result, will reduce the cash flow.

           However, FIFO will generate a higher net

           income, making the financial statements

           more favorable and thereby attracting

           outside investors.

FIGURE 2.13

11

APPENDIX

NOTE:

An identification page may precede the Appendix. The word is centered
vertically and horizontally. Page numbers of the appendix title page
may be centered on line 3 or 4 from the bottom of the page or typed
on line 3 or 4 from the top of the page (flush with the right margin).

12

APPENDIX A
(Triple Space)
Tabulated Questionnaire

NOTE:

The section and title are centered vertically and horizontally.

FIGURE 2.14

2.6 FORMAT

The appearance and readability of a report are affected by the width of the margins and the location of page numbers, as well as by the internal spacing.

MARGINS

A report may be unbound, bound at the left (or assembled in a cover attached at the left), or bound at the top (or assembled in a cover attached at the top). The following margins are suggested for each situation:

	Unbound	Left Binding	Top Binding
Top Margin	2″	2″	2½″
Preliminary pages with centered headings			
First page			
Text pages with major division headings centered at top			
Bibliography page	2″	2″	2½″
Type heading on line	13	13	16
Left Margin	1″	1½″	1″
Right Margin	1″	1″	1″
Bottom Margin	1″	1″	1″
Last line of type	7	7	7
Top Margin	1″	1″	1½″
Second page of a preliminary part			
Body pages without centered headings			
Start typing on line	7	7	10

PAGE NUMBERS

Page numbers are neither preceded nor followed by symbols. All preliminary pages are counted in the numbering system; but the first numbered page is usually the one containing the table of contents. Small roman numerals identify the preliminary pages. Consecutive arabic numbers identify the body pages and continue through the supplementary pages.

The side on which the report is bound determines the location of the page numbers. The method of numbering unbound reports and those bound at the left is shown below:

Report Part	Page Number
Preliminary pages (roman numerals)	Centered on line 3 or 4 from bottom of page
*Body (pages with headings: first page, pages with centered major division headings)	Centered on line 3 or 4 from bottom of page
Body (pages without centered major division headings)	Line 3 or 4 from top; flush with right-hand margin
*Supplementary pages (bibliography, appendix title pages)	Centered on line 3 or 4 from bottom of page
Supplementary pages (without headings)	Line 3 or 4 from top; flush with right-hand margin

  * An alternative plan is to type the page numbers of the body and all succeeding pages on line 3 or 4 from the top and flush with the right-hand margin.

For top-bound reports, all page numbers may be centered or typed flush with the right margin on line 3 or 4 from the bottom of the page.

SPACING

The body of a long report may be single- or double-spaced; however, a double-spaced report can be read more rapidly. A double space is always used between paragraphs. The first line of each paragraph is indented a minimum of five spaces. The spacing preceding and following headings of various degrees is illustrated under Headings, p. 114).

CHAPTER THREE

Memorandum and Letter Reports

Memorandum and letter reports are classified here as short reports. Normally they do not include supplementary pages; however, they may include one or more, but not all, of the preliminary pages shown in a long report (Chapter Two). Also, any report classified as long (Chapter Two) is considered a short report if it does not include the typical preliminary pages shown in a long report.

3.1 PURPOSE

A letter or memorandum is used to treat a topic of lesser magnitude (depth and scope) than that covered in a long report. The purpose of most short reports is to communicate about the various day-to-day activities and operations of the organization.

3.2 CHARACTERISTICS

Memorandum and letter reports may be requested by a superior, or their preparation may be a regular part of the writer's job. A short report is usually prepared by one person, and it may be read by one person or more (all employees). Also, it may be routed to several employees who have a need to know the information.

A memorandum format is used only for communications directed to a reader(s) within an organization. A letter format, considered more formal, is used for communications directed (1) to a reader outside the organization or (2) to an inside reader if the topic, the reader's level, or the writer's level justify greater formality.

Short reports are usually written in the first person; however, the writer may decide to use the third person, depending on the formality of the reporting situation.

3.3 WRITER'S FUNCTION

The writer's function depends upon the report problem and upon the reason for which the report is being written.

The writer needs to define the problem (mentally, at least) that is the basis of the report. In many instances, the background may be familiar; if not, the writer will need to gather the necessary facts. These facts are then organized (1) to meet the requirements of the reporting situation and (2) to accommodate the reader's interests, needs, and background.

A memorandum or letter report may be entirely in narrative form. In some instances, however, the writer may need to analyze the information quantitatively and even include brief, informal graphic aids to enhance the clarity and readability.

A short report may require conclusions and recommendations. In many reporting situations, the decision to include a recommendation is optional.

3.4 REPORTING SITUATIONS

Because any employee at any level in the organization may initiate a short report, the topics upon which such a report may be based are numberless. These reports may be classified by type according to the purpose for which they are written. Three common types are operational reports, justification reports, and progress reports.

OPERATIONAL REPORT

Many short reports are written to transmit information to one or more persons in an organization. These reports usually inform the reader about current operations, policies, and procedures, for example. The reader may only abstract data from a report (and then destroy it or keep it for a record), or the reader may act upon it.

Examples:

> **1.** Weekly report from a quality control manager to a plant superintendent about defects in work in process.
>
> **2.** Report from the personnel manager to all employees about the outcome of a survey to determine the need for an on-premises cafeteria.

The plan for an operational report depends upon the writer's assessment of the report's effect upon the reader, that is, whether the reader will consider the report as routine, as favorable, or as unfavorable.

1. Routine Report (Fig. 3.1, p. 39). The writer's assumption is that the reader will be neither pleased nor displeased. The information received contributes to the reader's job or to the reader as an employee. This plan (paragraph order) is used for routine letter or memorandum reports:

    a. Main idea (one paragraph)

    b. Explanation and details (one or more paragraphs)

    c. Appropriate closing (one paragraph)

2. Favorable Report (Fig. 3.2, p. 40). The writer assumes the reader will be pleased to get this information and uses a direct plan:

    a. Favorable information (one paragraph)

    b. Details (one or more paragraphs)

    c. Appropriate (e.g., forward looking) closing (one paragraph)

3. Unfavorable Report (Fig. 3.3, p. 41). The writer's assumption is that the reader will be displeased to get this information. An indirect plan is used:

    a. Pleasant or neutral statement (one paragraph)

    b. Reasons to support the negative idea

    c. Negative idea stated in positive manner

    d. Alternative, or compromises, if possible (one paragraph)

    e. Appropriate closing—friendly and positive (one paragraph)
Parts b and c may be combined in one paragraph.

JUSTIFICATION REPORT, (Fig. 3.4, pp. 42–43)

A justification report makes and justifies a recommendation. Usually this report is originated by a resourceful employee who has determined how costs can be reduced, how an improvement can be made,

```
                    FLASH ELECTRONICS, INC.

                                    DATE:  10 July 19--

TO:       J. R. Fox, Plant Superintendent
(Double Space)
FROM:     Barry Logan, Manager, Quality Assurance Department
(Double Space)
SUBJECT:  Weekly Report on Defects in Work in Process

(Triple Space)

    Of the 1500 items inspected, 75 (5%) were found to have defects.

Sixty (75%) of the defects were due to errors in assembling the components,

as shown below:
```

No.	Item	Comment	Number of Defects M	T	W	T	F	Total
1214	Answer panel	Attached upside down	10	6	2	1	1	20
1220	Case	Dented	8	2	0	0	0	10
1247	Transistors	Incorrectly assembled	10	2	0	2	1	15
1410	Function panel	Incorrectly wired	7	2	1	0	0	10
1810	"On" button	Loose	12	2	1	0	0	15
1259	Recharger plate	Apertures too large	1	1	1	1	1	5
			48	15	5	4	3	75

1" (left margin)   1" (right margin)

```
Our tolerance requirements limit weekly defects to 1 (one) percent.  The

exceptionally large number of defects found during the past week is

the result of hurried training given to three part-time employees.

After these employees received additional training and closer super-

vision, the number of defects decreased from 48 to 3.

BL/lw

NOTE:

The date may be shown anywhere above the body except (1) below the subject
line and (2) between the To and From elements.
```

FIGURE 3.1

RAMPART FOODS, INC.
2917 Locust Street
Madison, Wisconsin

July 5, 1979

TO: All Employees

Subject: Mid-year Bonus

At its June 30 meeting, the Board of Directors approved a 3 percent mid-year
bonus, which will be included in your July 31 check.

Dealer sales in the retail grocery industry have increased 2 percent over
the same period last year. Rampart Foods sales have increased 4 percent.
Over 10 percent more customers have purchased their food and nonfood items
at Rampart's this year. This increase in the number of customers can be
traced to our pricing policy, to clean, attractive displays, and to the
courteous, friendly service extended by our employees.

Because Rampart purchases most of its food items regionally, shipping and
related costs are less than if the managers purchased through an intermedi-
1" ate channel. In addition, produce is not damaged or wasted because of   1"
transportation schedules, and lead-time for deliveries is well coordinated.

Each of the four area stores has clean, attractive displays of food and
nonfood items. This aspect of merchandising influences the buying public.

I thank you sincerely for cooperating to make Rampart Foods, Inc., the
success that it is. Continued effort by each of us will bring a Christmas
bonus equally as good.

Sincerely,

John Alpers, President

NOTE:
In this letter report from the president to all employees, the inside
address is replaced by a phrase. A salutation is not used. The complimentary closing could also have been omitted.

FIGURE 3.2

```
                          SECURITY BANK

                                        DATE:  July 11, 19--

TO:       All Employees, Security Bank, Branch 52
(Double Space)
FROM:     Harley Smith, Administrative Vice President
(Double Space)
SUBJECT:  Response to Petition Requesting Installation of a Cafeteria

(Triple Space)

I have considered very carefully your petition to convert the employees'
lounge into a full-service cafeteria.
(Double Space)
Each Security Bank Branch is expected to gain sufficient revenue to pay for
its operating expenses and to make a percentage of profit on transactions.
As Branch 52 was opened just two months ago, certainly it could not be
expected to be self-sufficient (and garner a profit, too) at this time.
Converting the lounge into a full-service cafeteria would cost about $75,000
($35,000 for remodeling, $20,000 for installation of equipment, and a mini-
mum of $20,000 for salaries, plus a substantial amount for food items).
An additional $30,000 can be estimated for each year's operation.  If Branch
52 could produce the revenue for the conversion and meet operating expenses,
I would be glad to approve the request.

Branch 52 is in a unique position--the volume of demand deposits is high,
but their total cash value is small.  This situation requires more personnel
than in other branches where the opposite condition exists.  I realize that
waiting in line for elevators and in neighborhood restaurants is frustrating
and time-consuming.  Therefore, I offer these two alternatives:
(Double Space)
1.  Purchasing four vending machines for packaged items and fruit from
    Vendors' Associates.  Employees would receive 10 percent of the
    revenue, and the remainder would be used to purchase the items.

2.  Hiring Bruce Catering Service to provide cafeteria service two days
    per week.

Another possibility is to contact the other five tenants in the Murray
Building to determine the possibility of their being interested in a build-
ing cafeteria.  In this instance, costs would be shared proportionately.
The rental agency informs me that 400 to 500 people work in the Murray
Building and that no tenant has constructed a cafeteria.  With a positive
response from the other tenants and a feasible operating plan, the rental
agency would contract the job immediately.

Please complete the attached questionnaire, indicating the type of service
you prefer.  If you are interested in my investigating the possibility of a
building cafeteria, also complete the second page of the questionnaire.
Return your questionnaire to the branch manager by August 1.
HS/sj
Attachment:  Questionnaire
```

1"   1"

FIGURE 3.3

1

TURNER SCIENCE EDUCATIONAL KITS, INC.

March 29, 19--

TO: Carl Belmont, Administrative Vice President

FROM: Leslie Reed, Personnel Director

SUBJECT: Flexible Scheduling Would Save Labor Expense in the Assembly
         Department.

Recommendation--To recapture 2500 hours of unproductive, compensated labor
expense, I recommend that flexible scheduling be implemented in the Assembly
Department.

Cost and Savings--Under flexible scheduling, the additional utility expense
would be approximately $7,500 a year, which would be offset by an increase in
the unit selling price of the kits. The 2500 recaptured hours is equivalent
to $20,000 in labor expense which would then be paid for productive time.

Implementation--Employees would agree with their respective supervisors on
which eight hours (beginning and ending time) between 7 a.m. and 6:30 p.m.
they want to work. They would also agree to retain the one-hour lunch period
and two 15-minute break periods daily or to name other options. Supervisors
1" would remain on the 8:30 a.m. to 5:30 p.m. schedule.   1"

Conclusions--The company would receive four benefits by converting to
flexible scheduling:

1. Recapture 2500 labor hours equivalent to $20,000.

2. Increase production.

3. Improve employee relations.

4. Enhance the company's image.

Justification of Conclusions

1. The traffic congestion (Highway 2, Blake Street, Pine Street, and Mae
    Boulevard) caused by cars, vans, buses, and bikes approaching Baker High
    School and this company from 8 a.m. to 8:30 a.m. has resulted in many
    employees' arriving late. At the request of the Assembly Department
    manager, I made a one-month survey and found that approximately one-
    fourth of the 160 Assembly Department employees are an average of 15
    minutes late daily. If this tardiness continues, it will cause 2500
    unproductive labor hours per year, as shown below:

Total minutes lost per day	600
Total hours lost per day	10
Total labor days per year (less vacation)	250
Total labor hours lost per year	2500

FIGURE 3.4

Assembly Department employees are paid an average of $8 per hour. The total cost of the nonproductive time would be $20,000.

The extended hours would create additional utility costs of about $7,500 ($30 a day). As a business expense, this utility cost would increase the unit cost of the kits and therefore the unit selling price.

2. The educational kits are complex, and each assembler is a capable technician who performs a specialized job. When two or more unit assemblers are late, the total unit assembly function slows down. One kit can be assembled in about 30 minutes. In the 2500 hours that would be gained, 5,000 kits could be assembled.

3. The supervisor of each assembly group polled the assemblers and found that 90 percent (140) would like to change to a flexible schedule. Numerous employees have made suggestions concerning lunch hours and break periods, resulting in even more participation by employees in establishing their work environment. By adopting flexible scheduling and considering the employees' suggestions, we would develop greater rapport between the employees and management.

4. Minor accidents have already occurred in the congested area. The high school principal can hardly change the official starting time of Baker High School. The Turner Company, however, can alleviate the congestion and improve traffic safety by adopting flexible scheduling. The company's effort will enhance its image in the minds of educators, students, parents, and others in the community.

LR/js

1"   1"

FIGURE 3.4 (Continued)

or how some other benefit can be derived. In some instances, this report is requested by a superior.

Examples:

> **1.** How in-house microfilming would reduce the cost of filming records.
>
> **2.** Justification for hiring two part-time clerks to reduce the overtime pay in the Data Processing Unit.

Tabulations, enumerations, and representative headings set off the data and facilitate reading of the report. Whether the recommendation is pleasant or unpleasant to the reader, it should be stated, along with an associated benefit, at the beginning of the report.

If implementing the recommendation involves costs and/or savings, these should be stated early in the report. Generally, the costs and savings include factors such as money, materials, and time, and therefore can be stated in figures. The writer is responsible for outlining briefly the procedure for the implementation of the recommendation.

One method of organizing the remainder of the report is to present each conclusion with its justifying explanation in a separate paragraph. Another method is to enumerate the conclusions under one heading and to justify and explain each in a correspondingly numbered paragraph under the next heading.

Another type of justification report (sometimes called a recommendation report) also makes and justifies a recommendation, but this recommendation does not usually involve direct costs or savings. Also, the implementation procedures need not be mentioned because they are part of the operating procedures of the organization.

Examples:

> **1.** Recommendation from a manager to the personnel director to retain (or not to retain) a trainee.
>
> **2.** Recommendations that one of three interviewees be hired for a job.

PROGRESS REPORT (Fig. 3.5, pp. 45–46)

The purpose of the progress report is to inform the reader of the writer's progress toward the completion of a project. The writer describes the progress made to date and outlines future plans. Prob-

ERIE SAVINGS & LOAN ASSOCIATION

MEMORANDUM

TO: Charles Waller, President

FROM: Jerry Yost, Manager, Administrative Services

DATE: August 1, 19--

SUBJECT: Progress Report on Completion of the Perry Park Building

Current Status

The Perry Park Building is almost ready for occupancy; the following
work still needs to be done:

1. Signs: The electrical signs in the lobby have been installed and are
   functioning. All gold-lead signs on the doors have been completed. One
   sample decal which had been installed on the 16th Street doors was
   rejected. The Ohio Sign Company is redesigning it so that it can be
   installed on the inside of the glass without creating air bubbles.

2. Air Conditioning: The trouble spots are being monitored. The additional
   units for the security room and for the teller work area are being
   installed and should be operating next week.

3. Lighting: Fixtures on the tellers' cages have been delivered and will be
   installed next week.

4. Maintenance: The Jason Building Maintenance Company has been put on
   notice that its work is not satisfactory. If the company does not meet
   our standards by the end of the month, I will terminate our contract and
   use Allied Maintenance Services.

Future Plans

1. Trucks from Metropolitan Office Moving Company will begin arriving at the
   service elevator entrance at 7 p.m., August 13. Each department manager
   and one department employee will be present when the furniture and equipment is removed from their respective department and when it is installed
   in the Perry Park Building. The attached schedule shows the time each
   department is to be moved.

2. Baylor Armored Car Service will provide two cars for moving cash, nego-
   tiable instruments, and vital records. The cars will pick up these
   items at 10:30 a.m. on Sunday, August 15, and deliver them directly
   to the vault in the Perry Park Building, where they will be identified

FIGURE 3.5

and separated by two employees selected by the financial vice president.

3. When the last department is moved to the new building (approximately
    4:30 p.m. Sunday), Jason Building Maintenance Company will send its crews
    to clean the entire building.

4. Barring any problems, the building will be ready to open at 9:30 on
    August 16.
(Double Space)
JY/pt
(Double space)
Attachment: Moving Schedule

FIGURE 3.5 (Continued)

lems encountered or those anticipated should be explained. The writer may make recommendations for their solution or request instructions. Also, the writer should make a specific statement about meeting the project deadline.

This report may be required by the person who assigned or contracted a project, or it may be initiated by the person who is responsible for the work:

Examples:

1. Progress Toward the Completion of Plant Maintenance at Six Beet Receiving Stations.

2. Progress Toward the Completion of a Marketing Study to Determine the Location of a Retail Outlet.

A progress report may begin with an introductory statement reviewing the project. This feature serves to refresh the reader's memory about the project.

Headings can be used to label the paragraphs describing the progress made and those outlining the future plans. If problems encountered or anticipated are not explained under either of these headings, they may be explained under separate headings.

3.5 ORGANIZATION

The physical organization of a letter and a memorandum report is traditional. However, minor variations occur because of differing organizational standards and policies and because of the writer's ideas regarding the appropriate presentation for the specific occasion.

LETTER

A letter may include all or most of these parts:

1. *Date.* Use the style approved by the organization.
2. *Inside address.* For a letter to an individual, use:
    a. the addressee's courtesy title, complete name, and job title
    b. the addressee's section, unit, or department
    c. the name of the organization
    d. the organization's street address (and the building name or room number, if necessary)

e. the city, state, and ZIP code

If the reader and writer are located at the same address, the name of the organization and all following parts of the address may be omitted.

If the letter is directed to all employees, the inside address is omitted, and the writer may use "To All Employees" or a similar phrase in its place.

3. *Salutation.* The salutation is the greeting. It is selected to correspond to the name shown in the inside address.

A letter directed to all employees does not usually include a salutation.

4. *Subject Line.* A subject line is not required, but its use is encouraged. Although it need not be a sentence, the subject line should be sufficiently complete to identify the content of the report.

5. *Body.* The letter may transmit an enclosed or attached report, or the content of the letter may itself be the report.

6. *Complimentary Closing.* Some letter reports do not include a complimentary closing; others have one that is appropriate for the circumstances and reflects the writer's relationship with the reader.

The simplified letter (originally recommended by the National Office Management Association) does not include either a salutation or a complimentary closing.

7. *Signature Element.* The writer's typed name and title are shown in the signature element. The department may be included, particularly if it is not shown elsewhere or is not known by the reader.

The writer signs his or her name above the typed signature. A courtesy title does not precede the written or typed signature of a man. The trend is for women not to use a courtesy title.

8. *Initials.* When the writer's initials are used, they precede those of the typist. A symbol separates the two sets of initials.

9. *Enclosure.* An enclosure (or attachment) notation is placed below the initials when an item is enclosed (or attached) with the letter.

MEMORANDUM

The order and arrangement of the elements in the heading of a memorandum depend on the company policy or the writer's decision.

At the minimum, a memorandum heading includes these elements: DATE, TO, FROM, and SUBJECT.

1. DATE. Use the style approved by the organization.

2. TO. Use the name and location of the reader. The name is not preceded by a courtesy title (unless the writer would use one in speaking with the reader). The larger the organization, the more location information is needed to facilitate delivery. For reports directed to a branch or site, the city and state may also be needed.

3. FROM. Use the name and location of the writer. The name is not preceded by a courtesy title. Under the circumstances mentioned above, more information regarding the writer's location may be needed. The phone number may be included as a courtesy.

4. SUBJECT. A memorandum always includes a subject line. Its purpose is to identify the report content. The memorandum body contains the report. Below the body are the initials of the person who composed the report and the initials of the typist. An enclosure or attachment to the memorandum is indicated by a notation below the initials.

3.6 FORMAT

Typical letter and memorandum formats are shown in the illustrations in Part One. These additional comments cover variations in format.

SUBJECT LINE

A subject line in a letter or memorandum may be presented as follows:

1. All in uppercase (capital) letters.

2. In lowercase and uppercase, and with or without underscoring. Short prepositions, conjunctions, and articles (a, an, the) are not capitalized.

SECOND PAGES

The second and succeeding pages of a memorandum and a letter have an identification line containing this information and arranged as the writer deems appropriate: name of recipient, page number, and date (on line 7 from the top of the page). The text continues a triple space below the identification line.

MEMORANDUM MARGINS

The left margin is usually aligned with the first letter of the first word in the heading elements. The right margin is the same width as the left margin, usually 1 inch.

The first line of the body begins a triple space below the subject line. The last line of type on the page should be no lower than line 7 from the bottom.

LETTER PLACEMENT

Many variations are acceptable in letter format. A short letter (less than half a page) may be double-spaced.

The following table shows suitable line lengths for letters in three categories:

Approximate Words	Line Length
Less than 100	4 inches
Between 100 and 200	5 inches
More than 200	6 inches

The current trend is to use a 5-inch line for letters of any length and to vary the spacing in the top elements and signature element to give the letter a balanced, framed appearance on the page.

When the date is centered, the first line of a paragraph may be indented or blocked flush with the left margin. When the date is flush with the left margin, the first line of each paragraph must also be flush with the left margin.

PART TWO

Special Reporting Situations

The following communications are used for special reporting situations:

1. Handbooks, house organs, job descriptions, minutes, labor contracts, directives, policy statements, and staff manuals—all transmit information that helps personnel to understand the organization, to adapt to it as employees, or to recognize the scope of their job.

2. Legal briefs, staff reports, proposals, and audit reports—all require intensive prior investigation and analysis. They are usually internal reports; however, under certain circumstances, they may be directed to a person outside the organization.

3. Procedures—these communications are prepared for a subordinate(s) who needs to follow a certain set of steps to complete a job.

Part Two explains and illustrates legal briefs, minutes, policy statements, procedures, and proposals. Because each communication can be organized differently and also presented in a variety of formats, the examples are included only to serve as a guide to the reader.

2

CHAPTER FOUR

Legal Briefs

In general, a legal brief is a written summary or condensed statement of a series of arguments that apply legal theory to a particular factual circumstance.

4.1 PURPOSE

The purpose of a legal brief is to provide a condensation of legal principles and citations for evaluation, analysis, or study.

4.2 WRITER'S FUNCTION

The writer's function is to provide a legal summary of a case, consisting of a statement of the law and the pertinent facts, with applicable arguments upon both.

All legal briefs require the writer to:

1. Gather the relevant facts.
2. Identify the appropriate legal issues.
3. Apply the issues to the facts.
4. Establish and support a conclusion with reasoning and proper analysis.

4.3 CHARACTERISTICS

Preparing a brief usually requires secondary research and a thorough analysis of the facts. However, the actual length depends upon the complexity of the case and the depth of the analysis. A brief is written in the third person.

4.4 EXAMPLES

These are some situations for which a brief may be prepared:

1. By a lawyer for a plaintiff or defendant to explain the party's position to a judge.

2. By a trial lawyer to provide a complete analysis for bringing a case before the court.

3. By a student to summarize a hypothetical situation, a series of legal ideas, or a published opinion of a case.

4.5 ORGANIZATION

The content of a brief is organized in a logical order (see Fig. 4.1, p. 55). A brief prepared for a board or regulating body, such as the National Labor Relations Board, will differ to some extent from a brief prepared for the court. A court's decision is based on precedent(s), and a regulatory body's decision generally depends upon the facts presented in evidence. The following is one method of organizing the information:

1. *Facts.* A complete summary of the facts relevant to the problem.

2. *Issues.* The question(s) of law relevant to the facts, which have been presented to the court for determination.

3. *Rule.* The decision of the court in regard to the question(s) before the court.

4. *Reason.* The reasoning and analysis supporting the rule established by the court governing the application of the law to the facts.

WHITE V. MARYLAND
373 U.S. 59 (1963)

FACTS: Defendant was arrested and brought before a Maryland magistrate
         for preliminary hearing. Defendant entered a plea of guilty
         during this hearing while he was not represented by counsel.
         Later the defendant entered a plea of not guilty in another
         arraignment hearing. During the subsequent trial, the earlier
         action of entering a plea of guilty was allowed to be intro-
         duced into evidence. Defendant was convicted in this trial.

ISSUE: Is a defendant entitled to be represented by counsel at any
         and all stages of the criminal proceeding?

RULE: Yes.

REASON: Every defendant must be represented by counsel at all stages
         of a criminal proceeding in order to protect every defendant's
         constitutional rights. Only the presence of counsel can enable
         a defendant to be aware of all the defendant's rights and
         immunities in a criminal proceeding. Counsel enables a defen-
         dant to plead in his best interests, and lack of counsel is a
         denial of a defendant's constitutional rights.

FIGURE 4.1

CHAPTER FIVE

Minutes

Minutes are a concise, accurate, well-organized description of the proceedings in a meeting.

5.1 PURPOSE

Minutes serve as an official record of the proceedings.

5.2 WRITER'S FUNCTION

The writer records the proceedings during the meeting and prepares the minutes from this record. All discussion is considered, but only pertinent discussion is condensed and included. The writer must record verbatim all amendments, motions, and resolutions. The person who records the proceedings may be an officer of the group, a person who has been designated to do so, or a person with the job title of "secretary." On the other hand, the proceedings may be machine-recorded, and then the writer or a secretary summarizes them from the recording.

5.3 CHARACTERISTICS

Minutes are written in the third person. Statements are attributed to the person who made them. Courtesy titles may be used before a name, if appropriate. Copies of minutes are distributed to the members of the group holding the meeting and to others who have a need to know the content.

5.4 EXAMPLES

Minutes may reflect the proceedings of a routine and regular meeting or of one called for a special purpose (e.g., to discuss the budget).

5.5 ORGANIZATION

The heading includes an identification of the group and the circumstances surrounding the meeting: date, time, location (see Fig. 5.1, pp. 58–59).

This identification is followed by a list of present and absent members, or by a statement that a quorum is present. The proceedings may be based on a previously distributed agenda, or they may be determined by the chairperson of the group. In either case, they are recorded in the order discussed. Following the discussion, the next meeting date may be named. Lastly, the time of adjournment is recorded.

Minutes include a complimentary closing and the name and title of the recorder. To facilitate reading, the topics discussed may be enumerated, and captions may be shown in the margin.

Note:

Because minutes serve as an official record of the proceedings that occurred in a meeting, their accuracy is important. During various stages of their existence, they have these values:

1. *Operating.* Immediately after publication, they serve as guides for action by members of the convened group and perhaps for others in the organization.

2. *Administrative.* Members of management may make decisions and determine policy on the basis of information.

3. *Legal.* In some instances, the minutes are the basis upon which designated persons are required to pursue specified actions.

4. *Research.* After a period of time, minutes have research value since they provide a record of previous actions, recommendations, and results, thereby becoming a guide for future actions.

MINUTES

Board of Directors

Belmont Farm Land Corporation

July 18, 19--

The Board of Directors of Belmont Farm Land Corporation met in the conference room of the Belmont Building, 52 & O Streets, Lincoln, Nebraska,
on July 18, 19--, at 2 p.m.

The meeting was called to order by the president. All members were
present: Alice Benson, President
          Martin Strang, Vice President, Farm Operations
          Joseph Barbane, Treasurer
          Mark Murchison, Secretary
          Ellen Duval, Controller
          Parker Klopp, Vice President, Administration
          Simon Schulberger, Vice President, Acquisitions

The minutes of the June 17, 19--, meeting were approved as distributed.

1. President Benson requested a meeting with Joseph Barbane, Mark Murchison, and Ellen Duval to prepare a cash flow analysis and an income projection for next year.	1. FINANCIAL PROJECTIONS
2. Mr. Strang reported that the farm manager, Ben Alcot, requested permission to build a rentention pond on the north section of the Reese farm. The pond would permit construction of facilities, such as grain storage bins and livestock shelters, in areas which had previously been designated as a flood plain. Mr. Murchison moved that Ben Alcot be permitted to build a retention pond upon the approval of plans and costs by the Board. Ms. Duval seconded the motion. All members voted in favor of the motion.	2. REESE FARM RETENTION POND APPROVED
3. Simon Schulberger reported that on April 10, 19--, he had contacted all Board members requesting authorization to enter into negotiation for the purchase of the Grant farm and to deliver a Specific Performance Contract and check in escrow for $30,000. The Board approved and authorized Mr. Murchison to prepare a Secretary's Certificate, which is incorporated into these minutes. State inspectors later found the water content to be unsatisfactory. Therefore, the Specific Performance Contract was canceled and the escrow check was returned to Belmont.	3. GRANT FARM PURCHASE CANCELED

FIGURE 5.1

4. Mr. Schulberger then reported on a farm adjacent to the Patton farm, which might be available. The 320-acre Bradshaw farm borders the Patton farm to the north and would therefore be convenient from the standpoint of operations. After discussion, Mr. Schulberger agreed to investigate the purchase of the Bradshaw farm and report to the Board.

In connection with the purchase of additional farm land and upon a motion duly made and seconded, all members voting, it was

RESOLVED: to authorize the president, vice president of acquisitions, and secretary to enter into negotiations and execute and deliver all documents necessary to the purchase of additional farm land, under conditions prescribed by the Belmont Board of Directors.

5. The Board discussed the possibility of selling the Lecter farm for two reasons: (1) it is 23 miles from the nearest Belmont operation and is inconvenient and costly for farm management, and (2) the contour of the land does not lend itself well to the implementation of irrigation. After a motion duly made and seconded, all members voting, it was

RESOLVED: to authorize the vice president of acquisitions to enter into negotiations to sell the Lecter farm, under conditions prescribed by the Board of Directors.

6. Mr. Klopp reported that Ben Alcot, Rock Creek area farm manager, had requested a cost-of-living increase. Replacing Mr. Alcot with a person of equal experience and ability would be difficult. Joseph Barbane made a motion that Mr. Alcot be given a $600 cost-of-living increase and a 7 percent salary increase. The motion was seconded by Mr. Murchison. All members voted in favor of the motion.

The meeting was adjourned at 4:15 p.m.

Respectfully submitted,

Mark Murchison
Secretary

FIGURE 5.1 (Continued)

CHAPTER SIX

Policy Statements

A company's philosophy and a professional organization's code of ethics represent policies to which employees or members are expected to subscribe. Some policy statements form the basis for regulations and represent constraints within which personnel must perform their jobs.

6.1 PURPOSE

The purpose of a policy statement is to provide boundaries for managerial and organizational action. It is the basis for establishing procedures to carry out the work of the organization or a unit within it.

6.2 WRITER'S FUNCTION

Policy statements are written by staff personnel who are responsible for the work to which the policy pertains. Statements for managerial personnel and organizational activities are presented in a broad, general manner that permits considerable latitude and flexibility. Those for nonmanagerial personnel and for tasks are presented in a more specific, factual manner that permits minimum latitude.

6.3 CHARACTERISTICS

A policy statement is a formal declaration and is written in the third person. Its dissemination may be limited to the person to whom it applies and to that person's superiors who need to be aware of it. Some policies affect an entire organization and are placed in a handbook or manual.

A policy statement is in effect until it is revised or superseded by a new policy.

6.4 EXAMPLES

A policy may be broad, restrictive, or narrow:

1. Broad policy

   Management Guide for Savings and Loan Branch Manager

2. Restrictive

   Policies for Admission of Students to an M.B.A. Program

3. Narrow

   Mailroom Policies to Comply with Federal Requirements

6.5 ORGANIZATION

A policy may be written in paragraph form or it may be shown with headings and enumerations. Headings vary with the content of the policy (see Figs. 6.1 and 6.2, pp. 62 and 63).

MANAGEMENT GUIDE

College of Business Dean

I. Identification

As a line administrator in the University, the Dean of the College of Business reports to the Academic Vice President on curriculum and personnel requirements, use of capital and other budget allowances, student enrollment, and other pertinent activities.

II. Responsibilities

Acting within the boundaries of the University Code and College of Business Code, the Dean is delegated the authority to carry out the responsibilities of the office to meet the goals of the University and of the College. The Dean may delegate certain responsibilities, along with commensurate authority, to the associate dean and to department chairpersons, and to other subordinates having the knowledge and experience to carry them out.

III. Activities

To assure the enlightened and well-organized operation of the College, the Dean will perform these activities:

1. Encourage excellence in instruction, provide opportunities for innovative teaching methods, and discern areas which can become "spheres of excellence" for the College.

2. Monitor the curriculum development to assure compliance with the policies of the accrediting associations and the requirements of the certifying associations.

3. Encourage scholarly writing for dissemination to the public, professional publications, and technical journals.

4. Approve faculty, staff, and student recruiting in compliance with federal and University Affirmative Action guidelines.

5. Approve faculty and staff salaries objectively with emphasis on merit.

6. Direct and encourage department chairpersons to develop their faculty members' ability to carry out instructional and professional obligations.

FIGURE 6.1

```
┌─────────────────────────────────────────────────────────────────┐
│                                                                   │
│                  TRAINING DEPARTMENT POLICY                       │
│                                                                   │
│            For In-service and Cross-training Classes              │
│                                                                   │
│  The Training Department follows these policies in conducting in-service
│  and cross-training classes:                                      │
│                                                                   │
│  1.  Classes are held in one of the 15 classrooms on the first floor of
│      Complex B, with these exceptions:                            │
│                                                                   │
│      a.  Students need to use stationary equipment or items that cannot
│          be moved from the department easily.                     │
│                                                                   │
│      b.  Students need to use materials in conjunction with equipment in
│          a department.                                            │
│                                                                   │
│  2.  Classes will meet on company time during the hours enrolled employees
│      are assigned to work, with the following restrictions:       │
│                                                                   │
│      a.  When two shifts overlap, the instruction for the two groups may
│          be held at the end of one shift and the beginning of the next
│          shift.                                                   │
│                                                                   │
│      b.  A training session for operating and supervisory personnel is not
│          to exceed 2 hours a day, 6 hours a week, or 16 weeks a year.
│                                                                   │
│      c.  Employees must be given a 5-minute break between the hours of a
│          two-hour session.                                        │
│                                                                   │
│  3.  Class instructors will be qualified company employees, with these
│      exceptions:                                                  │
│                                                                   │
│      a.  If a qualified employee cannot be located or does not want to
│          assume the instructional responsibilities, a professional
│          instructor can be hired.                                 │
│                                                                   │
│      b.  If no training material exists, professional instructors will
│          prepare an outline that coincides with the requirements of the
│          Training Department.  If the outline is acceptable to the
│          training director, the professional instructor can be hired.
│                                                                   │
│  4.  Class instructors will be paid a sum dependent upon the level of the
│      material and the length of the course.                       │
│                                                                   │
└─────────────────────────────────────────────────────────────────┘
```

FIGURE 6.2

CHAPTER SEVEN

Procedures

A procedure is a step-by-step plan for the completion of an activity or a task. All procedures are based on policies and show how these policies are to be implemented.

7.1 PURPOSE

The purpose of a procedure is to provide the user with easy-to-follow directions so that this person can accomplish the activity or task. A well-written procedure can be an excellent training tool, enabling the user to complete a job without asking numerous questions.

7.2 WRITER'S FUNCTION

The person who writes a procedure is familiar with how an activity or a task should be performed; that is, the sequence of steps and the information the user needs to complete each step. To prepare an acceptable procedure, the writer must consider the user's level of knowledge concerning the activity or task. Where necessary, the writer includes explanations and graphic aids to clarify a step.

7.3 CHARACTERISTICS

The characteristics of a procedure depend upon the user's level (managerial or operating) or location (employee, customer, etc.). Procedures prepared for use by management personnel may be written in the third person and may represent only a guideline for completing an activity. Procedures prepared for operating personnel, however, are specific directions leaving no (or minimal) opportunity for the employee to deviate. Operating procedures are usually written in the second person.

The steps in a procedure may be performed by one person (IRS procedure for completion of Form 1040) or by two or more persons (company procedure for handling an employee grievance). Some procedures affect all employees and are included in an employee handbook or manual. Other procedures affect only the operation of a department or unit within an organization, and are placed in that department's manual.

7.4 EXAMPLES

Any step-by-step presentation that leads to the completion of an activity or a task is a procedure. These examples illustrate the diverse activities and tasks for which procedures can be used:

1. Preparing a report for an accrediting organization

2. Entering transactions on line from a branch savings and loan to the home office

3. Operating a piece of equipment

4. Answering the telephone

5. Requesting reimbursement for travel

6. Conducting a meeting (the agenda)

7. Recruiting executive-level personnel

8. Handling requests for information under Freedom of Information and Privacy Acts

9. Testing employees

10. Selecting trainees

7.5 ORGANIZATION

A procedure may be written in paragraph form, with or without headings and enumerations, or it may be highly structured and include illustrations. An operating procedure may be prefaced by the policy it implements. The procedure is named, and the job title of the user is given. Any additional information that prepares the reader to begin the task needs to be included (see Figs. 7.1 and 7.2, pp. 67, 68, and 69).

For easy reading and understanding, the writer may organize an operating procedure in a manner similar to this:

1. Identify the steps by number, using only one action or task in each step.

2. Identify substeps by letter.

3. Use concrete verbs to begin each itemized step.

4. Place in parentheses the explanations that some users might need to know.

5. Use branching to allow for exceptions.

6. Show illustrations of forms, equipment, and so on, to which the procedure pertains.

7. Code illustration segments to correspond to the applicable steps.

8. Use colors, lines, or arrows to direct the reader's attention to specific points.

```
POLICY:
  As the sole agent to register a voter, the county clerk (and the deputy
responsible for voter registration) must be responsive to the potential
voter.  By performing this job conscientiously and responsibly, this
office provides a citizen his most precious right--THE RIGHT TO VOTE.

PROCEDURE TITLE:  Registration of a voter
JOB TITLE:  Registration Clerk (Deputized)

SITUATION:  Potential registrant stands at counter in front of the "Voter
            Registration" sign.

CLERK:      Have you ever registered to vote before?

PERSON:     (Will probably give one of the following answers:)
            a.  Yes, but I didn't vote in the last election.
            b.  Yes, but not here.
            c.  I don't remember.
            d.  No, I don't think so.
            e.  No.

REGARDLESS OF ANSWER:  GO TO STEP 1.

1.  Ask the person's GIVEN name.
    (Mrs. Jones is not acceptable; must be Eloise Black Jones.)

2.  Search the MASTER VOTER REGISTRATION LIST for this name.
    (List is in alphabetical order--clip board, Drawer #1.)

    a.  Find name?  Go to Step 3.
    b.  Don't find name?  Go to Step 10.

3.  Verify spelling of the name on the MASTER VOTER REGISTRATION LIST

    a.  Spelled correctly?  Go to Step 4.
    b.  Not spelled correctly?  Go to Step 11.

4.  Verify the political affiliation.
    Designated by:  D--democratic
                    R--republican
                    N--nonpartisan

    a.  Correct affiliation?  Go to Step 5.
    b.  Incorrect affiliation?  Go to Step 12.

5.  Verify the residence address.

    a.  Correct address?  Go to Step 6.
    b.  Incorrect address?  Go to Step 13.
```

FIGURE 7.1

6. Tell person he/she is registered to vote in Laramie County.

7. Tell person that Wyoming voters remain registered as long as they vote in a general election every two years.

8. Give the person a voter registration card.

9. Tell the person
   a. When the next election will be held.
   b. Where to vote.

   (Steps 10-13 provide additional information.)

FIGURE 7.1 (Continued)

```
┌─────────────────────────────────────────────────────────────────┐
│                      (Partial procedure)                          │
│ POLICY:  A Common Stock Worksheet is prepared to show comparisons │
│          of data on stocks being considered for investment by     │
│          customers.                                               │
│                                                                   │
│ PROCEDURE TITLE:  Common Stock Worksheet Preparation              │
│ JOB TITLE:        Clerk Trainee                                   │
│                                                                   │
│                         PREPARATION                               │
│                                                                   │
│ 1.  Obtain the three-ring notebook labeled Value-Line Investment  │
│     Service (Vice president's office).                            │
│                                                                   │
│ 2.  Open notebook to the alphabetical listing of stocks.          │
│     (designated by tab).                                          │
│                                                                   │
│ 3.  Locate the name of the stock on which information is needed   │
│     (page number is to the left of the stock name).              │
│                                                                   │
│ 4.  Turn to the page shown in Step 3.                            │
│                                                                   │
│           COMPLETION OF WORKSHEET IDENTIFICATION SECTION           │
│                                                                   │
│ 5.  Transfer the following data from this page to the Worksheet:  │
│                                                                   │
│     a.  Write name of stock (Value-Line 1a) on Worksheet          │
│         (Blank No. 1).                                            │
│     b.  Write stock symbol (Value-Line 2a) on Worksheet           │
│         (Blank No. 2).                                            │
│     c.  Record date on which Worksheet is being prepared          │
│         (Blank No. 3).                                            │
│     d.  Write the number of common stock shares outstanding       │
│         (Value-Line 4a) on Worksheet (Blank No. 4).               │
│     e.  Write the word "Blank" in spaces in which no data is      │
│         recorded.                                                 │
│                                                                   │
│                COMPLETION OF COLUMNAR INFORMATION                  │
│                                                                   │
│ 6.  Write the high and low stock price for each available year    │
│     (Value-Line 5a) in the spaces on the Worksheet (Blank 5).     │
│                                                                   │
│ 7.  Write the Earnings Per Share (EPS) for each year              │
│     (Value-Line 7a) on the Worksheet (Blank No. 7).               │
│                                                                   │
│ 8.  Calculate the high and low P/E ratios.                        │
│                                                                   │
│     a.  Calculate:  High yearly P/E = high stock price ÷ EPS.     │
│     b.  Calculate:  Low yearly P/E = low stock price ÷ EPS.       │
│                                                                   │
│ 9.  Record P/E ratios (Blanks 8a & b).                           │
│                                                                   │
│ (An illustration of the Worksheet and the page from Value-Line    │
│ Investment Service would help to expedite completion of the       │
│ task.)                                                            │
│                                                                   │
└─────────────────────────────────────────────────────────────────┘
```

FIGURE 7.2

CHAPTER EIGHT

Proposals

A proposal is a specific offer to perform an activity or pursue a project. If accepted, it becomes a contractual obligation. The offer may be to carry out a plan or provide a service, for example.

8.1 PURPOSE

The purpose of a proposal is to prove to the reader that the writer can perform a specific activity or pursue a project (initiate an operation or change a current operation) to the reader's satisfaction, or better than competitors.

8.2 WRITER'S FUNCTION

The writer outlines the activity and shows how it would be pursued to completion. The proposal implies that the writer (or the writer's company or department) is being recommended for selection to perform the outlined activity.

8.3 CHARACTERISTICS

A proposal is usually directed to a member of upper-middle management or top management. As a contract, it is a formal document and is usually written in the third person. A proposal written for an internal reader may be transmitted by letter or memorandum. A letter usually transmits a proposal to a reader outside the organization.

The length of a proposal depends upon the complexity of the project or activity being outlined. A proposal is concise, but sufficiently explanatory to convince the reader that the writer can perform the activity. Tables, charts, and diagrams may be appended to the proposal to clarify or emphasize the data.

Although one person is usually responsible for preparing a proposal, others may assist by contributing information in their areas of expertise. Even though a proposal is directed to one person, it may be discussed with others, particularly in the case of one that requires considerable expenditure or extensive operational changes.

8.4 EXAMPLES

A proposal may be an offer to make a minor improvement or change, or it may be prepared in response to an offer by the government soliciting a bid on a complex project. The cost of the project may be minimal, or it may run into hundreds of thousands of dollars. In some instances, a department manager may be expected to prepare a proposal to support a request to institute an operational change.

Examples:

1. Proposal to establish a continuing education program for accountants
2. Proposal to initiate an integrated corporate records management program
3. Proposal from a vendor to install and service a computer system
4. Bid (in response to a government offer) to manufacture a training plane for the Air Force

8.5 ORGANIZATION

A proposal may include headings to identify the topics. The amount of explanation under each heading depends upon the reader's organizational level and extent of understanding or upon the reader's requirements (see Fig. 8.1, pp. 73–77). The organization may vary, but at a minimum, the writer may want to include most of these sections:

1. Introduction (reason for proposal)

2. Description of the proposed activity or project

3. Benefits to be derived from implementing the proposal

4. Costs of development and implementation

5. Methods of implementation (how, when, where, and so on)

6. Remarks: may include evidence that the writer (or the writer's department or company) has knowledge, experience, employees, or money to pursue the project

Note

In an educational environment, the proposal prepared as a basis for a research topic usually includes most of these parts:

1. An explanation of the problem (or topic) to be pursued.

2. The purpose of the research.

3. The research methods to be used, usually supported by some secondary sources to indicate that sufficient preresearch has occurred.

4. A schedule for completing the research phases.

CONSOLIDATED RECORDS CONSULTANTS, INC.
2105 Random Boulevard
Denver, Colorado 80202

August 10, 19--

Mr. Harley Hunt, Vice President of Administration
Solaradd Energy Corporation
1892 Drake Circle
Denver, Colorado 80220

Dear Mr. Hunt:

The accompanying proposal is submitted in response to your request, made during our July 16 meeting.

During the past three weeks, two of my consultants and I visited each department in Solaradd, observed the operations, and interviewed administrative personnel, researchers, managers, and operating employees. The consensus is that the problem of obtaining, abstracting, reproducing, storing, and retrieving information affects almost everyone at every level.

An initial survey revealed that, in addition to generating records for its ongoing operations, the corporation has a heavy reporting burden created by all levels of government. About 30 percent of the records are created to meet the federal agencies' reporting requirements: Office of Safety and Health Administration, Environmental Protection Agency, Housing and Urban Development, and the Equal Opportunity Employment Commission. In addition, complete, accurate records must be maintained for federal and state Internal Revenue Services.

State statutes, county planning and development guidelines, city ordinances and zoning codes--all must be complied with and a record of compliance maintained. These records account for approximately 10 percent of the corporation's reporting burden.

Although the reporting burden cannot be decreased, the management of records in all media can be improved through the implementation of an integrated records management program. The benefits of such a program are explained in the proposal.

Thank you for giving Consolidated Records Consultants, Inc., an opportunity to study the information flow and develop this proposal.

Sincerely,

Margo Moore
President

FIGURE 8.1

PROPOSAL

PLACE: Denver, Colorado   DATE: August 10, 19--

SUBMITTED TO: Mr. Harley Hunt, Vice President of Administration,
               Solaradd Energy Corporation

SUBMITTED BY: Margo Moore, President, Consolidated Records Consultants,
               Inc.

Purpose

After having studied the records, media, and systems, Consolidated
Records Consultants, Inc., recommends that Solaradd Energy Corporation
establish an integrated records management program.

This proposal describes an integrated program for the management of information (from creation to disposition) and outlines the plan by which
Consolidated Records Consultants would implement this program.

Description of Program

An integrated program for the management and organization of records in
all media has these features:

1. Records inventory--to determine what records are maintained, where
    they are located and how they are classified.
2. Records appraisal--to evaluate the administrative, legal, operational,
    research, and historical value of each record series (group).
3. Retention and Disposition Schedule--to show the time a record series
    should be maintained; where, how, and under what authority it
    should be disposed of.
4. Vital records program--to identify vital records and protect them
    in the event of a catastrophe, permitting the business to continue
    operations.
5. Records management manual--to describe for users the procedures for
    maintaining, storing, retrieving, and disposing of records.
6. Records centers--to store active and inactive records, located
    according to their need of accessibility.
7. Centralized control--to be provided by a corporate records manager
    who would direct the program and give continuity to the activities.
8. Qualified personnel (information specialists, technicians, and
    analysts)--to handle the activities pertaining to records in all
    media--paper, tape, film, and so on).
9. Equipment and supplies evaluation--to identify current equipment
    and determine applicability of equipment for records stored.
10. Forms program--to identify forms and plan for elimination, combina-
    tion, or revision.

FIGURE 8.1 (Continued)

Benefits of an Integrated Program

Centralized control of the records function will result in reduction of long-term costs for equipment, labor, space, and materials, as shown:

1. No duplication of equipment and materials.
2. Only necessary duplication of records.
3. Quicker retrieval of information.
4. Less space through scheduled disposition and the destruction of unnecessary records.
5. Fewer, but better-trained, personnel.
6. Quantity purchases of materials and supplies.
7. Integrated systems to take better advantage of existing equipment and personnel.

An intangible benefit is better service to the user and less frustration for both the user and operating personnel. The goal of the program would be to provide the right information in the right form to the right person at the right time and at a minimum cost.

Estimated Costs of Implementing the Program

Equipment and Supplies   -0-
The amount budgeted for equipment and supplies does not need
to be increased. After a complete analysis of all systems,
however, the consultants may recommend some of the line
items be replaced by others more compatible with the
changed system.

Construction and Remodeling   -0-
Sufficient storage space is available within the corporate
complex for use in storing the inactive records and those
requiring climate control.

Personnel $25,000
The total efforts of 26 personnel are now devoted to the
records function. The integrated program would require
the addition of a corporate records manager; however,
the consultants estimate that 19 trained specialists could
perform the work now handled by 26. Therefore, the
records manager's salary would eventually be absorbed by
a reduction of personnel through attrition.

Consulting Service $20,000
This cost covers the services of two consultants for 45
days. These consultants would implement the program,
make recommendations, and train personnel.
                                                          _____
                                                             $45,000

FIGURE 8.1   (Continued)

Method of Implementing the Program

Consolidated Records Consultants, Inc., estimates that the following work could be accomplished in these time frames:

August 15-31:   Records inventory and appraisal completed, and records retention and disposition schedule established.

September 1-15:   All systems and forms analyzed and recommendations made.

October 15:   Complete report presented to Vice President of Administration.

This method of implementing the program assumes that company personnel can be used and trained during each phase. Additional training sessions would be held for two weeks (October 1-15) at a time convenient to company operations.

Remarks

A vita for each of the participating consultants is attached, along with a list of firms for which Consolidated Records Consultants, Inc., has performed consulting activities. Each firm is listed by permission of the corporate officers.

Signed

_____   _____
Margo Moore   Date

Attachments

1. Vita--Edward Carter
2. Vita--Paul Francis
3. List of clients

FIGURE 8.1 (Continued)

```
                                    Vita


                              EDWARD CARTER


Associate Consultant, Consolidated Records Consultants, Inc., specializing
in consulting work for firms in various fields of energy development
(since 1978).

EXPERIENCE

1975-1977:   Corporate Records Manager, Carbon Company, Tulsa, Oklahoma.
             Conducted surveys, established the corporate records management
             program, as well as programs for two divisions; initiated an
             in-house microfilming program; and developed standards for a
             technical research library.

1970-1974:   Manager, Information Systems, Locktyron, Incorporated,
             Houston, Texas.
             Directed programmers, systems analysts, and management analysts
             in applying data processing principles and techniques to various
             business situations, as well as to those unique to a manufacturer
             of oil well drilling equipment.

1968-1970:   Technical Information Specialist, Intercontinental Oil
             Development Corporation, Denver, Colorado.
             Prepared general records management manuals and procedure
             manuals for finance, marketing, production, land lease, site
             operations, and distribution functions.

EDUCATION

M.S.     Information Systems  Colorado State University  Fort Collins,
         Colorado  1968

M.S.     Business Administration  University of Nebraska  Lincoln, Nebraska
         1966

ORGANIZATIONS

Association of Record Managers and Administrators
Association for Systems Management
Data Processing Management Association
Society for Management Information Systems
Beta Gamma Sigma (Business Administration Honorary)

(Served on a variety of committees in each professional organization.)


The clients for whom I have performed consulting service, along with the
names of the contact persons, are listed on the attached sheet.
```

FIGURE 8.1 (Continued)

PART THREE

Preparing
the Report

To make a favorable impression, a report should be accurate, concise, and complete. It should also be presented in an interesting, readable style and tell the reader what he or she needs to know.

   Report preparation is a decision-making process. At least three-fourths of the time spent in preparing a report is devoted to planning the project, evaluating the information, and organizing the content. These mental tasks are especially time consuming, but the more carefully they are performed at each stage of preparation, the better the first draft will be.

CHAPTER NINE

Defining the Problem

The preparation of a business report begins when the problem has been defined and continues through the outline, research, analysis, and interpretation phases. The written report, complete with the necessary preliminary and supplementary pages and organized with headings and subheadings, shows the writer's approach to the problem.

To prepare the report, the writer follows a carefully developed plan sufficiently flexible to allow for adjustments in implementation. The first step in the plan is to define the problem.

A problem must be properly defined so that it can be solved to the reader's satisfaction. Before defining a problem, the writer needs to learn as much as possible about it, sorting out all the facts, determining their importance, and weighing their contribution to the solution.

Memorandum and letter reports are often based on day-to-day problems that, depending upon the writer's experience, may only require a mental definition. Long reports and special reports, however, require a carefully conceived definition.

This definition is the basis upon which the written research objective is formed; it, in turn, becomes the purpose of the report.

Illustrations and further explanation of problem definitions and purpose statements are located under Writer's Function (see Long Reports, p. 8, and Memorandum and Letter Reports, p. 37) and Reporting Situations (see Long Reports, pp. 8–10, and Memorandum and Letter Reports, pp. 37–47).

CHAPTER TEN

Outlining the Information

An outline is an orderly presentation of the major topics and subtopics upon which a report is based. It gives the writer direction in performing the research and organizing and writing a report, and it is the reader's road map through the body of the report.

10.1 DEVELOPING THE OUTLINE

Developing the outline is a continuous task, beginning after the problem is defined and ending when the table of contents is constructed.

PLANNING OUTLINE

The planning outline is made after the problem is defined. At this point, the outline is likely to consist of only main divisions and perhaps some subdivisions, depending upon the writer's grasp of the problem. A single word or phrase may be the only identification the writer can give each part of the outline prior to beginning the in-depth research.

INTERIM OUTLINE

After the research is started and more background is obtained, the writer will add, change, or drop subtopics and perhaps even a major topic. With continued research, the writer expands the outline: it becomes longer and the original words denoting topics and subtopics may become sentences, clauses, phrases, or meaningful captions. Reorganizing the outline is a natural, desirable activity performed concurrently with the research task.

WRITING OUTLINE

The writing outline is the basis upon which the first draft of the report is written. When the research has been completed, the writer evaluates the last outline to determine if (1) it conforms to the approach that will be used to present the data and (2) each main topic and subtopic is in proper order. The points at which the graphic aids will appear are marked, and the aids are prepared in proper form. At this time the decision is made that this outline can be used as the writing outline or that it should be improved.

TABLE OF CONTENTS (Fig. 2.6, pp. 19–20)

The writing outline is refined and becomes the table of contents (with the addition of the appropriate preliminary and supplementary pages). The table of contents headings may be in sentence, clause, phrase, or caption (meaningful words) form. Consistency in construction is important; that is, each major division heading should be parallel (for example, all verb, preposition, or noun phrases; all clauses; all captions; or all questions). Also, all lettered headings, such as A and B under the same main division heading, should be parallel.

Regardless of the type of report, the writer must prepare major and subdivision headings that carry the message to the reader and show the approach to the problem. One-word or two-word headings may be used in the planning outline, but in the table of contents these short headings are usually insufficient to carry the message or reflect the approach.

10.2 DESIGNATING THE DIVISIONS

The headings and sequence of outline divisions may vary, depending upon the nature of the report and the requirements of the reader. However, principles of outline construction for long reports require that if a major division is divided, two or more subdivisions must result. In other words, the writer cannot have an A subdivision without a B, or a 1 without a 2, and so on.

The sequence of outline headings in most business reports is designated by roman numerals, capital letters, arabic numbers, and lower case letters. In long, complex technical reports, the divisions may be designated by an arabic number followed by a decimal point and additional numbers to the right (for example: 1; 1.1; 1.11) representing each succeeding subdivision.

10.3 ORGANIZING THE OUTLINE

The order, length, and number of topics are considered in organizing the outline.

ORDER OF TOPICS

An outline shows how the information will be organized in the written presentation. Often the information can be presented in more than one sequence; therefore, the writer must choose the sequence that best meets the reader's needs. A report may be organized with the topics presented (1) in chronological order, (2) in order of importance, (3) according to phases of development in the project, (4) in relation to the present and proposed activity, or in other logical ways.

In addition, the writer should determine how the reader will accept and use the data by answering questions such as these:

1. If the recommendations are negative, should the reader see the supporting facts before reading the negative portion?

2. If the reader extracts data from the report, should the organization be governed by the order in which the data are extracted?

LENGTH OF TOPICS

Logically, more important topics (those headed A) will require more space than supporting topics (1, 2, and so on, in descending order). However, no major division should be out of proportion (much longer or much shorter) compared with any other major division. If a major division is much longer than others, the information may be overemphasized, or it may actually involve more than one topic and thus reflect poor organization. On the other hand, a major division much shorter than others may contain information that should be part of another major division, may belong in the background, or may not be essential to include in the report.

Too many divisions distract the reader; headings are emphatic and direct the reader's eyes to a short line in the center or at the margin. The reader is slowed down and can remember neither the many points nor the order of their importance.

If too few headings are used, the reader may not be sure where a particular segment fits into the continuity of the report without looking back to find a division heading.

Reports with few headings often have long paragraphs; a paragraph that requires most of a page (or more) does not present an appealing appearance. The reader may be discouraged by the mass of information.

10.4   SELECTING DIVISION HEADINGS

Each major division heading represents a topic of primary importance to the report. A subdivision heading represents content that supports the major heading under which it is located. Two examples of headings for a planning outline and its counterpart in the table of contents follow.

The outline upon which a comparative analytical report is based may have the criteria as major division headings.

Example of problem statement:

> The purpose of this report is to compare Jay Model 7 and Kay Model 9 typewriters to determine which is the better to purchase for the Claims Department. The solution will be based on cost, features, and maintenance.

Headings in planning outline:

    I.   Introduction
    II. Cost
    III. Features
    IV. Maintenance

Headings in table of contents:

    I.   Introduction
    II. Cost for Jay Model 7 and Kay Model 9 Is Comparable
         A.   Original Cost Is Similar
         B.   Quantity Cost Favors Kay Model 9

III. Features of Jay Model 7 Are More Applicable to Claims Department Procedures

IV. Maintenance Would Be Better on Jay Model 7
    A. Better Maintenance Contract Offered by Martin Company
    B. Better References Presented by Martin Company

The criteria (cost, features, and maintenance) become major division headings. With this format the writer can measure each typewriter against the same criterion at the same time and in the same report location. However, if Jay Model 7 and Kay Model 9 were major division headings, the writer would be restricted to a discussion of the three criteria under Jay Model 7 and to a repetition of those criteria under Kay Model 9. The two machines could not be compared unless the writer used a third major division for comparison and repeated the information from the two preceding divisions. Such a format is lengthy, repetitious, and confusing.

This example shows a planning outline for an informational report and a part of and its final presentation in the table of contents.

Example of problem statement:

How are underground pipelines used as channels of distribution for various products?

    I. Introduction
   II. Water
  III. Oil
  IV. Natural Gas
   V. Steam
  VI. Grain
 VII. Miscellaneous Products

Table of Contents:

  I. Introduction

 II. Water Systems Require More Pipeline Mileage
    A. Conduit Systems Carry Water from Source
    B. Intake Systems Carry Water to Destination
    C. Sewer Systems Remove Water and Refuse

III. Oil Pipeline Usage Is Increasing Rapidly
    A. Domestic Usage: Lines Extended from 1975 to 1980
    B. Foreign Usage: Field-to-Terminal Lines Added from 1975 to 1980

IV. Natural Gas Pipeline Construction Is Controversial

The informational report statement gives the researcher key words ("used as a channel of distribution") that help to determine the major division headings. Additional research provides the background to develop the major and subdivision headings shown in the table of contents.

10.5 OUTLINING SHORT REPORTS

Regardless of the length of a communication, it should be based on an outline. Often outlining is considered a task applicable only to a long report; however, in a memorandum or letter (even without headings), the information must be presented in an order appropriate for the content and acceptable to the reader.

In short reports and special reports, the headings are brief; often one or two words will suffice to tell the reader what the content contains. These headings may be underscored, enumerated, or set off in some other way. The headings do not follow the formal outline construction, organization, and format prescribed for headings in long reports.

CHAPTER ELEVEN

Performing the Research

The decision to use primary or secondary research is determined by the nature of the problem, the kind of information needed, its availability, its current value, the cost to obtain it, and the time to devote to the search.

11.1 SECONDARY RESEARCH

Secondary research is performed in libraries; the information is obtained from published (secondary) sources. This type of research is always undertaken before primary research, when the investigator personally collects original data. Secondary research reveals what has been written about the topic in question, the age of the information, and its relevance to the current problem. Having this background eliminates the possibility of duplicating the efforts of previous researchers.

Secondary research requires five steps: (1) locating the sources, (2) preparing a bibliography, (3) using the card catalog, (4) establishing a notetaking system, and (5) recording the notes.

LOCATING THE SOURCES

Specialized indexes list publications on a variety of subjects in many disciplines. Part Six includes an annotated bibliography of sources—such as indexes, handbooks, services, and newsletters—that are especially useful for persons researching topics in business and economics. Most of these sources can be found in academic, business, technical, community, and private libraries.

In many instances, a person must be able to locate government sources that lead to the appropriate publications or documents. Some of the most commonly used sources are explained and illustrated in Parts Five and Six. Any library designated a "depository library" contains copies of all government publications and documents.

PREPARING A BIBLIOGRAPHY

To save time and to select useful sources, the researcher needs to make two lists: (1) a subject-clue list—words, phrases, or names that will serve as clues to information about the topic and (2) a bibliography—the complete documentation of publications (articles and books, for example) that may contain useful information.

The subject-clue list may contain synonyms, commonly used terms that apply to the topic, and words naming similar concepts or activities. For a report on training programs in banks, this subject-clue list might be constructed:

> *banks*
> *bankers*
> *certification*
> *continuing education*
> *financial institutions*
> *human resources management*
> *recruiting*
> *training*
> *training programs*

This procedure can be followed to develop a bibliography from the subject-clue list:

1. *Select an Appropriate Index.* Use the card catalog to locate the call number of an index that is likely to contain the subject clues (see Indexes to Books, Periodicals, p. 193, and Indexes to Articles, p. 195).

2. *Search the Index Subject List.* Look first for the most specific and relevant subjects on the subject-clue list; then search for the other listed subject clues, and finally note applicable clues shown in the index.

3. *Compile a Bibliography.* On a full sheet of paper, copy the complete information shown for each publication of potential value. Number each publication on this list consecutively (see Fig. 11.1, p. 91).

By first looking in an appropriate index under the most relevant subject clues—such as "banks" or "bankers"—the researcher may find one of the other subject clues shown. Publications found by searching for the most relevant clues are likely to contain specific information about training programs in banks, as well as examples. If one of the other subjects is selected, the publications about training programs in general will be found. Some of these publications may contain examples of training programs in banks. The two articles listed in the bibliography (see Fig. 11.1, p. 91) were found in the *Business Periodicals Index* (see p. 196).

USING THE CARD CATALOG

At a minimum, a library card catalog contains three sets of 3 × 5 cards for the items in the library collection: (1) author cards, (2) title cards, and (3) subject cards. Each card should provide complete bibliographic information and show the call number, which identifies the location of the publication within the library.

The researcher locates the first publication from the bibliography in the card catalog and records the call number. This publication is then scanned to determine if it contains useful information. If it does not, it is checked off, and a notation regarding its value is made (for example, n.p.—not pertinent). If it does contain useful information, the researcher takes notes and marks this publication on the list (perhaps with an X) to show that it has been used. This procedure is repeated for each publication in the bibliography.

Meaningful symbols are used to indicate the value of a publication. These same symbols should be used consistently throughout the research phase.

For some assigned topics, the researcher may be required (or may desire) to compile an annotated bibliography—a brief description of the content and value of each publication (see Annotated Bibliography, p. 155).

ESTABLISHING A NOTE-TAKING SYSTEM

Any note-taking system is acceptable as long as it is easy to use and logical. The system selected should be used consistently throughout the research phase.

```
1.  Credit investment (a training program).  E. E. Pace & D. G.
    Simmson.   J Comm Bank Lending 59:3-8 My '77


2.  It's time to stop trial & error training for new install-
    ment lenders.  W.J. Fiorentini.  Banking 69:34+ Mr '77
```

FIGURE 11.1

This system is given as an example:

> The researcher can transfer each entry from the bibliography to a 3 × 5 card, assigning it a number (see Fig. 11.2).
>
> Then a set of 5 × 8 cards can be numbered to correspond to the numbers on the first set of cards; the researcher uses this set to record the notes (see Fig. 11.3).
>
> Because the numbers correspond to those on the 3 × 5 cards, the complete documentation does not need to be copied a second time.

If a publication provides considerable useful information and more than one card is needed, each can be numbered consecutively. Enough information, such as page numbers, sections, and chapters,

FIGURE 11.2   3 × 5 bibliography card.

```
                                                              1*

    Grilli, Enzo R.   The Future for Hard Fibers and Competition

    from Synthetics.   World Bank Staff Occasional Papers, No. 19.

    Baltimore:   Johns Hopkins University Press, 1975.
      ↑
(Documentation of publication)


      *Number corresponds to the first publication on the
  bibliography list.
```

_____

_____

_____

    *1 corresponds to the number on the 3 x 5 card; 2 indi-
cates that this is card #2 of two or more cards containing
notes from this source.

FIGURE 11.3 5 × 8 bibliography card.

for example, should be shown on the card so that the researcher
does not need to waste time relocating the source to obtain this
information at a later date.

Before the writing outline is prepared, the researcher should
evaluate the notes on the 5 × 8 cards and designate them with
numerals or letters to indicate the major sections (II) and subdivisions (A) to which they apply. This step helps to filter out old,
repetitive, unauthoritative, and questionable information and makes
the report more concise and relevant.

RECORDING THE NOTES

The researcher often has the urge to "take down everything" when
"everything" is not needed; in fact, much of the information in the
source may even be superfluous. To avoid painstaking copying effort, the researcher should read the pages pertinent to the outline
topics and decide which of the following methods best fits the material and the topic.

1.   A verbatim quotation consists of the exact words of the original
author in the same order and with the same punctuation as in the
original passage. This quotation is placed within quotation marks
(see Quotation Marks, p. 297). The author of the original passage
must be given credit in a reference note (see Reference Notes, p.
123).

2.   A verbatim quotation with ellipsis marks inserted in lieu of a
word, phrase, clause, sentence, or paragraph is also placed within

quotation marks (see Ellipsis, p. 290). The author of the original passage must be given credit in a reference note (see Reference Notes, p. 123).

3. A paraphrase is a restatement of a passage. Even though the writer's own words are used, the author of the original passage must be given credit in a reference note (see Reference Notes, p. 123).

4. A summary is a sentence or paragraph condensation of a partial or entire publication. The author of the original publication must be given credit in a reference note (see Reference Notes, p. 123).

5. Dates, figures, names, or other pertinent useful facts may be abstracted from a source. If the facts are not generally known, they should be credited to the original author in a reference note (see Reference Notes, p. 123).

3

11.2 PRIMARY RESEARCH

Primary research is "first-hand" research. A report may be based entirely on primary research; or primary research may be used to update, supplement, or support secondary research (or previous primary research). The writer bases the choice of a primary research method on the nature of the information needed. Even though the evidence gathered by means of primary research may not be shown in a reference note, it must be fully explained in the methods section of the report. Commonly used primary research methods are observation, investigation, experimentation, and survey.

OBSERVATION

Observation is literally gathering data "on the spot."

Examples:

    1. Watching—a report may be based on a superior's "watching" an employee to determine that person's ability to get along with coworkers.

    2. Counting—a restaurant owner may hire a person to count and record the number of people who pass the restaurant during each of its open hours for one week.

INVESTIGATION

Although all research can be termed "investigation," the use of company records provides an example of this method. The researcher must investigate the records and select the one(s) that will supply the facts or figures needed. These facts (or figures) may be manipulated and reconstructed into another format that will help the researcher obtain additional information.

Example:

> The researcher gathers the figures to construct a balance sheet, income statement, cash flow statement, or stock analysis.

3 EXPERIMENTATION

This method is probably the least commonly used to obtain data for business decision making. It requires one control group and one or more experimental groups; a variable (treatment) is applied to the experimental group(s). The hypothesis to be tested is that the variable is responsible for the difference between the controlled and the experimental situations.

Example:

> A training department has been using the traditional method (text and instructor) to train the company machine transcribers in English fundamentals. The training director has decided to evaluate the programmed method. The experiment involves two classes, one taught by the traditional method and one using a programmed text on the same subject. Prior to the study, the classes are evaluated for English aptitude and given a test for qualitative ability and a course pretest. At the end of the experiment, a posttest is given; and assuming all data remain constant, the difference in the scores between the two classes is assumed to be due to the one variable: different instructional method.

The experimenter must use care not to bias the results through the selection of the members of the groups or to bring in any other unrelated variables.

SURVEYS

A survey investigates a group of persons, items, or actions for the purpose of obtaining answers to specific, predetermined questions. This handbook contains only a brief description of survey methods.

A more complete description can be found in textbooks on research methods or applied statistics.

When the population of the entire "universe" being surveyed (people, items, actions) cannot be surveyed, the writer must use a sampling technique. To be reliable, the sample must be large enough to represent each type of characteristic in the relevant population. In addition, the sample must be randomly chosen, meaning that each entity in the population (person, item, action) has an equal opportunity to become a part of the sample. For some situations, the population may be stratified and a random sample taken from each area; that is, the sample is broken into subgroups, each having a designated characteristic.

Example:

> A college population may be divided (1) according to the schools within the college, (2) then by the class level, (3) then by sex, and so on. In this way, the researcher can take a random sample of each category (sex, level, and school).

Systematic sampling can be used to observe items, people, or actions according to a unit's predetermined position in the scheme of things.

Example:

> The sample may include: (1) Every tenth item that comes off the assembly line, or (2) every third customer who visits a cosmetic counter.

In batch sampling, a group of randomly selected items from the population is used to determine some characteristics of the batch.

Example:

> One hundred identical machine parts can be examined to determine the percentage of defective parts.

This type of sampling may be the basis for applying quality control measures.

A survey instrument may be an interview sheet, a telephone questionnaire, or a mail questionnaire. A properly constructed, well-designed survey instrument facilitates obtaining, tabulating, and analyzing the data. Therefore, the researcher needs to be aware of the principles involved in constructing a survey instrument:

1. Group all questions on the same subject, rather than scattering them throughout the survey instrument.

2. Place the spaces to be marked in a format that facilitates manual or machine tabulation.

3. Do not ask a respondent to rank more than five items.

4. If doubtful that all possible answers are set forth, add "other" with a blank(s) following so a response can be added.

5. Phrase each question so that only one answer is required; do not ask for two answers within one question.

6. Use concrete and common words so the respondent cannot misinterpret the question.

7. Phrase questions in such a way that the respondent is not "led" to give a certain (or desired) answer.

8. Do not ask questions that might embarrass the respondent. If the respondent's name is not requested or if the final data are grouped, a personal question may be asked, since the respondent will not be identified.

9. Do not request information that is available from printed sources.

10. Do not use overlapping ranges for quantitative data; for example, do not show age ranges in this way: 21–30; 30–40; 40–50, and so on. The respondent who is 30, 40, or 50 does not know which range is applicable. Show these ranges as 21–30; 31–40; 41–50.

1. Personal Interview

The researcher should make the request for an interview either in writing or by telephone. The interviewee can be informed of the topic to be discussed, the reason for the interview, and the approximate time to be consumed by the interview.

The interviewer should write as little as possible in the presence of the interviewee in order not to distract him or her. An interview sheet, containing the questions and spaces for responses, should be prepared and used by the interviewer during the interview. If this sheet is sent to the interviewee prior to the interview, this person can become aware of the topic and will understand the interviewer's reasoning and approach. This additional step expedites the interview and shows good organization on the part of the interviewer.

Following the personal interview, a letter of appreciation should be sent to the interviewee. Not only is this action a business courtesy, but it also reflects favorably upon the researcher.

2. Telephone Interview

Persons who receive unsolicited calls from unknown people, and not always at the most convenient times, are often not eager to answer the caller's questions. A pleasant voice giving identifying information immediately, along with the reason for the call and the time required, can sometimes change the interviewee into a cooperative person. Due to the nature of the interview, the questions should be short and easy for the average person to comprehend without repetition. If multiple choice questions are used, the answers should be short enough so the listener does not become confused.

3. Mail Questionnaire

A mail questionnaire is always accompanied by a transmittal letter. The letter is a persuasive type that (a) arouses the reader's interest, (b) explains the basis of the problem and how the reader can assist, and (c) requests that the questionnaire be returned by a specific time. Letters requesting a response "as soon as possible (or at your earliest convenience)" do not bring good results from busy readers.

If the writer can provide a benefit, such as a copy of the synopsis, for the respondent, this benefit should be mentioned along with the request.

Enclosing a stamped, addressed envelope for the respondent's use will facilitate the response and is usually worthwhile. The letter and questionnaire are the writer's ambassadors and should reflect the writer's diligence, subject-matter knowledge, and ability to communicate.

CHAPTER TWELVE

Preparing the Graphic Aids

3

A graphic aid is an illustration, such as a table, chart, map, pictogram, flowchart, or diagram.

When facts and figures are integral parts of the data, graphic presentation is desirable. A graphic aid can (1) display detailed data in an ordered, easy-to-grasp format; (2) show the reader at a glance the relationships between the factors being measured; and (3) support and clarify the content.

12.1 PLACEMENT

A graphic aid is first introduced, then shown, and then interpreted for the reader.

INTRODUCTION

A graphic aid is used for a purpose; therefore, it should be introduced by a significant statement about the content, thereby directing the reader's attention to the aid. Reference to the aid should be at the end of the sentence or in a subordinate position within the sentence. Constructions such as the following may be used to introduce a graphic aid: (1) "as shown in Table 3," (2) "(see Table 3)," (3) "(Table 3)," or (4) "according to Table 3." To decide on a significant point to introduce this aid, the writer examines the data presented in the aid to determine such facts as these: the greatest or the least (in some relevant category), differences, similarities, or trends. Even the fact that no difference exists may be significant.

PRESENTATION

A graphic aid is located as close as possible to the sentence in which it is introduced. If the aid is shown two or more pages after it is introduced, that page should be mentioned in the introductory statement. Aids should not be split between pages. A lengthy table requiring two or more pages can be taped together and the pages neatly folded. Such an aid may be more appropriately displayed in the appendix rather than in the body, particularly if the data are primarily supportive.

INTERPRETATION

It is the writer's job, not the reader's, to interpret aids in the report. Calling attention to isolated facts or figures is rarely sufficient; a fact or figure is usually understood more clearly by its relationship to another. The writer can interpret by (a) using percentages to compare raw figures, (b) giving ratios and fractions, (c) using words, such as "ten times more," and (d) showing trends over time (see Fig. 12.1, pp. 100–101). To discern these relationships, the writer must scrutinize the data carefully. Without performing diligent analyses and interpreting the results accurately, the writer may make an inaccurate or illogical statement.

12.2 TABLES

A table shows an orderly arrangement of data and provides for easier assimilation of facts than a presentation of those same facts in a prose text. Headings, rows, and columns structure the data and show natural relationships (see Fig. 12.2, p. 102). A table is preferable to a chart if numerous, exact figures are to be shown (see Fig. 12.3, p. 103).

A table in a long or short report may be formal or informal. Formal tables may include all or most of the following features:

NUMBERS

A formal table (usually boxed, lined, and with structured headings) is identified by an arabic number above or to the left of the title. Succeeding tables are given consecutive arabic numbers. If the report contains many chapters, each including several tables, the chapter and table number may be shown like this: Table 10.3 (Chapter Ten, Table 3).

Of the total daily oil supply required by the United States (18,860 barrels), 43% (8,143 barrels) is imported. The ten largest suppliers of foreign oil account for approximately four-fifths (81.3%; 6,775 barrels) of the oil imported by the United States, as shown in Table 1.

TABLE 1

THE TEN LARGEST SUPPLIERS OF FOREIGN OIL, RANKED BY
AVERAGE FIGURES FOR THE FIRST FOUR MONTHS OF 1979

Supplier	Thousands of Barrels per Day	Percentage Share of Imports
1. Saudi Arabia	1,479	17.8
2. Nigeria	1,102	13.2
3. Venezuela	719	8.6
4. Libya	678	8.1
5. Algeria	634	7.6
6. Canada	548	6.6
7. Virgin Islands	484*	5.8*
8. Mexico	413	5.0
9. Indonesia	409	4.9
10. United Arab Emirates	309	3.7
	6,775[a]	81.3[a]

[a]The figures do not equal 100 percent because (1) 16.8% (1,368 barrels) of the imported oil is supplied by numerous other countries, none of which exports more than 3.7% to the United States, and (2) 1.9% represents the discrepancy resulting from averaging the figures.

*Virgin Island totals represent refined products that are produced elsewhere.

Source: U.S. Department of Energy; American Petroleum Institute.

(Interpretation)

Six of the ten largest suppliers (Saudi Arabia, Nigeria, Libya, Algeria, Indonesia, and the United Arab Emirates) are located in the Eastern Hemisphere. These nations export over half the foreign oil used by the United States daily (55.3%; 4,611 barrels). Their contribution is 68% greater than the total supplied by the four remaining nations.

FIGURE 12.1

PART THREE   PREPARING THE REPORT

Suggested Typewritten Format for a Vertical Placement on Page with Text

(1) Triple-space between the last line in a paragraph and the table number.
(2) Single-space the lines in the title; center the title and type it in all capital letters, or capitalize the first letter of each word except articles, prepositions, and conjunctions.
(3) Double-space after the title and center the column headings over the respective columns.
(4) Underscore the headings or draw a line horizontally across the page under the headings and spaces between.
(5) Double-space between the headings and the first entry.
(6) Single or double-space the body; consider the amount of data and the ease of reading.
(7) Double-space after the last entry and draw a line part (or all) of the way across the page.

FIGURE 12.1 (Continued)

<u>Company Identification</u>

Eighty-four percent (101) of the responding companies employ fewer than 25,000 people (Table 2).

TABLE 2

APPROXIMATE TOTAL NUMBER OF EMPLOYEES
IN RESPONDING ORGANIZATIONS
(Headings in Thousands)*

| Division of Business | Number of Employees | | | | | Total | Percent |
	-5	5-10	10-25	25-50	50+		
Manufacturing	8	15	18	8	5	54	45.0
Insurance	10	3	1	-	-	14	11.7
Banking	7	6	1	-	-	14	11.7
Utilities	4	6	1	-	-	11	9.2
Retailing	-	1	5	-	-	6	5.0
Transportation	-	2	1	2	-	5	4.2
Diversified Investments	-	1	-	1	1	3	2.5
Other	6	3	2	2	-	13	10.8
Total	35	37	29	13	6	120	100.1
Percent	29%	31%	24%	11%	5%		

  * Ranges: under 5,000; 5,000 to 10,000; 10,001 to 25,000; 25,001 to 50,000; over 50,000.

FIGURE 12.2

TABLE 3

PROFITS IN MAJOR INDUSTRIES, AS ABSTRACTED FROM REPORTS OF REPRESENTATIVE CORPORATIONS

	2nd Quarter 1978	2nd Quarter 1979	Percent Change
Aircraft, Missiles	$ 346,449,000	$ 431,536,000	+ 24.6
Airlines	472,647,000	405,827,000	- 14.1
Banks	1,344,825,000	1,662,630,000	+ 23.6
Building materials	717,999,000	841,089,000	+ 17.1
Chemicals	944,586,000	1,252,956,000	+ 32.6
Coal mining	18,348,000	21,574,000	+ 17.6
Computers, office equipment	1,083,434,000	1,141,107,000	+ 5.3
Drugs	720,021,000	844,706,000	+ 17.3
Electric utilities	967,563,000	1,036,097,000	+ 7.1
Electrical equipment	525,791,000	615,781,000	+ 16.9
Food, beverages	546,789,000	616,157,000	+ 12.7
Gas utilities	247,040,000	322,304,000	+ 30.4
Motor vehicles, parts	1,760,707,000	1,842,879,000	+ 4.7
Nonelectrical machinery	374,769,000	413,269,000	+ 10.3
Nonferrous metals	366,437,000	658,440,000	+ 79.7
Paper	349,769,000	413,269,000	+ 10.3
Personal care	151,482,000	170,392,000	+ 12.5
Petroleum	3,143,043,000	4,961,080,000	+ 57.8
Printing, publishing	163,597,000	198,005,000	+ 21.0
Railroads	412,801,000	530,880,000	+ 28.6
Restaurants, lodging	87,127,000	104,688,000	+ 20.2
Retail food stores	100,073,000	112,791,000	+ 12.7
Rubber	132,339,000	113,740,000	- 14.1
Steel	310,228,000	404,686,000	+ 30.4
Telephones	1,502,628,000	1,657,555,000	+ 10.3
TV, radio broadcasting	229,731,000	244,540,000	+ 6.4
Textiles, apparel	89,253,000	101,747,000	+ 14.0
Trucking	94,586,000	84,755,000	- 10.4

Source: U.S. News & World Report, Economic Unit.

FIGURE 12.3

3

An informal table (a short tabulated presentation without lines and a title) does not require a number.

TITLE

The title is concise and identifies the content of the table.

COLUMN HEADINGS

These headings are concise labels for the data below; they are shown horizontally across the table and above the corresponding data. Headings containing letters in vertical format are difficult to read and should be used only as a last resort.

Units by which the data are measured (dollars, barrels, etc.) need to be shown in the column headings. To save space, the author may abbreviate these units or use symbols to represent them.

BODY

The data on the table are arranged systematically and neatly under the column headings and across from the factor on the stub. If no data exist for a column entry, (1) two hypens may be typed in the space, or (2) sufficient periods may be added to equal the column width, or (3) the letters "n.a." may be used to show that the stub heading is "not applicable." If the table shows dollar amounts, a dollar sign is placed before the first number in the amount column; its placement should correspond to the dollar sign that will be typed before the total.

STUBS

The left column of a table is the "stub." Each row entry under the stub title names the factor to which the data across from it correspond. In a table with several columns, the stubs may also be shown to the right of the body.

LINES

A table must be easy to read. Whether to line or underscore at certain places depends upon the size of the table (length and width) and the amount of data it contains. These points can be used as guidelines:

1. Headings should be immediately obvious to the reader. Each heading can be underscored, or a line can be drawn horizontally across the page under the headings and the spaces between.

2. If several columns are shown, lining between the columns clarifies the identity of the data within these columns.

3. A horizontal line below the table can be used to separate the table from footnotes and the source information. This line can extend part or all the way across.

4. If neither footnotes nor source information is shown, the table need not be followed by a line.

5. Boxing a table (lines on all four sides) is the extreme in formality; most graphics prepared in-house but not in a reproduction department are not presented in this way.

3

SYMBOLS

To explain an item on the table, the writer can use an asterisk, dagger, lowercase letter, or number beside the item to call the reader's attention to a corresponding symbol below the table. This explanation is a footnote only to the table; therefore, it is not placed at the bottom of the page in footnote format. If the table consists entirely of numerical data, a letter indicating a table footnote is preferable to a number.

SOURCE NOTE

If the table is based on data gathered in primary research, the source note may be omitted, or it may be shown as, "Source: Primary."

12.3 GRAPHS AND CHARTS

Relationships between the measurable factors on a graph or chart are indicated by lines, bars, or pictorial representations. Because a graph or chart shows approximate relationships, it is sometimes supplemented by a table that gives the exact figures. Another way to provide the exact figures for significant relationships is to place them within the graph or chart.

A chart is identified with an arabic number. If several charts, maps, and diagrams are used, the writer can identify each group separately (Chart 2, Map 4, Diagram 1) or can consider all illustrations other than tables as one category and label them Figure 1, 2, 3, and so on.

A title, preceded by an identifying number, is usually placed below an aid. The title should be comprehensive, yet concise. It can be shown entirely in capital letters, or the first letter of each word except prepositions, conjunctions, and articles can be capitalized.

The most frequently used visual representations of data are the line chart, bar chart, and pie chart.

LINE CHART (Figs. 12.4 and 12.5, pp. 106–107)

A line chart shows changes in a series of data over a period of time—for example, changes in the population of a country, retail sales volume in a city, demand deposit volume in a bank, and sales of a company.

The vertical axis (Y) identifies the factor and quantity being measured, and the horizontal axis (X) identifies the time period under observation. These axes form the grid upon which the data are recorded.

Care must be taken not to distort the graphic representation. An equal amount of space must be allowed between each horizontal

FIGURE 12.4 Line chart

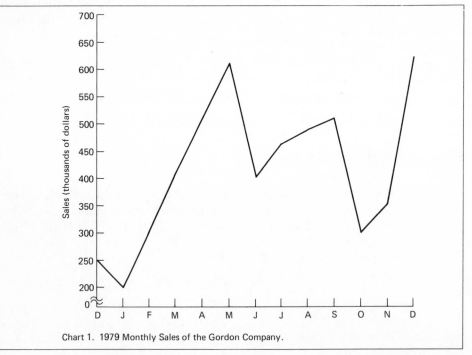

Chart 1. 1979 Monthly Sales of the Gordon Company.

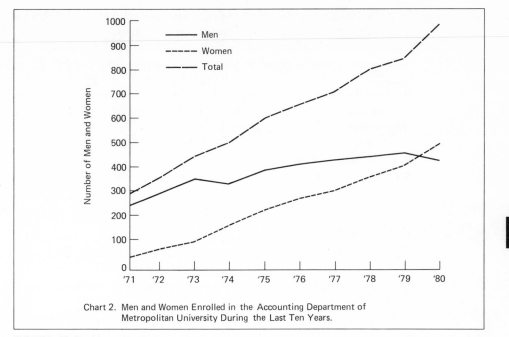

Chart 2. Men and Women Enrolled in the Accounting Department of Metropolitan University During the Last Ten Years.

FIGURE 12.5 Line chart

line, and an equal amount of space must also be allowed between each vertical line. The closer the intervals on the horizontal axis and the wider the intervals on the vertical axis, the more violent the changes appear.

The angle where the axes meet is labeled zero, and each interval point above it is labeled with an ascending equal value; that is, the second point is labeled 100; the third, 200, and so on. If a wide range (or distance) exists between zero (0) and the next quantity, two close short parallel lines are drawn between the horizontal axis and the first horizontal line to "break" the vertical axis at this point. To determine the intervals between the quantities on the vertical axis, the writer locates the least and the greatest quantities that are to be shown (200 and 600), subtracts the former from the latter (400), and decides upon realistic, logical intervals for this type of data.

The factor, for example, "Sales (thousands of dollars)," may be shown vertically at the left of the quantities on the vertical axis. Each time period is labeled below the horizontal axis.

To record data, the writer places a dot on the first vertical line to show the approximate quantity that is given for a specific point in time. After a dot has been inserted for each quantity, a line is drawn to connect the dot on the first vertical line with the dot shown at the intersection of the next vertical and horizontal line.

More than one factor can be measured on a multiple line chart—for example, the change in a nation's population over ten years shown by one line indicating the male population and another indicating the female population. The writer can use as many lines as necessary as long as the factors are logically related and the data are clearly and easily distinguishable.

Colored lines, shading between lines, broken lines, dots, and other devices can be used to make the lines clearly identifiable and to distinguish each from the other. A legend is included within the graph to identify the lines.

3 BAR CHART (Figs. 12.6, 12.7, and 12.8, pp. 108–110)

A bar chart shows equal-width bars in a horizontal or vertical pattern to represent quantities in relation to a factor—for example, state population according to ethnic groups or sales by retail outlets of a company.

The bar titles are shown on one axis and the scale values on the other axis. A caption identifies the scale values, for example, "thou-

FIGURE 12.6 Bar chart

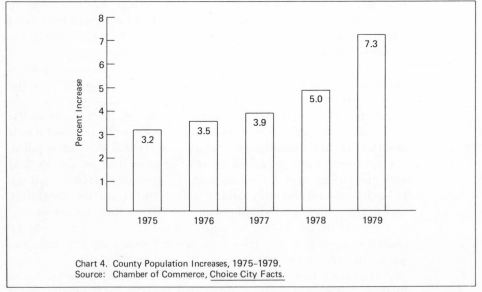

Chart 4. County Population Increases, 1975–1979.
Source: Chamber of Commerce, <u>Choice City Facts.</u>

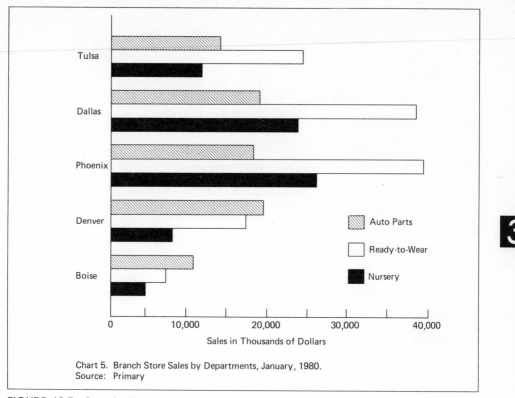

Chart 5. Branch Store Sales by Departments, January, 1980.
Source: Primary

FIGURE 12.7 Bar chart

sands of dollars," or "percentage increase." The chart number is shown to the left of the title, which is placed below the chart. Explanations are placed below the title and above the source note. Data taken from primary research do not require a source note. The entire bar graph is placed within a box.

For clarity, the specific value represented by a bar may be shown within the bar or in proximity to it.

A multiple bar chart shows two or more factors or variables, thus permitting comparisons against a quantitative value. (Example: Branch Store Sales by Departments). Charts containing multiple bars or single bars that are divided into parts are accompanied by a legend that identifies the bars and parts, such as color, diagonal lines, vertical lines, dots, or left and right vertical lines (cross hatches).

A single vertical or horizontal bar may be divided into parts, each representing some part of the entire factor.

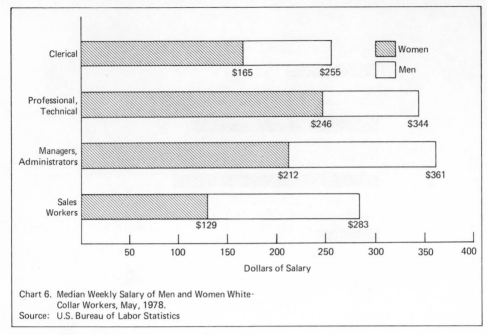

Chart 6. Median Weekly Salary of Men and Women White-
         Collar Workers, May, 1978.
Source: U.S. Bureau of Labor Statistics

FIGURE 12.8 Bar chart

PIE CHART (Fig. 12.9)

A pie chart shows wedges of various sizes corresponding to the quantities that make up the whole (100%). Each wedge on the pie should represent the corresponding quantity of each factor as closely as possible. A compass can be used to draw a circle and to identify points indicating the boundary of each wedge. The first line drawn on the pie extends from the center to the 12 o'clock position. The remaining lines are drawn clockwise from the center to the designated points to show the percentages (and wedge sizes) in decreasing order. The percent figure is shown within the wedge, if possible. The factors are typed or lettered horizontally, adjacent to the wedge each represents.

PICTOGRAMS

Symbols rather than bars represent the quantitative data and the factor being measured: people, coins, bags of grain, and so on.

Each symbol represents a specific number of units. Partial symbols are shown to represent fewer than a designated number of units.

Because this type of presentation is very imprecise, the exact

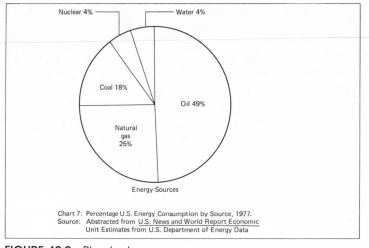

FIGURE 12.9   Pie chart

FIGURE 12.10   Sales districts of Rayburn Publishing Company, 1979.

NOTE: For some illustrations such as flowcharts, templates
can be used to draw the symbols.

Care must be taken not to include more information
than can be properly and clearly presented on the aid.
Crowded letters or symbols reduce the effectiveness
of the aid.

number of units may be shown to the right of or below each symbol line, or the aid may be accompanied by a table that shows the figures.

The pictogram can be presented vertically or horizontally on the page. The decision is based on the length and width of the aid, the amount of data, and the degree of readability.

If this type of aid is prepared by the writer (as opposed to an in-house graphics department), a template can be used to draw the symbols. Because a pictogram is difficult to construct, it is usually used only by writers who have access to a graphics department.

12.4 MISCELLANEOUS GRAPHIC

Maps, organizational charts, schematic diagrams, drawings, flow charts, and other such aids are often used in a business report. The placement and presentation of the number, title, footnote, and source are the same for these aids as for charts (see Fig. 12.10, p. 111).

Horizontal lettering is used to identify the subjects in the illustration. When possible, the lettering should be within boundaries of the geometric figure or illustration (maps and organizational charts, particularly). If a part is too small to include the lettering, a line or arrow can be drawn from the part to the margin where the lettering can be shown clearly.

CHAPTER THIRTEEN

Presenting the Information

To guide the reader through the report, the writer chooses a method to designate the importance of topics and then shows the approach within each topic.

13.1 HEADINGS

Style manuals show various methods of presenting headings; the major differences are in heading location and capitalization. The writer must choose one method and use it consistently throughout the report.

Placement on the page and method of capitalization determine the degree of importance accorded to a heading and therefore to the topic it designates. Rarely are more than five degrees of headings used in a report. A suggested format is shown here for five degrees of headings (see Fig. 13.1, p. 114).

13.2 TOPICS

The topic of a major division makes a significant contribution to the report. Particularly in a long report, this topic should be introduced, discussed, and summarized. To provide continuity, the writer makes a transitional statement relating this topic to the next one (see Text in Chapter Two, p. 29).

FIRST-DEGREE HEADING

(Triple Space)

The first-degree heading is reserved for the title of a report. A first-degree heading is usually shown in capital letters. A triple space follows a first-degree heading. The next line of type may be the first line of a paragraph or the heading of the first major division in the report.

(Triple Sapce)

Second-Degree Heading
(Double Space)

A second-degree heading represents a major division designated by a roman numeral--I, II, and so on--in the outline. This heading may be presented with or without an underscore; the decision must be consistently applied to all headings of this degree. The first letter of each word (except prepositions, conjunctions, and articles) is capitalized. A triple space precedes a second-degree heading, and a double space follows it.

1½"   (Triple Space)   1"

Third-Degree Heading
(Double Space)

A third-degree heading represents the outline divisions designated by capital letters. The first letter of each word (except prepositions, conjunctions, and articles) can be capitalized, or the writer may choose to capitalize only the first letter of the first word. This heading is usually underscored so that it stands out from the following material. A triple space precedes a third-degree heading, and a double space follows it.

(Double Space)

Fourth-degree heading. A fourth-degree heading represents the outline division designated by an arabic number. This heading is underscored and indented the same number of spaces as the report paragraphs are indented. It is followed by a period and two spaces or set off in some other way from the first sentence. A double space precedes a fourth-degree heading.

(Double Space)

A fifth-degree heading represents the outline division designated by a lower-case letter. This heading is underscored and consists of the first word(s) in the sentence. A double space precedes the paragraph that includes this heading.

FIGURE 13.1

LEAD-IN

A lead-in sentence or paragraph is used at the beginning of a main division to introduce the topic to the reader. It also relates the forthcoming sections to the background of the report and the previous topics.

DISCUSSION

Each subdivision of a major division is preceded by a heading that reflects the content of the subdivision. The discussion of the topic may consist of one paragraph or more. Each discussion paragraph should include a topic sentence. If this sentence is the first in the paragraph, it presents the gist of the paragraph and is followed by supporting information. If the topic sentence is the last one in the paragraph, it is preceded by the supporting information which leads to this conclusion.

SUMMARY

The preceding discussion on all topics in this main division is summarized in a sentence (separate from the last discussion paragraph) or short paragraph. The summary is actually a brief conclusion pertinent to the preceding topics.

TRANSITION

The transition from one major division to the next major division may be in the same sentence or paragraph as the summary or in a different sentence or paragraph. The purpose of the transition is to bridge the gap between the two major divisions.

PART FOUR

Documentation

Documentation consists of reference notes identifying the sources from which information has been taken. The entire list of sources presented in a specific, ordered format becomes the bibliography. The documentation of reference sources is a necessary process in research and report writing. Not only is documentation essential under copyright law and common law, but it also lends credibility to the paper.

CHAPTER FOURTEEN

Requirements for Documentation

Passages containing words, ideas, or interpretations not originated by the author must be documented; that is, the author must support these statements with a written reference note giving credit to the originator. Any material taken verbatim, verbatim with omission, paraphrased, condensed, or abstracted from a publication must be supported by a reference note.

14.1 OTHER MEDIA

The process of footnoting and documenting sources used in a report, paper, or thesis is not limited to books and periodical articles. Proper credit must also be given for any information taken not only from published sources but also from sources such as television, radio, lectures, letters, and personal interviews.

14.2 COPYRIGHT LAWS

Copyright law has become an important and controversial subject. What action constitutes a violation of copyright has been uncertain for several years. Until January 1, 1978, when the Copyright Act of 1976 became effective, all copyrighted works were under the protection of the antiquated Copyright Act of 1909.

Copyright is a form of protection for authors of literary works, music, plays, and the like. Thirteen classes of items, as listed in Title 17, *United States Code,* can be copyrighted:

Books
Periodicals
Lectures or other productions to be presented orally
Dramatic and dramatico-musical compositions
Musical compositions
Maps (cartography)
Works of art including jewelry, paintings, weavings, and sculpture
Drawings of a technical character
Photographs
Prints
Pictorial illustrations and commercial prints
Motion-picture photoplays
Motion pictures other than photoplays

To be copyrighted, a work need not be in published form such as an item that is for sale or made available to the public. When the work, such as a company report or student paper, is created, it is protected by the common law literary property form of copyright. This form of protection is effective while the work is unpublished.

The other form of protection is the statutory copyright. Only these specific items can be afforded the statutory copyright protection:

Musical compositions
Dramas
Art works
Drawings and sculptures of a scientific or technical nature
Photos
Motion pictures
Oral works

To be under the statutory copyright, however, the item must be registered in the Copyright Office.

14.3 FAIR USE

Perhaps the most recognized judicial doctrine pertaining to the copyright is that of "fair use." Fair use is a rather nebulous term which enables certain copyrighted works to be used without the use being deemed an infringement. However, extensive use of copyrighted materials in educational instruction and some other applications calls for a more definitive concept of fair use.

Title 17 of the *United States Code*, Section 106 (17 U.S.C. Sec. 106 (1976)) outlines the exclusive rights given the copyright holder. Section 107 outlines the exemptions to those rights. The most critical exemption is that pertaining to photocopying of published items such as periodicals. Basically, Section 108(d) allows for one copy to be made of the copyrighted works only if the copy becomes the property of the user for use in private research or study. Also included in this one-copy fair use doctrine are such items as television newscasts and documentaries.

The one exemption to the single-copy rule involves classroom or face-to-face teaching. In this limited situation, the teacher may make one copy of the copyrighted item per student in the class.

14.4 INFRINGEMENT, PLAGIARISM, AND PIRACY

Infringement of a copyright is defined as the copying or appropriating of "original" work of the author or copyright proprietor (*Weitzenkorn v. Lesser*, 50 Cal. 2d 778, 256 P.2d 947). Title 17, Sections 101, 134, 135 and 154–156, of the *United States Code* provide that anyone who infringes the copyright of any work protected by the Copyright Law is subject to injunctive relief restraining the infringement. He or she is liable for damages suffered by the copyright holder due to the infringement, as well as for profits which the infringer may have made from the infringement. It also levies criminal charges for willful infringement resulting in profit.

Another term often associated with copyright is piracy. Piracy is the willful stealing of another's work for the purpose of turning it into one's own property. The act of piracy often occurs with short stories of publication quality and musical recordings. Money or monetary advancement is generally involved.

Piracy is rather difficult to prove because original work papers and notes are usually discarded by the author when the product is finished and put in final form. Without proof, such as work papers and rough drafts, it is hard to prove rightful ownership. However, if the piece under question were publishable and the author had submitted an outline or other similar paper relating to the contents of the item to an editor, the rightful ownership possibly could then be proved.

Plagiarism is the practice of wrongfully using a publication or an idea in literature, music, or art as one's own. This practice often occurs in report writing. To avoid plagiarizing material, one should document and footnote properly any sentence, parts of sentences, and any ideas which are not the author's own.

14.5 SUMMARY

Plagiarism, infringement, and piracy are often used interchangeably. Perhaps the main differences among the three are:

1. Plagiarism is the copying of someone's work which either has or has not been given protection by the Copyright Law. Generally, plagiarism occurs when a sentence, part of one, or even a whole paragraph or more is "lifted" from a source and used in a paper without being footnoted.

2. Infringement is the copying of someone's work (either part or whole) without permission from the copyright holder. The most common type of infringement is that dealing with photocopying articles without the holder's permission.

3. Piracy is the willful stealing of a whole work. This theft usually involves the "stealing" of an article or short story from the original author and passing it on as one's own.

All three are punishable in the courts.

CHAPTER FIFTEEN

Reference Notes

A reference note gives details which identify a source the author has used. A reference note placed at the bottom of the page on which the reference occurs is a "footnote." If the reference is placed on a separate page at the end of the report, it is called an "endnote" or "note."

Footnotes and endnotes may be used in these forms: (1) as reference notes to identify primary and secondary sources, (2) as content notes to explain a term, concept, or statement in the text, (3) as acknowledgment notes to credit a source that was omitted in the acknowledgments section or to explain the contribution more specifically, and (4) as a consolidated reference note to present two or more references more concisely.

15.1 NUMBERING FOOTNOTES AND ENDNOTES

Each passage to be documented is designated by an arabic number, and a corresponding arabic number identifies its footnote or endnote. Consecutive arabic numbers (beginning with 1) are used throughout the report, with these exceptions: (1) if the chapters are long, reference notes may be numbered consecutively (beginning with 1) within each chapter or report part; (2) if numerous content notes are used in the report, they may be designated on each page by asterisks, daggers, or letters.

To identify the word, phrase, clause, sentence, or paragraph that is to be documented, an arabic number is placed in a superior position (raised slightly above the line) and as close as possible to the passage it identifies. This number follows all end-of-sentence punctuation and all internal punctuation. The arabic number follows the punctuation after a quotation within the text and follows the punctuation after the last sentence in a block quotation.

An arabic number should not be placed in any position where it will distract the reader; for example, (1) between the subject and verb, (2) after a colon preceding the material to be documented, or (3) after an author's name.

Style manuals for various disciplines illustrate footnotes and endnotes differently. The author must select one style and use it consistently.

The following sections illustrate (1) reference notes, (2) content notes, (3) acknowledgment notes, and (4) consolidated notes.

REFERENCE NOTES

Reference notes in the form of footnotes and endnotes provide a complete identification of the source. At the minimum, a first reference note gives the name of the author(s), title of the publication, publishing information, and page number(s) (see Fig. 15.1).

Endnotes are gaining in acceptance and popularity as a documentation method for all but the most formal reports and academic degree research papers (see Fig. 15.2).

CONTENT NOTES

A content footnote contains one or more complete sentences of explanation (see Fig. 15.3).

ACKNOWLEDGMENT NOTE

By using an acknowledgment note, the author accomplishes two goals: (1) calling attention to a specific contribution, and (2) eliminating distracting information from the text, thereby making it more concise and readable (see Fig. 15.4).

to determine the demographics of the population in the region

identified as the Pacific Northwest.[2]
(single space)
(double space)

[1]Ronald W. Hasty and R. Ted Will, Marketing (Scranton: Harper
& Row, 1975), p. 47.
(double space)

[2]John R. Stuteville, Marketing in a Consumer-Oriented Society
(Belmont, Calif.: Wadsworth Publishing Co., 1975), p. 82.

1½"

1"

7
6
5
4
3
2
1

1"

FOOTNOTE PLACEMENT

1. Single-space after the last typed line on the page.
2. Type a 1½" line.
3. Double-space.
4. Indent the same number of spaces that the text paragraphs are indented.
5. Type the arabic number in a superior position.
6. Type the footnote single spaced.
7. Double-space between footnotes.
8. The last line of the footnote should be no lower than line 7 (one inch) from the bottom of the page.

If absolutely necessary, part of a footnote may be carried over to the next page. Under these circumstances, it is continued (without indenting) a double space below the typed line.

The footnote should be placed at the bottom of the page even if the page contains only a few lines of type.

Two or more short footnotes may be typed on the same line but must be separated by at least three spaces.

FIGURE 15.1

4

CONSOLIDATED REFERENCE

This type of reference eliminates the need for two or more references, each documenting the same passage or item of information. A semicolon separates each complete reference (see Fig. 15.5).

Endnotes

(Double Space)

[1]Ivan Flores, <u>Data Structure and Management</u>, 2nd ed. (Englewood Cliffs, N.J.: Prentice-Hall, Inc., 1977), p. 105.

(Double Space)

[2]Thomas R. Prince, <u>Information Systems for Management Planning and Control</u>, 3rd ed. (Homewood, Ill.: Richard D. Irwin, Inc., 1975), p. 97.

1½"   1"

FIGURE 15.2

---

of the more recent developments has been the establishment of facili-

ties management groups which perform a systems analysis function.[1]

(Single space)

(Double space)

[1]A facilities management group serves in the capacity of an outside consultant, establishes the function, staffs it temporarily, and trains the company employees to take over the activities.

1½"   1"

1"

FIGURE 15.3

(Single space)

(Double space)

[1]The author is indebted to Josephine Weaver, librarian at Ft. Devons, Ayer, Massachusetts, for providing the statistics on the typical library categories selected by Army personnel enrolled in degree programs.

1½"   1"

1"

FIGURE 15.4

FIGURE 15.5

At least three recent books are used both as classroom texts in junior

colleges and as supplementary reference in business training programs.[5]

---

[5]Arnold Rosen and Rosemary Fielden, <u>Word Processing</u> (Englewood Cliffs, N.J.: Prentice-Hall, Inc., 1977); Paula B. Cecil, <u>Word Processing in the Modern Office</u> (Menlo Park, Calif.: Cummings Publishing Company, 1976); Joyce Kupsh et al., <u>Word Processing in American Business</u> (New York: John Wiley & Sons, 1978).

1½"   1"

1"

15.2 OTHER REFERENCE NOTES

Under certain circumstances, a passage may be documented within the text rather than in a footnote or endnote.

PARENTHETICAL NOTE

Parenthetical notes may be used if the author has only a few sources to document. This method is used primarily in papers of a scientific or technical nature. The parenthetical note (or note plus text) should include the same information that would be included in a footnote for this source. The order of the items in the parenthetical note depends on the part of the documentation that is included in the text itself. Therefore, the style of parenthetical note is not uniform.

Because the author's names are used in the text, the remainder of the information is placed within parentheses.

Example 1:

> Barbara N. Weaver and Wiley L. Bishop (The Corporate Memory, New York: John Wiley & Sons, 1974, p. 37) describe. . . .

A second reference to a source may be documented with only the authors' names and the page number. The "p." can be omitted.

Example 2a:

> The multinational corporation with its world-wide interests and complex communications network is subject to regulation at all levels of government as well as by foreign governments; it cannot survive without accurate, immediate documentation of all transactions, events, and activities (Weaver and Bishop, 28).

If more than one publication written by the same authors is used, a shortened title or the date of the publication is included.

Example 2b:

> . . . immediate documentation of all transactions, events, and activities (Weaver and Bishop, Memory, 28).

Example 2c

> . . . immediate documentation of all transactions, events, and activities (Weaver and Bishop, 1974, 28).

The writer may use a numbering system to designate a source. In this system, the bibliographic items are numbered, and each documented passage is given a number that corresponds to the bibliographic entry. Following the comma after this number is the page number(s). The numbering system is adaptable to a variety of uses.

Example 3:

> ... immediate documentation of all transactions, events, and activities (12, 28).

CROSS REFERENCES

A cross reference is used (1) to refer the reader to another part of the paper and (2) to introduce or reintroduce an illustration or an example. The note is placed in parentheses located within the sentence or following it (see Parentheses, p. 293). Cross reference notes are used throughout this book to direct the reader's attention to other portions. In the second sentence of this paragraph, the cross reference directs the reader to a section which contains an explanation and illustration of parentheses enclosing cross references.

The use of "above" or "below" is discouraged because in the final draft of the paper, the information to which the writer refers may be on a preceding or succeeding page rather than above or below the point where this statement is made.

4

CHAPTER SIXTEEN

First Notes

First notes for books, periodicals, and other sources are as complete as possible so that the reader can locate the source and find within it the passage that is being documented.

16.1 BOOKS

The items to be included in a first reference note can usually be found on the front and back of the title page. In a reference note, these items are separated by commas with one exception: no comma precedes the left parenthesis shown before the facts of publication. Reference note items are usually shown in this order:

  1. Author

  2. Title

*3. Name of editor, compiler, or translator

*4. Name of Preface, Introduction, or Foreword author(s)

*5. Name of series, its volume and number

  6. Name or number of edition other than the first one

*7. Total number of volumes

  8. Facts of publication (city, publisher, date)

*9. Volume number

10. Page number

* These items are used only if the passage or nature of the source requires this identification. Items not found on the title page (or the reverse side) may be located on other pages in the front matter or in the card catalog.

The standard form for documentation of books follows. The code in parentheses is keyed to a representative reference note in section 16.1, Books: Examples, pages 135 to 138.

1. *Author(s).* The author's first name, middle initial or name, and surname are listed in this order (see Example 1, p. 135). Initials are shown in lieu of the first name and the middle name only when the author is better recognized by the initials than the names. For a book written by two or three authors, the names are recorded in the same order in which they are shown on the title page (see Examples 2 and 3, p. 135).

If a book is prepared by four or more authors, the name of the author shown first on the title page is listed first in the reference note. This name is followed by "et al." or the English translation "and others" (see Example 4, p. 135).

A book may be prepared by a group of people representing a governmental body, a business firm, an institution, a committee, an association, or like entity. Such a book is said to have corporate authorship. The name of the corporate author may be shown on the title page or elsewhere in the front matter. Occasionally, the corporate author is also the publisher. A book by a corporate author may be cited in more than one way (see Example 5, p. 135).

2. *Titles.* The title of the book is copied from the title page. Regardless of the type in which the title is set, in the reference note it is capitalized according to the rules for the capitalization of titles (see Titles, p. 267).

On the title page, a title is sometimes shown on two lines and without punctuation. The writer needs to punctuate the title so that it is readable and logical. For example, a title may be shown on the title page as follows:

CONTROLLING COSTS
A Management Approach

In the reference note, the title should appear like this (two spaces follow the colon):

Controlling Costs: a Management Approach

Both the title and subtitle are underscored (including all spaces and punctuation). A comma follows the title unless the next item is shown in parentheses.

In rare circumstances, if a title is extremely long, three dots (ellipsis) may be inserted in place of the omitted words; however, the complete title must be shown in the bibliography.

A chapter title is needed only when the writer refers to an entire chapter. This title is shown in quotation marks following the comma after the author's name. The comma following the title is placed inside the last set of quotation marks. The words in the title are capitalized according to the rules for the capitalization of titles (see Titles, p. 267).

"Constructing Short and Special Reports,"

3. *Editor, Compiler, or Translator.* The name of the editor, compiler, or translator should be included in a reference note if this individual's name and title are printed on the title page. In a reference note, an abbreviation is used to designate the title.

The name of an editor, compiler, or translator is shown in the authorship position of the reference note when

a. The book does not have a named author, such as a book of reading (see Example 6, p. 136).

b. The writer is citing from a contribution made by an editor, compiler, or translator or that person's contribution is emphasized (see Example 7, p. 136).

If the writer cites a passage by the book author, the name of the editor, compiler, or translator follows the book title (see Example 8, p. 136).

A book containing readings or cases includes contributions by many authors, although the book itself does not have a named author. A reference to an article in this book lists the article author's name first. Names of editors, compilers, or others precede the facts of publication (see Example 9, p. 136).

4. *Preface, Foreword, or Introduction Author.* The name of the preface, foreword, or introduction author is included in the reference note if this author is named on the title page (see Example 10, p. 137). If, however, a passage from this person's contribution is cited, this person's name is placed first in the reference note (see Example 11, p. 137).

5. *Series; Multivolume Work*

a. A series is infinite because a publisher (or corporate entity) can continue to publish successive books, pamphlets, or monographs in series as long as economically feasible and justifiable. An entire series may be prepared on one topic, or each part may be devoted to different topics pertinent to a discipline. The identification of a series may be a name, title, and number, or only a number. In a reference note, the series identification follows the source title (see Examples 12 and 13, p. 137).

b. A multivolume work is finite; the publisher and author(s) have determined at the outset the number of volumes to be included. The volumes are usually pertinent to the same topic. The author(s) and titles of each volume may vary; that is, (1) each volume may be written by the same author and have the same title (see Example 8, p. 136), (2) each volume may be written by the same author but have a different title (see Example 15, p. 138), or (3) each volume may be written by a different author and have a different title. The entire work may be cited (see Example 14, p. 138), or one volume may be cited (see Example 15, p. 138).

6. *Edition.* The edition of a book is shown on the title page or the copyright page. An edition may be designated by a number, by revision information, by a name, or as a paperback publication. Because the content of different editions is not the same, the first reference note must list the edition (other than the first numbered edition) being cited.

In a book, a numbered edition may be designated as "second edition," "third edition," "fourth edition," and so on, but in a reference note, the identifying words are abbreviated to "2d ed.," "3d ed.," and "4th ed." The edition is listed immediately preceding the facts of publication (see Example 2, p. 135).

Some books are designated as revisions. The revision information may include such phrases as "revised edition," "second revised edition," and others. In a reference note, these words are abbreviated; for example, "rev. ed." and "2d rev. ed." This information is listed immediately preceding the facts of publication (see Example 16, p. 138).

For a paperback book which the writer has cited (as opposed to its hardback counterpart), the paperback publisher is listed after the hardback publisher within the facts of publication segment (see Example 17, p. 138).

7. *Number of Volumes.* A reference note that cites a multiple-volume work lists the number of volumes immediately preceding the facts of publication (see Examples 7 and 14, pp. 136 and 138).

8. *Facts of Publication.* The facts of publication include the city where the source was published, the name of the publisher, and the date of publication. This information is printed on the title page or on the copyright page. In a reference note, each item is separated from the next by a comma, and the entire segment is enclosed within parentheses. A period follows the right parenthesis if the citation does not include any more items. If the citation includes a page number or a volume and page number(s), a comma follows the right parenthesis.

a. City of Publication. If more than one city is named, select the first one as the city of publication. The name of the city is followed by a colon and two spaces.

(New York:

If the name of the city is not well known, follow it with a comma, the standard abbreviation of the state name, a colon, and two spaces:

(Fort Collins, Colo.:

Should neither the title page nor the copyright page show a city of publication, list "n.p." (no place) as the first item after the left parenthesis. Follow the abbreviation with a colon and two spaces if the publisher is named next and with a comma if the publisher is not named next.

(n.p.:   Albers Publishing Company, Inc.,

b. Name of Publisher. In the reference note, the publisher's name may be listed as it appears on the title page, or it may be abbreviated for conciseness. In addition, the word "The" is omitted when it is the initial word; "Inc." and "Ltd." following the publisher's name may also be omitted. The word "Company" may be abbreviated as "Co.," and the ampersand (&) may be used in place of "and."

(Chicago: (The) Univ. (ersity) of Chicago Press,
(Cambridge, Mass.: (The) M.I.T. Press,

For a book that has been printed by a subsidiary of another publisher, the reference note should list first the publisher, and then the subsidiary.

(Beverly Hills: Benziger Bruce & Glencoe, Inc., Glencoe Press,

Should the title page or the copyright page not show the name of a publisher, use "n.p." (no publisher) after the colon following the city of publication.

(Denton, Tex.: n.p.,

c.   Date of Publication. The date (year) of publication is usually shown on the title page or the copyright page. If more than one date is shown, use the latest one. When neither page carries a copyright date, use the abbreviation "n.d." (no date).

(Cincinnati: South-Western Publishing Co., n.d.),

9.   *Volume Number.* In citing a volume of a multivolume work, list the volume number after the comma following the right parenthesis that encloses the facts of publication.

Omit the abbreviations "vol.," "p.," and "pp." when both the volume and page numbers are listed in adjacent positions. Use a colon after the volume number to distinguish it from the page number (see Example 7, p. 136).

10.   *Page Number(s).* The page number on which a passage appears must be included in the reference note. The page number follows the comma after the right parenthesis (unless a volume number precedes it). As the page number ends the citation, it is followed by a period. Use the abbreviation "p." to refer to a passage on one page and "pp." to refer to a passage that covers two or more pages. Inclusive pages are listed as follows:

pp. 9–99.   pp. 87–88.   pp. 672–73.   pp. 401–2.

[1]Peter Ferdinand Drucker, Management: Tasks, Responsibilities, and Practices (New York: Harper & Row, 1974), pp. 309–10.

If a page being cited does not show a number, use "n. pag." (no page).

), n. pag.

Pages that contain preliminary matter (foreword, preface, acknowledgments, and so on) are often numbered with small roman numerals. Show the complete roman numeral.

), pp. viii–ix.

These examples are keyed to the explanations in section 16.1, Books: Standard Form, pages 130 to 134.

In typewritten footnotes, one space follows a period and a comma, and two spaces follow a colon—with these exceptions: No space is used after a period within an abbreviation (s.v.) or after a period that is immediately followed by a comma (Bros.,) or by a colon (Colo.:). No space follows a colon that immediately precedes a page number (2:11).

1. *One Author*

> ¹Frederick Winslow Taylor, <u>The Principles of Scientific Management</u> (New York: Harper & Bros., 1911), p. 29.

2. *Two Authors.* Separate the names by "and"; use a comma after the name of the second author.

> ²Robert N. Corley and Robert L. Black, <u>The Legal Environment of Business,</u> 3d ed. (New York: <u>McGraw-Hill,</u> 1973), pp. 310–11.

3. *Three Authors.* Separate the first author's name from the second author's name by a comma. Use a comma before "and." Follow the third author's name with a comma.

> ³William W. Pyle, John Arch White, and Kermit D. Larson, <u>Fundamental Accounting Principles,</u> 8th ed. (Homewood, Ill.: Richard D. Irwin, Inc., 1978), p. 87.

4. *Four or More Authors.* Use the term "et al." or "and others" after the name of the author who is listed first on the title page. Follow the term with a comma.

> ⁴Joyce Kupsh et al., <u>Machine Transcription and Dictation</u> (New York: John Wiley & Sons, 1978), pp. 63–67.

5. *Corporate Author.* Cite either the name of the corporate author or the book title first. If the name of the corporate author is cited first, follow it with a comma and the book title. If the book title is cited first, follow it with a comma, the word "by," and the name of the corporate author. When the complete name of the corporate author is included in the book title, use it only once—in the authorship position or in the title.

⁵AICPA, APB Accounting Principles in Effect as of June 1973, 2 vols. (Chicago: Commerce Clearing House, 1973), 1:110–11.

6. *No Named Author; the Editor, Compiler, or Translator Is Cited.* Show the editor's, compiler's, or translator's name in the authorship position. Show this person's title in abbreviated form (ed., comp., trans.) followed by a comma. If two or more persons having the same title are involved, add an "s" to the abbreviation.

⁶Henry L. Tosi, Robert J. House, and Marvin D. Dunnette, eds., Managerial Motivation and Compensation (East Lansing, Mich.: Bureau of Business and Economic Research Studies, Michigan State University, 1972).

7. *Named Author; the Editor, Compiler, or Translator Is Cited.* If the citation is from an editor's, compiler's, or translator's contribution, show the name of this person in the authorship position. Show the author's name preceded by the word "by" following the book title.

⁷Joseph Stiglitz, ed., The Collected Scientific Papers of Paul A. Samuelson, by Paul A. Samuelson, 2 vols. (Cambridge, Mass.: M.I.T. Press, 1966), 2:10.

8. *Named Author and Book Has an Editor, Compiler, or Translator.* List the book author and the title; then show the appropriate abbreviation (ed., comp., trans.) followed by the name of the contributor. The abbreviation in this location means "edited by," "compiled by," or "translated by"; therefore, do not show it in plural form.

⁸Paul A. Samuelson, The Collected Scientific Papers of Paul A. Samuelson, ed. Joseph Stiglitz, 2 vols. (Cambridge, Mass.: M.I.T. Press, 1966), 1:75.

9. *Named Article Author in Book Containing a Collection of Articles.* List the article author's name followed by a comma. The title of the article is in quotation marks; a comma precedes the last set of quotation marks. The title of the book is preceded by "in." List the editor (compiler or translator), if any, and the edition number, if any, preceding the facts of publication.

⁹V. F. Ridgway, "Dysfunctional Consequences of Performance Measurement," in Managerial Motivation and

Compensation, ed. Henry L. Tosi, Robert J. House, and Marvin D. Dunnette (East Lansing, Mich.: Bureau of Business and Economic Research Studies, Michigan State University, 1972), pp. 147–49.

10. *Preface, Foreword, or Introduction Author.* Show this author's contribution and name following the comma after the book title. The words "with a" may be inserted before the contribution.

[10]Steven P. Zell, Unemployment Insurance: Programs, Procedures, and Problems, with a Foreword by Roger Guffy (Kansas City, Mo.: Research Division, Federal Reserve Bank of Kansas City, 1977).

11. *Preface, Foreword, or Introduction Author is Cited.* Show this person's name as the first item in the reference note. Follow it with the contribution surrounded by commas. The book author's name preceded by the word "by" follows the book title.

[11]Roger Guffy, Foreword to Unemployment Insurance: Programs, Procedures, and Problems, by Steven P. Zell (Kansas City, Mo.: Research Division, Federal Reserve Bank of Kansas City, 1977).

12. *Named Series.* Show the series title following the comma after the book title. Capitalize the words in the title according to the rules for capitalization of titles (see Titles, p. 267). If the series has an editor, name the person(s) after the comma following the series title.

The names of some series include the publisher's complete name (especially if a corporate agency is the publisher). Under these circumstances, do not repeat that name in the facts of publication.

[12]C. William Emory, Business and Research Methods, Irwin Series in Information and Decision Sciences, ed. Robert Fetter and Claude McMillan (Homewood, Ill.: Richard D. Irwin, Inc., 1976), p. 175.

13. *Named and Numbered Series.* Show the series number (with "number" abbreviated as "No.") after the comma following the series title. If the series has only a number, show the number after the comma following the book title.

[13]Enzo R. Grilli, The Future for Hard Fibers and Competition from Synthetics, World Bank Staff Occasional Papers, No. 19 (Baltimore: Johns Hopkins University Press, 1975).

14. *Entire Multivolume Work Cited.* Show the number of volumes immediately before the facts of publication. Use an arabic number to designate the number of volumes in the set. Abbreviate "volumes" as "vols." Note that the volumes in the example were published in different years.

> [14]Alfred E. Kahn, The Economics of Regulation: Principles and Institutions, 2 vols. (New York: John Wiley & Sons, Inc., 1970–71).

15. *One Volume of a Set Is Cited; Each Volume Has Different Title.* List the name of the volume author and then the name of the cited volume preceded by a comma. Show the number of the volume followed by "of" preceding the multivolume title, which is underscored.

> Alfred E. Kahn, Institutional Issues, vol. 2 of The Economics of Regulation: Principles and Institutions, 2 vols. (New York: John Wiley & Sons, Inc., 1971), pp. 47–56.

16. *Revised Edition.* List the edition in abbreviated form preceding the facts of publication.

> [16]Doris E. Whalen, The Secretary's Handbook, rev. ed. (New York: Harcourt Brace Jovanovich, Inc., 1973), p. 141.

17. *Paperback Edition.* List the publisher of the paperback edition and its publication date after the comma following the name of the hardback publisher.

> [17]Robin Moore, The Fifth Estate (New York: Doubleday & Co., Bantam Books, 1974), p. 90.

16.2 PERIODICALS

A periodical is published on a regular basis: daily, weekly, monthly, bimonthly, quarterly, or at other regular intervals.

STANDARD FORM

The standard form for the first reference to an article includes all or most of these items:

1. Author's name
2. Article title
3. Periodical title
4. Volume number
5. Volume date
6. Page number

The listing of the volume number, date, and page number is not consistent for different types of publications. Note the publications listed in the section Periodicals: Examples, pages 140 to 141.

1. *Author.* The name of the author(s) is shown on the same page as the article title or at the end of the article. The name is listed in the customary order and followed by a comma (see Books: Standard Form—Authors, p. 130).

> Adam Smith,
> William W. Pyle and John A. White,
> C. Robert Patty, Albert Haring, and Harvey L. Vredenberg,

An article prepared by more than three authors is cited with the first named author as the first item in the reference note followed by "et al." or "and others."

> Deane Carter et al.,

If the article does not have a named author, it was probably prepared by a staff writer. Under these circumstances, begin the reference note with the title of the article.

2. *Article Title.* The article title is placed within quotation marks and followed by a comma, which is placed inside the last set of quotation marks (see Books: Standard Form—Title, pp. 130 to 131). The title is capitalized according to the rules for the capitalization of titles (see Titles, p. 267).

If a title appears on two lines and is not punctuated, insert the proper punctuation to make it meaningful.

> The Human Resource Center Concept
> The AT&T Experience
> *change to*
> "The Human Resource Center Concept:
> The AT&T Experience,"

3. *Periodical Title.* The periodical title is underscored and follows the comma after the article title. It is capitalized according to the rules for capitalization of titles (see Titles, p. 267). A comma follows the title unless a volume number is listed.

U.S. News & World Report,

4. *Volume Number.* If a periodical is identified by a volume number, that number is shown after the periodical title. Some writers, however, do not insert the volume number if the periodical is a nationally circulated popular magazine. When a periodical has both a volume number and an issue number, only the volume number need be listed in the reference note.

5. *Volume Date.* The date of issue is shown in parentheses after the volume number, if any. No comma precedes the left parenthesis. If the publication does not show a volume number, the date is listed after the periodical title. Dates are not listed in the same way for all publications that are issued periodically.

Volume number: 42 (May 1979),
No volume number: U.S. News & World Report, 7 July 1979,

6. *Page Numbers.* When a volume number precedes the parentheses enclosing the date, a colon is placed one space after the right parenthesis and immediately preceding the page number(s). The abbreviations "vol.," "p.," and "pp." are omitted.

42 (September 1979):14–17.

If the volume number is omitted, the date identifies the issue and is not placed in parentheses.

December 1979, pp. 14–17.

EXAMPLES

This section provides examples of reference notes for various publications that are issued on a regular basis.

1. *Weekly Magazine; Author Given.* Place a comma after each item of identifying information and a period at the end of the reference note.

[1]Caroline Mayer, "Accountants—Cleaning up America's Mystery Profession," U.S. News & World Report, 19 December 1977, pp. 39–42.

2. *Weekly Magazine; No Author Given.* Begin the reference note with the article title.

[2]"A Partial Recovery by the Cities," Business Week, 22 January 1979, pp. 94–96.

3. *Monthly Publication.*

[3]Robert Rush, "MIS Planning in Distributed Data Processing Systems," Journal of Systems Management 30 (August 1979):17–27.

4. *Bimonthly Publication.*

[4]William L. Trombetta, "Product Liability: What New Court Rulings Mean for Management," Business Horizons 22 (August 1979):67–72.

5. *Quarterly Publication.*

[5]Seymour J. Pomrenze, "The Freedom of Information Act and the Privacy Acts and the Records Manager—Some Considerations," ARMA Records Management Quarterly 10 (July 1976):5–9, 14.

6. *Daily Newspaper.* In newspapers that have two or more city editions as well as editions for suburban areas, identify the edition after the name of the newspaper. Then list in order the date, section, page, and column. If the city of publication is not included in the name of the newspaper, list it in parentheses following the name. If the newspaper has a large national circulation, such as *The Wall Street Journal,* the city name may be omitted.

[6]Michael Weinstein, "The Crowded World of Urban Supermarkets," New York Times, Late City Ed., 18 December 1977, sec. 8, p. 1, col. 1.

7. *Weekly Newsletter.* Follow the order for a magazine, including a volume number if one exists.

[7]Moody's Investors Service, "An Encouraging Signal from Consumer Credit Data," Moody's Bond Survey 71 (13 August 1979):934.

16.3 MISCELLANEOUS SOURCES

Many sources from which a researcher gathers information do not fall into the category of books or periodical publications. Examples of such sources are brochures, cassettes, microfilms, and computer programs. However, when these sources are used to provide evidence or support, they must be documented.

STANDARD FORM

The format of reference notes for books and periodicals has become standardized to a great extent. On the other hand, for most of the nonpaper media, the documentation is shown differently in various style guides. Therefore, the writer should follow one style guide consistently and document similar sources uniformly. Also, the writer must use some creativity and judgment in determining what information is essential to identify a source sufficiently for the reader.

Although an explanation accompanies the examples, these guidelines can be used in making decisions regarding the items to include and the order in which they should be listed.

1. *Author.* List the author's name first. Do not use a term such as "letter," "lecture," or "interview" in the first position. When possible, avoid naming an author more than twice—in the first position, in the title, and in the facts of publication.

For some sources, such as films and cassettes, the first item listed may be the name of a lecturer or speaker, especially if that person is prominent.

2. *Title.* Generally speaking, the title of a complete published work is underscored, and the title of a part is placed within quotation marks. When no title exists and the writer provides one, it is capitalized according to the rules for capitalization of titles (see Titles, p. 267), but it is not placed within quotation marks. The title of an unpublished work is placed within quotation marks.

3. *Facts of Publication.* For some media, the producer, distributor, or manufacturer's name is used in lieu of "publisher."

4. *Additional Information.* The nature of some sources requires that additional information such as special features, catalog number, or other significant data be provided to identify the source fully, particularly if the reader may need the information.

The examples given here cover most of the nonprinted sources and some specialized printed sources commonly used in business.

1. *Brochure.* List the items in the standard format for a book: author, title, facts of publication, and page number. If an item is not shown, list the next item in order. When a brochure is identified by a number, list the number after the comma following the title. To avoid redundancy when the corporate author is also the publishing agency, use the name in the authorship position only.

> [1]Consumers Union, <u>Consumer Reports</u>, No. BR21 (Orangeburg, N.Y., n.d.).

2. *Cassette (Audiotape or Videotape).* For one cassette (or more than one, none of which is separately named or numbered), List the items in the standard format for a book, substituting applicable items as shown here:

- a. Editor, speaker, or lecturer, if named
- b. Cassette title, underscored
- c. Producer, director, or other manager, if named
- d. Facts of publication in parentheses
- e. Catalog numbers
- f. Physical features in parentheses

> [2]Chris Argyris, <u>Argyris on Organization</u> (San Jose: Lansford Publishing Co., 1978), 942NN (4 videotape cassettes).

Items (e) and (f) may be omitted when the information is expected to be of little value to the reader. Under these circumstances, the writer should show the reference note as follows so that the reader is aware of the medium:

> [2]Chris Argyris, <u>Argyris on Organization</u> (San Jose: Lansford Publishing Co., 1978) (videotaped).

3. *Cassettes: An Alternate Documentation.* If the occasion when the cassette was shown is more important than the facts of publication, catalog number, and features, place the appropriate information within parentheses in lieu of the former facts.

[3]Freda Clark, <u>Management Techniques for Women</u> (2 videotaped cassettes shown at the national convention of student chapters, Administrative Management Society, New Orleans, 17 August 1978).

4. *Cassette Guidebook.* A guidebook providing narrative description or verbatim dialog may accompany a cassette. List the items in the standard format for a book, inserting the producer's or director's name before the facts of publication.

[4]Karen Sterkel, ed., <u>A Viewer's Guide: A Dialog between Harold Koontz & C. West Churchman</u>, dir. Morton Kotlar (Fort Collins, Colo.: Videodocumentary Clearing House, College of Business, Colorado State University, 1978), p. 7.

5. *Cassette Series (Named or Numbered) with Separate Titles for Each Cassette.* The title of the entire collection is underscored and followed by a comma. The title of the series is neither underscored nor in quotation marks, but it is followed by a comma. If an individual cassette is numbered, list the number (followed by a colon) before the individual cassette title, which is placed within quotation marks. Omit the catalog number and special features if the reader is not expected to need them.

[5]<u>Motivation and Personal Skills Development</u>, The Smile of Success, Tape 5: "Personal Development: Time Use" (Roanoke, Tex.: Cassettes Unlimited, n.d.), #299 (12 videotape cassettes).

6. *Computer Program.* The title and description of a computer program is given in the methods section of a report. If, however, data from various sources need to be distinguished within the report body, use this form.

[6]Statistical Package for the Social Sciences (SPSS) (documentation by McGraw-Hill Publishing Co.; produced and distributed by Northwestern University, 1975).

7. *Dictionary (General).* Do not list the page number in a source that is compiled with entries in alphabetical order. The city of publication and name of the publisher are usually omitted on well-known reference works of a general nature. The year of a first edition is shown in parentheses. For second and succeeding editions, the edition number or year is shown without parentheses.

List the items in this order: dictionary title; edition; s.v.—sub verbo, meaning "under the word"—and dictionary entry in quotation marks. No punctuation separates s.v. from the entry.

> [7]The American Heritage Dictionary of the English Language, 1975 ed., s.v. "account executive."

8. *Dictionary (Specialized).* For a specialized dictionary, use the standard format for a book and add the s.v. entry at the end.

> [8]Donald Moffat, Economics Dictionary (New York: Elsevier Scientific Publishing Co., 1976), s.v. "duopoly."

9. *Dissertation (Unpublished).* The titles of unpublished works are enclosed within quotation marks. The word "dissertation" may be abbreviated "diss."

List the items in this order: author; title; in parentheses—the degree for which the dissertation was written, the university that conferred the degree, and the year the dissertation was approved; and the page number.

> [9]Ruebens da Costa Santos, "Relative Product Evaluation: An Experimental Study" (Ph.D. diss., University of Texas at Austin, 1977), p. 18.

10. *Dissertation Abstracts (DA)* and *Dissertation Abstracts International (DAI).* This named entry is included among the sources because it is widely accepted by scholars and business researchers as a concise guide to completed research in educational institutions.

The title was *Dissertation Abstracts* prior to 1969; with the 1969 issue, the title was changed to *Dissertation Abstracts International.* This multivolume work is divided into two series: "A" covers humanities and social sciences; "B," the sciences. The first volume of the divided series is No. 27.

List in this order: author, dissertation title, *DA* or *DAI,* volume number, year in parentheses, page number, degree-granting institution in parentheses.

> [10]Aaron Samuel Gurwitz, "Local Taxation and the Dynamics of Metropolitan Property Values," DAI 38 (1977) 5620A (Stanford University).

11. *Encyclopedia.* Omit the page number and volume number for a work that is compiled in alphabetical order. Use s.v. (*sub verbo*— "under the word") to identify an entry. List the entry author (see Dictionary, p. 144).

List in this order: title of work, edition, s.v. and the entry in quotation marks, the word "by" and the entry author (if given).

[11]International Encyclopedia of Statistics (1978), s.v. "Bayesian Statistics," by Bruno de Finetti.

12. *Equipment Specifications.* Specifications may be printed on a single sheet (often called a "spec sheet" or "specs"), in a brochure, or in a pamphlet. When specifications are changed or models are introduced, new sheets are printed. To assist the reader in locating a specific sheet, give the name of the equipment as the title, plus the number, if any, that identifies the sheet. Normally page numbers are not shown on equipment specification sheets. To eliminate redundancy when the corporate author is obviously the publishing agency, the writer may eliminate the name in the facts of publication. List the items in the standard format for a book.

[12]Remington Rand Systems Division, Sperry Rand, Remkard, F-698 (104) (Marietta, Ohio, n.d.).

13. *Film.* In the business environment, a film is usually shown for one of these reasons: (1) the speaker or lecturer is an authority or (2) the circumstances shown represent the application of principles or concepts.

List the items in this order: name of featured speaker or lecturer, if any; film title underscored; series title, if any; in parentheses—the city, publishing agency or distributor, and date of release.

The catalog number and information regarding the special features may be omitted if they are not expected to be of interest to the reader. To distinguish this note from one for a book, the word "film" in parentheses should follow the facts of publication, as shown in this example:

[13]Peter F. Drucker, Effective Decisions, Peter Drucker Series (Washington: Bureau of National Affairs, 1964) (film).

14. *Handbook (General).* Use the standard format for a book.

[14]J. W. Haslett, ed., Business Systems Handbook (New York: McGraw-Hill Book Co., 1979), p. 44.

15. *Handbook (Special Usage Reference).* In the card catalog, a special usage reference book is usually shown under the name of the corporate author and also by the title. In many cases, the corporate author is also the publishing agency. Standard & Poor's Corporation is both the corporate author and the publishing agency, and the title of the book is Standard & Poor's Register of Corporations, Directors and Executives. To eliminate redundancy, use the name of the corporate author (publishing agency) only once, preferably in the authorship position. This handbook, like many special usage reference books in business, is compiled with the entries listed in alphabetical order. Because the content of the report will name the alphabetical entry (in this case, the corporation being studied), do not use s.v. and the entry. Also, some of these reference books have page numbers and others do not; omit the page number when the entries are alphabetized.

> [15]Standard & Poor's Corporation, Register of Corporations, Directors and Executives (New York, 1979).

16. *Interview.* Interviewing is a primary research method, and as such, the type, number, and circumstances surrounding the method are explained in the methods section of a report. Randomly selected telephone interviews are not documented; the information is usually grouped for presentation in the report. Calls made to specific individuals whose responses contribute to the report are documented. However, in grouped data, individual responses are no longer identifiable. As a business courtesy, the writer should ask if the interviewee may be named in the report.

List in this order: name of interviewee; title, organization, and location; in parentheses—the type of interview; the date.

> [16]Sandra Dose, Program Director, WTOP-TV, Baltimore (personal interview), 1 September 1979.

17. *Lecture.* List in this order: lecturer, title within quotation marks, the occasion, the date.

> [17]Eleanour V. Stevens, "Unfair Union Labor Practices" (lecture in BP 491, Labor Relations and Collective Bargaining, Colorado State University, Fort Collins), 10 February 1980.

18. *Letter.* List in this order: letter writer; title, organization, and location of writer separated by commas; in parentheses—the word "letter"; the date.

[18]Leonard Kruk, Editor, John Wiley & Sons, Inc., New York (letter), 19 December 1979.

19. *Microforms.* A microform is a photographic image of a document. The film may be in any one of these configurations:

a. Roll film

b. Microfiche

c. Microjackets

d. Ultrafiche

e. Aperature cards

Many widely circulated publications, such as *The Wall Street Journal,* are available on film in public and private libraries. Because the film copy is exactly the same as the original, the report reader has no reason to care that the writer obtained information from the filmed copy rather than from the original. Therefore, the reference note for an item taken from film is exactly the same as it is for the original work.

For unpublished material, the circumstances are different. A micrographics system is implemented in many organizations in the public and private sectors to retain copies of original documents because the originals: (a) have been moved to another location for safe keeping, (b) have been moved to a remote location to save space, (c) have been destroyed under the organization's retention schedule and in accordance with government regulations, or (d) have been subpoenaed by the court.

Should a writer need to refer to the microfilmed document to provide evidence supporting a statement, a content reference note would be the best method of documentation. The reference note should concisely identify the filmed document. At the minimum, it should describe the document(s), give the film location, and show the authority under which the document was filmed.

For example, a corporation's compiled profit figures by product line may be unavailable for any one of the four preceding reasons. The writer might document the filmed record in this way:

[19]"Compiled Product Line Income Statements, 1970–75," microfiche series, Retention Schedule Item No. 15.

20. *Microfilmed Dissertations.* If an institution requires that the student indicate in a reference note whether the original dissertation or a filmed copy has been used, the reference note can be constructed in this way:

> [20]Robert Lee Vigeland, "Statement of Financial Accounting Standard Number 2 and Market Equilibrium" (Ph.D. diss., Columbia University, 1977), p. 99 (Ann Arbor, Mich.: University Microfilms, No. 7802317, 1978).

21. *Pamphlet.* List the items in the standard order for a book:

> [21]Marvin Duncan, Farm Real Estate Values: What's Happening & Why, with a Foreword by Roger Guffy (Kansas City, Mo.: Research Division, Federal Reserve Bank of Kansas City, 1979), p. 36.

22. *Proceedings (Published).* The reference note may apply to the book containing the published proceedings, consisting of papers presented, seminars, panels, the official minutes, and so on; or it may apply to one of these segments within the book. In addition to the author and title, this note should identify the segment fully. Usually these elements are included in the note: nature of the segment; year, location, and date of the meeting (if not included in the title); facts of publication; and page(s).

> [22]Ralph V. Switzer, "Changing Attitudes toward Law," paper presented to the American Business Law Association, Proceedings of the Fifty-fourth Annual Meeting, Lansing, 7 August 1978 (n.p.: American Business Law Association, 1978), p. 31.

23. *Radio Program.* List in this order: most logical name under which the program could be found, usually the call letters of the local station and/or of the national network; title of program underscored; other facts that may be of interest to the reader—name of broadcaster, commentator, producer, or performer; date of broadcast.

If the program is part of a named or numbered series, list such information after the title of the program, capitalizing it according to the rules for capitalization of titles (see Titles, p. 267).

> [23]KOA, Market Reports, 1 September 1979.

24. *Report (Published).* List in the standard format for a book (see section 16.1, Books: Examples, p. 135).

> [24]AICPA, Report of the Study Group on the Objectives of Financial Statements (New York, 1973).

25. *Taped Recording.* List in this order: speaker, topic title in quotation marks, description of the occasion, date.

> [25]Terry L. Lantry, "Introduction to Contract Law" (videotaped lecture in BG 260, Legal Environment of Business, Colorado State University, Fort Collins), 8 March 1980.

26. *Television Program.* List in the order for a radio program.

> [26]CBS, Evening News, commentator: Roger Mudd, 29 August 1979.

27. *Unpublished Works.* An unpublished work may be a paper presented at a meeting, minutes of meetings, material prepared for forthcoming publication, unpublished reports and proceedings, class handouts, and other such material. Most unpublished material is prepared for the benefit of an individual or for a group of persons with a common interest. The reference note should contain sufficient information to identify the source.

> [27]Jennifer Bacon, "Advertising Mix Recommended for Barton Enterprises" (consultant's report to J. R. Bloom, president, Division 6, Tulsa), 4 January 1980.

28. *Yearbook.* If a yearbook contains a history of events that occurred during the year, list the items in the standard format for a book.

For a yearbook containing a compilation of articles published for the first time, use this format: article author; article title in quotation marks; yearbook title followed by "in" and the remainder of the title; editor, if any; yearbook part, if any; facts of publication; page(s).

> [28]Bernard Newton, "Economic Contributions of Smith, Malthus, Ricardo, and Marx," Foundations of Education for Business, in Thirteenth Yearbook of the National Business Education Association, ed. Gladys Bahr and F. Kendrick Bangs, pt. 1 (Reston, Va.: National Business Education Association, 1975), pp. 1–13.

CHAPTER SEVENTEEN

Second Reference Notes

Reference notes for second and succeeding citations of the same source should be presented in a shorter form than the original reference note. This handbook follows the current style for documenting sources and omits the usage of "op. cit." (in the work cited) and "loc. cit." (in the place cited). The following sections illustrate the use of two methods to present second and succeeding reference notes: (1) for consecutive references and (2) with intervening references.

17.1 CONSECUTIVE REFERENCES

For a second reference note to the source in the immediately preceding note, use the word "ibid."

GUIDELINES

Follow these guidelines when using "ibid.":

1. Use "ibid." to replace all or part of the immediately preceding reference.

2. Use "idem," not "ibid." to replace only the author's name.

EXAMPLES

These examples show how "ibid." is used:

¹Barbara N. Weaver and Wiley L. Bishop, The Corporate Memory (New York: John Wiley & Sons, 1974), p. 9.

²Ibid.

³Ibid., pp. 40–51.

17.2 INTERVENING REFERENCES

If one or more intervening reference notes occur between two reference notes documenting the same source, "ibid." cannot be used.

GUIDELINES

Follow these guidelines where intervening reference notes occur.

1. Use the author's last name followed by a comma and the page number of the original reference (see Examples 8 and 13, p. 153).

2. If two or more authors have the same name or if two or more works by the same author have been used, include a brief title after the comma following the author's name (see Example 9, p. 157).

3. For unpublished sources, list only the last name of the author or contributor and that person's contribution in parentheses (see Example 11, p. 157).

4. Always list the name of a corporate author and the publication title in a second reference (see Example 10, p. 157).

5. If a book has two or three authors, list the last name of each (see Example 12, p. 157).

EXAMPLES

These examples illustrate second and succeeding reference notes when intervening references occur.

For spacing in typewritten footnotes, see the Examples in section 16.1, p. 135.

¹John R. Stuteville, Marketing in a Consumer-Oriented Society (Belmont, Calif.: Wadsworth Publishing Co., 1975), p. 82.

²Raymond V. Lesikar, Basic Business Communications (Homewood, Ill.: Richard D. Irwin, Inc., 1979), p. 390.

³AICPA, APB Accounting Principles in Effect as of June 1973, 2 vols. (Chicago: Commerce Clearing House, 1973), I:110–11.

[4]Alberta Leake, "The Information Managers of Tomorrow," seminar, National Micrographics Association, Denver (lecture), 8 October 1979.

[5]Raymond V. Lesikar, Report Writing for Business, 5th ed. (Homewood, Ill.: Richard D. Irwin, Inc., 1979), p. 76.

[6]Ronald Hasty and R. Ted Will, Marketing (Scranton: Harper & Row, 1975), p. 47.

[7]Lois Meyer, "Machine Transcription," National Business Education Forum 40 (December, 1979): pp. 9–10.

[8]Stuteville, p. 97.

[9]Lesikar, Report Writing, pp. 409–10.

[10]AICPA, APB Accounting Principles in Effect as of June 1973, pp. 113–14.

[11]Leake (lecture).

[12]Hasty and Will, pp. 49–50.

[13]Meyer, p. 10.

4

CHAPTER
EIGHTEEN

Bibliography

4

A bibliography, usually the last supplementary page of the report, is an alphabetical listing of the sources that contributed to the report. The writer should choose a title from the following list to reflect the nature of the sources.

Bibliography—implies that the listing includes all or most of the published material available on a topic and cited in reference notes and source notes (for graphic aids). This term is used for a listing in a comprehensive report.

Selected Bibliography—includes only those published sources most pertinent to the topic, all of which have been cited in reference and source notes.

Sources Cited—includes published and unpublished sources (books, unpublished reports, and interviews) that have been cited in reference and source notes.

Sources Consulted—includes published and unpublished sources, all of which may or may not have been cited in reference and source notes.

If permissible or desirable, the writer may list all sources that have contributed to the report or have enhanced the search, thereby showing the scope of the research and providing a background for continued research. Listing all sources whether or not they have served these purposes results in an exaggerated bibliography, which gives an unfavorable impression of the researcher's honesty.

Annotated Bibliography—lists references followed by a comment on the value and content of each source. An annotated bibliography may be prepared during a library search to determine the nature and amount of material available on a topic, or it may be prepared for use in lieu of another type of bibliography. Meaningful fragments as well as complete sentences may be used in the evaluation. A period follows both types of construction.

National Microfilm Association, Introduction to Micrographics. Silver Spring, Md.: National Microfilm Association, 1973.

> An excellent introduction to microforms—their formats, production, and duplication. Each type of microform is explained and illustrated. Contains a microform flow chart which clarifies the various developments resulting from roll film. Extensive glossary is included.

STANDARD FORM

When numerous diverse sources are cited (books, periodicals, government publications, and interviews), the bibliography should be divided into categories that identify these sources. The categories, as well as the sources under each, are listed in alphabetical order (see Fig. 18.1, pp. 156–157).

Follow these guidelines to arrange a bibliography listing:

1. List the author's surname first.

2. If no name is given, list the title as the first item.

3. If two references by the same author are used, type a one-inch line (10 pica or 12 elite spaces) in the first position of the second entry in lieu of the author's name.

4. Show the title in the same manner as in the reference note (within quotation marks or underscored) and capitalized in the same way.

5. List the page numbers (inclusive numbers) only for references to articles and other sources which are a part of a whole publication.

REFERENCE NOTE AND BIBLIOGRAPHY ENTRY COMPARED

In a reference note, the author's first name is listed in normal reading order, but in a bibliography entry, it is listed in reverse order for alphabetizing purposes.

Sources Cited (line 13)

(Triple Space)

Articles
(Double Space)
"A Partial Recovery by the Cities." Business Week, 22 January 1979,
    pp. 94-96.

"An Encouraging Signal from Consumer Credit Data." Moody's Investor
    Service 71 (13 August 1977):934.
(Double Space)
Mayer, Caroline. "Accountants--Cleaning up America's Mystery
    Profession." U.S. News & World Report, 19 December 1977,
    pp. 39-40.

Pomrenze, Seymour J. "The Freedom of Information Act and the Privacy
    Acts and the Records Manager--Some Considerations." ARMA Records
    Management Quarterly 10 (July 1976):5-9, 14.

Weinstein, Michael. "The Crowded World of Urban Supermarkets." New
    York Times, Late City Ed., 18 December 1977, sec. 8, p. 1, col. 1.

(Triple Space)

Books
(Double Space)
Association of the Institute of Certified Public Accountants. APB
    Accounting Principles in Effect as of June, 1973. 2 vols.
    Chicago: Commerce Clearing House, 1973.

Corley, Robert N., and Black, Robert L. The Legal Environment of a
    Business. 3d ed. New York: McGraw-Hill, 1973.

Kupsh, Joyce; Anderson, Donna; Meyer, Lois; and Moyer, Ruth. Machine
    Transcription & Dictation. New York: John Wiley & Sons, 1978.

Samuelson, Paul A. The Collected Scientific Papers of Paul A.
    Samuelson. Ed. Joseph Stiglitz. 2 vols. Cambridge, Mass.:
    M.I.T. Press, 1966.

Tosi, Henry L.; House, Robert J.; and Dunnette, Marvin D., eds.
    Managerial Motivation and Compensation. East Lansing, Mich.:
    Bureau of Business and Economic Research Studies, Michigan
    State University, 1972.

Miscellaneous

Clark, Freda. Management Techniques for Women. 2 videotaped
    cassettes shown at the national convention of student chapters,
    Administrative Management Society, New Orleans, 17 August 1978.

FIGURE 18.1

Consumers Union. Consumer Reports, No. BR21. Orangeburg, N.Y.,
    Consumers Union, n.d., n. pag.

Drucker, Peter F. Effective Decisions. Peter Drucker Series.
    Washington: Bureau of National Affairs, 1964 (film).

Gurwitz, Aaron Samuel. "Local Taxation and the Dynamics of
    Metropolitan Property Values." DAI 38 (1977), 5620A (Stanford
    University).

Moffatt, Donald. Economics Dictionary. New York: Elsivier
    Scientific Publishing Co., 1976. S.v. "duopoly."

NOTE:

1. Start the first line of each entry at the left margin.
2. Indent the second and succeeding lines of each entry no fewer than
   5 spaces from the margin.
3. Double-space after the period following each item (but not after
   the period following an initial).
4. Start the second page of the bibliography listing one inch from
   the top of the page (line 7).
5. If the bibliographical entries are numbered, type the arabic
   number at the left margin, followed by a period and one space.
6. If categories of publications are used, triple-space from the last
   line of a reference and type the category title at the left
   margin in upper and lower case and underscored. Double-space
   after the category line.

1½"   1"

4

FIGURE 18.1 (Continued)

A comma separates each item of identifying information in a reference note, but in a bibliography listing, a period is used for this purpose. Parentheses are not used to enclose the facts of publication.

In a typewritten bibliography, two spaces follow the period after each segment, and one space follows other periods—with these exceptions: No space is used after a period within an abbreviation (s.v.) or after a period that is immediately followed by a comma (Bros.,) or by a colon (Homewood, Ill.:). Two spaces follow a colon except when the colon precedes a page number (2:11).

The spacing for typewritten footnotes is explained in section 16.1, p. 135.

Compare the entries:

> *Bibliography Entry*
> Drucker, Peter F. <u>Management: Tasks, Responsibilities, and Practices.</u> New York: Harper & Row, 1974.
>
> *Reference Note*
> Peter F. Drucker, <u>Management: Tasks, Responsibilities, and Practices</u> (New York: Harper & Row, 1974), pp. 309–10.

4

18.1 BOOKS

The general guidelines for bibliographical entries are given in the section Standard Form, pp. 155 to 157.

STANDARD FORM

The entries for books follow this order: author (name in reverse order), title, facts of publication.

EXAMPLES

These entries are coordinated with the reference notes under Books: Examples, pages 135 to 138.

1. *One Author*

> Taylor, Frederick Winslow. <u>The Principles of Scientific Management.</u> New York: Harper and Bros., 1911.

2. *Two Authors*

> Corley, Robert N., and Black, Robert L. The Legal Environment of Business. 3d ed. New York: McGraw-Hill, 1973.

3. *Three Authors.* Use a semicolon between each author's name.

> Pyle, William W.; White, John Arch; and Larson, Kermit D. Fundamental Accounting Principles. 8th ed. Homewood, Ill.: Richard D. Irwin, Inc., 1978.

4. *Four or More Authors.* Name all the authors represented by "et al." in the reference note. Separate each author's name by a semicolon.

> Kupsh, Joyce; Anderson, Donna; Meyer, Lois; and Moyer, Ruth. Machine Transcription & Dictation. New York: John Wiley & Sons, 1978.

5. *Corporate Author.* Always list the name of the corporate author. Do not use an initialism.

> American Institute of Certified Public Accountants. APB Accounting Principles in Effect as of June, 1973. 2 vols. Chicago: Commerce Clearing House, 1973.

6. *No Named Author; Editor, Compiler, or Translator Is Cited.*

> Tosi, Henry L.; House, Robert J.; and Dunnette, Marvin D., eds. Managerial Motivation and Compensation. East Lansing, Mich.: Bureau of Business and Economic Research Studies, Michigan State University, 1972.

7. *Named Author; Editor, Compiler, or Translator Is Cited.*

> Stiglitz, Joseph, ed. The Collected Scientific Papers of Paul A. Samuelson. By Paul A. Samuelson. 2 vols. Cambridge, Mass.: M.I.T. Press, 1966.

8. *Named Author; Book Has an Editor, Compiler or Translator.*

> Samuelson, Paul A. The Collected Scientific Papers of Paul A. Samuelson. Ed. Joseph Stiglitz. 2 vols. Cambridge, Mass.: M.I.T. Press, 1966.

9. *Named Article Author in Book Containing a Collection of Articles.*

> Ridgway, V. F. "Dysfunctional Consequences of Performance Measurement." In Managerial Motivation and Compensation. Ed. Henry L. Tosi, Robert J. House, and Marvin D. Dunnette. East Lansing, Mich.: Bureau of Business & Economic Research Studies, Michigan State University, 1972, pp. 147–149.

10. *Preface, Foreword, or Introduction Author.*

> Zell, Steven P. Unemployment Insurance: Programs, Procedures, and Problems. Foreword, Roger Guffy. Kansas City, Mo.: Research Division, Federal Reserve Bank of Kansas City, 1977.

11. *Preface, Foreword, or Introduction Author is Cited.*

> Guffy, Roger Z. Foreword. Unemployment Insurance: Programs, Procedures, and Problems. By Steven P. Zell. Kansas City, Mo.: Research Division, Federal Reserve Bank of Kansas City, 1977.

12. *Named Series.*

> Emory, C. William. Business Research Methods. Irwin Series in Information and Decision Sciences. Ed. Robert Fetter and Claude McMillan. Homewood, Ill.: Richard D. Irwin, Inc., 1976.

13. *Named and Numbered Series.*

> Grilli, Enzo R. The Future for Hard Fibers and Competition from Synthetics. World Bank Staff Occasional Papers, No. 19. Baltimore: Johns Hopkins University Press, 1975.

14. *Entire Multivolume Work Cited.*

> Kahn, Alfred E. The Economics of Regulation: Principles and Institutions. 2 vols. New York: John Wiley & Sons, Inc., 1970–71.

15. *One Volume Cited; Each Has a Different Title.*

> Kahn, Alfred E. Institutional Issues. Vol. 2 of The Economics of Regulation: Principles and Institutions. 2 vols. New York: John Wiley & Sons, Inc., 1971.

16. *Revised Edition.*

> Whalen, Doris E. The Secretary's Handbook. Rev. ed. New York: Harcourt Brace Jovanovich, Inc., 1973.

17. *Paperback Edition.*

> Moore, Robin. The Fifth Estate. New York: Doubleday & Co., Bantam Books, 1974.

18.2 PERIODICALS

The general guidelines for bibliographical entries are given in the section Standard Form, pp. 155 to 157.

STANDARD FORM

List the entries in the same format as book entries, with these exceptions:

1. When the volume number is given, place the date in parentheses.

2. Show the inclusive pages of the article.

3. Eliminate these abbreviations "vol.," "pp.," and "p." when the volume number is given.

EXAMPLES

These entries are coordinated with the reference notes in section 16.2, Periodicals: Examples, pp. 140 to 141.

1. *Weekly Magazine; Author Given*

> Mayer, Caroline. "Accountants—Cleaning up America's Mystery Profession." U.S. News & World Report, 19 December 1977, pp. 39–40.

2. *Weekly Magazine; No Author Given*

> "A Partial Recovery by the Cities." Business Week, 22 January 1979, pp. 94–96.

3. *Monthly Publication*

> Rush, Robert. "MIS Planning in Distributed Data Processing Systems." Journal of Systems Management 30 (August 1979):17–27.

4. *Bimonthly Publication*

> Trombetta, William L. "Product Liability: What New Court Rulings Mean for Management." Business Horizons 22 (August 1979):67–72.

5. *Quarterly Publication*

> Pomrenze, Seymour J. "The Freedom of Information Act and the Privacy Acts and the Records Manager—Some Considerations." ARMA Records Management Quarterly 10 (July 1976):5–9, 14.

6. *Daily Newspaper*

> Weinstein, Michael. "The Crowded World of Urban Supermarkets." New York Times, Late City Ed., 18 December 1977, sec. 8, p. 1, col. 1.

7. *Weekly Newsletter*

> Moody's Investors Service, "An Encouraging Signal from Consumer Credit Data." Moody's Bond Survey 71 (13 August 1979):934.

18.3 MISCELLANEOUS SOURCES

The general guidelines for bibliographical entries are given in the section Standard Form, page 155.

FORMAT

Some sources which are neither books nor periodical publications may be documented in the same format as a book or periodical, depending upon their nature. Others may require additional information for identification.

This section contains bibliographic entries for the reference notes in section 16.3, Miscellaneous Sources: Examples, pages 143 to 150.

1. *Brochure*

> Consumers Union. Consumer Reports, No. BR21. Orangeburg, N.Y., n.d.

2. *Cassette*

> Argyris, Chris. Argyris on Organization. San Jose: Lansford Publishing Co., 1978 (videotaped).

3. *Cassette; an Alternate Documentation*

> Clark, Freda. Management Techniques for Women. 2 videotaped cassettes shown at the national convention of student chapters, Administrative Management Society, New Orleans, 17 August 1978.

4. *Cassette Guidebook*

> Sterkel, Karen, ed. A Viewer's Guide: A Dialog between Harold Koontz & C. West Churchman. Dir. Morton Kotlar. Fort Collins, Colo.: Videodocumentary Clearing House, College of Business, Colorado State University, 1978.

5. *Cassette Series (Named and Numbered) with Separate Titles for each cassette*

> Motivation and Personal Skills Development. The Smile of Success. Tape 5: "Personal Development: Time Use." Roanoke, Tex.: Cassettes Unlimited, n.d. #299 (12 videotape cassettes).

6. *Computer Program*

> Statistical Package for the Social Sciences (SPSS). Documentation by McGraw-Hill Publishing Co.; produced and distributed by Northwestern University, 1975.

7. *Dictionary (General)*

The American Heritage Dictionary of the English Language. 1975 ed. S.v. "account executive."

8. *Dictionary (Specialized)*

Moffatt, Donald. Economics Dictionary. New York: Elsevier Scientific Publishing Co., 1976. S.v. "duopoly."

9. *Dissertation (Unpublished)*

Santos, Ruebens da Costa. "Relative Product Evaluation: An Experimental Study." Ph.D. diss., University of Texas at Austin, 1977.

10. *Dissertation Abstracts or Dissertation Abstracts International*

Gurwitz, Aaron Samuel. "Local Taxation and the Dynamics of Metropolitan Property Values." DAI 38 (1977), 5620A (Stanford University).

11. *Encyclopedia*

International Encyclopedia of Statistics, 1978. S.v. "Bayesian Statistics," by Bruno de Finetti.

12. *Equipment Specifications*

Remington Rand Systems Division, Sperry Rand. Remkard, F-658 (104). Marietta, Ohio, n.d.

13. *Film*

Drucker, Peter F. Effective Decisions. Peter Drucker Series. Washington: Bureau of National Affairs, 1964 (film).

14. *Handbook (General)*

Haslett, J. W., ed. Business Systems Handbook. New York: McGraw-Hill Book Co., 1979.

15. *Handbook (Reference)*

Standard & Poor's Corporation. Register of Corporations, Directors and Executives. New York, 1979.

16. *Interview*

Dose, Sandra. Program Director, WTOP-TV. Baltimore. Personal interview, 1 September 1979.

17. *Lecture*

Stevens, Eleanour V. "Unfair Union Labor Practices." Lecture presented in BP 491, Labor Relations and Collective Bargaining, Colorado State University, Fort Collins, 10 February 1980.

18. *Letter*

Kruk, Leonard. Editor, John Wiley & Sons, New York. Letter, 19 December 1979.

19. *Microforms*

"Compiled Product Line Income Statements, 1970–75." Microfiche series, Retention Schedule Item No. 15.

20. *Microfilmed Dissertation*

Vigeland, Robert Lee. "Statement of Financial Accounting Standard Number 2 and Market Equilibrium." Ph.D. diss., Columbia University, 1977. Ann Arbor, Mich.: University Microfilms, No. 7802317, 1978.

21. *Pamphlet*

Duncan, Marvin. Farm Real Estate Values: What's Happening & Why. Foreword, Roger Guffy. Kansas City, Mo.: Research Division, Federal Reserve Bank of Kansas City, 1979.

22. *Proceedings*

Switzer, Ralph V. "Changing Attitudes toward Law." Paper presented to the American Business Law Association. Proceedings of the Fifty-fourth Annual Meeting, Lansing, 7 August 1978 . N.p.: American Business Law Association, 1978, p. 31.

23. *Radio Program*

KOA. Market Reports. 1 September 1979.

24. *Report (Published)*

American Institute of Certified Public Accountants. Report of the Study Group on the Objectives of Financial Statements. New York, 1973.

25. *Taped Recording*

Lantry, Terry L. "Introduction to Contract Law." Video-taped lecture in BG 260, Legal Environment of Business, Colorado State University, Fort Collins, 9 March 1980.

26. *Television Program*

CBS. Evening News. Commentator: Roger Mudd. 29 August 1978.

27. *Unpublished Works*

Bacon, Jennifer. "Advertising Mix Recommended for Barton Enterprises." Consultant's report to J. R. Bloom, President, Division 6, Tulsa, 4 January 1980.

28. *Yearbook*

Newton, Bernard. "Economic Contributions of Smith, Malthus, Ricardo, and Marx." Foundations of Education for Business. In Thirteenth Yearbook of the National Business Education Association. Ed. Gladys Bahr and F. Kendrick Bangs. Pt. 1. Reston, Va.: National Business Education Association, 1975, pp. 1–13.

4

PART FIVE

Selected Government References for Business Writers

Business research and reports frequently require the use of a variety of public documents. Chapters Nineteen through Twenty-two present representative illustrations of the proper way to reference items from the public sector, as well as documents prepared by the United Nations.

5

CHAPTER NINETEEN

Federal Government References

References made to publications of the United States government frequently take a form that is different from those shown in Part Four.

1. The purpose and placement as a reference, content, acknowledgment, or consolidated note are the same as those for general references.

2. Unlike the general reference, government publications frequently do not have an author and appear as a publication of an agency or office.

3. The location of publication (country, state, etc.) is placed as the first item in the reference, for example:

> U.S. Civil Service Commission, The Role of the Civil Service Commission in Federal Labor Relations (Washington, D.C.: U.S. Government Printing Office, May 1971), pp. 46–47.

4. If the government publication has an author, it should be referenced as:

> F. J. Loevi, Jr., Collective Bargaining Under Executive Order 11491, Personnel Pamphlet Series No. 2 (Washington, D.C.: Department of Health, Education & Welfare, March 1973), p. 59.

1. *Orders*

   a.   Executive Orders are initiated by the President of the United States.

   b.   Each is assigned a number, preceded by "Executive Order" or "E.O."

   c.   The order may cover a wide variety of topics directing or "ordering" a person, office, or agency to conform.

   d.   Executive Orders may be found in the *Federal Register*.

   e.   Cite as:

   > U.S., President, Executive Order 12127 of March 31, 1979, "Federal Emergency Management Agency," <u>Federal Register</u> 44 No. 65, 3 April 1979, 19367.

2. **Proclamations**

   a.   Initiated by the President of the United States.

   b.   Each is assigned a number preceded by the word "Proclamation."

   c.   You may locate these in the *Federal Register*.

   d.   Proclamations should be cited as:

   > U.S., President, Proclamation 4643, "Cancer Control Month, 1979," <u>Federal Register</u> 44 No. 47, 8 March 1979, 12601.

3. **Agency Regulations**

   a.   Any department of the U.S. government may issue publications; e.g., Department of Labor, Department of Internal Revenue, Department of Commerce, Department of Defense, etc.

   b.   The publication may be instructional, regulatory, or informational.

   c.   Departmental publications should be cited as:

   > U.S., Department of Labor, <u>Federal Labor Laws and Programs</u>, Bulletin 262 (Revised September 1971), p. 33.

   d.   The Securities and Exchange Commission is a federal body established by the Securities and Exchange Act of 1934.

e. The purpose of the Commission is to protect the investing public from unethical practices in the buying and selling of securities and in the operation of financial markets.

f. A variety of publications are prepared by this body, typical of which is:

> Directory of Companies Required to File Annual Reports with the Securities and Exchange Commission under the SEC Act of 1934 (Washington, D.C.: U.S. Government Printing Office), published annually.

This publication is divided into two parts and gives an alphabetical listing of all industry groups, as well as a listing by Standard Industrial Classification (SIC).

19.2 LEGISLATIVE BRANCH

1. *Committee Reports*

a. Committee reports are prepared for each piece of legislation (called a bill) and are given consecutive numbers such as "H.R. Rep. No. _____" or "S. Rep. No. _____."

b. Cite reports as:

> H.R. Rep. No. 123, 93d Cong., 1st Sess. §12(1973)
>
> (House Report Number) (93d Congress, 1st Session) (Section 12) (year 1973)

2. *Bills*

a. Each house (U.S. House of Representatives and the U.S. Senate) reviews and votes on the acts or bills. When passed by both houses and signed by the President of the United States, the bills become statutes.

b. Each bill is assigned a number, with an indication of where the bill was introduced: "H.R. _____" for House of Representatives and "S. _____" for Senate.

3. *Debates*

a. The House and Senate separately debate the bill in question.

b. The debate transcripts are published in the *Congressional Record* as public information.

4. CONGRESSIONAL RECORD

a. The bill debate transcripts are published in the *Congressional Record*. Issued daily, it is a report of the Senate and the House activity and debates.

b. See Fig. 19.1, p. 172.

c. Cite bound volumes as:

121 Cong. Rec. 41103 (1975)

(Volume 121) (Congressional Record) (page 41103) (year 1975)

d. Cite daily issue as:

124 Cong. Rec. S14255 (daily ed. August 23, 1978) (Remarks of Senator Heinz)

(Volume 124) (Congressional Record) (page S14255) (date of daily edition) (person speaking)

e. The *Daily Digest* is included in each issue of the *Congressional Record* and highlights the important activities of Congress.

---

(1) [*August 23, 1978* **CONGRESSIONAL RECORD — SENATE** **S 14225**

Strengthening rural and urban infrastructure to support these development efforts will be highly demanding of investment funds in industry as well as in agriculture. This will require efforts on a large scale to mobilize domestic resources, including the reform of taxation systems, introducing **(3)** realistic prices for public sector products and services, restraint in government consumption expenditures, and increased incentives for private saving. It is, however, extremely difficult to raise domestic saving at these countries' very low levels of income. With their limited capacity to service external debt, these countries urgently require increased flows of concessional assistance if necessary investments are to be made. **(4)**

REDUCING ABSOLUTE POVERTY

A necessary condition for progress in reducing poverty is maintaining rapid economic growth, especially in the rural areas of Low Income countries where the majority of the poor live. But the elimination of absolute poverty by the end of this century seems impossible. Illustrative projections show that even if the trends projected above continue to the end of the century, about 17 percent of their populations would still be left in absolute poverty by the year 2000. With the rapid increases in population that now appear inevitable, this means 600 million people. Assumptions about future progress can, of course, be varied in innumerable ways. Nonetheless, it is disturbingly clear

efforts of developing countries to sustain rapid growth and alleviate poverty as rapidly as possible.●

---

(2) [U.S. POLICY IN RHODESIA

● Mr. HEINZ. Mr. President, much of the debate on our Rhodesian policy has revolved around points which I believe to be extraneous to the central issue. That central issue is, simply, what is the best path to a peaceful transition to majority rule.

It is unfortunate, in my view, that so much of the public debate on Rhodesia has been taken up with implicit moral commentaries on the various parties there. We often hear statements about which group represents our real friends there, which group promises a system of government closest to our own, or which group is most popular with the other African nations, particularly the Front Line states.

These are important questions, Mr. President, but by focusing on them, we miss the most important issue—how to avoid violence as Rhodesia moves to majority rule, as move it must.

To its credit, the administration makes its case clear in this respect. The crux of

ministration's. Rather we should be talking about what course of action will lead to a peaceful transition of power to black rule. There seems no longer to be basic disagreement on the final goal, only on how to get there, and how soon. One area of disagreement, however, is on how long to continue the economic sanctions against Rhodesia.

Opponents of the immediate lifting of economic sanctions contend that the best way to get there lies in the pursuit of further negotiations pursuant to the Anglo-American Plan, possibly an All Parties Conference, so that the Patriotic Front can be brought into the process.

This, of course, has been our policy objective since the Carter administration came into office. Presently negotiations seem to have reached the fundamental obstacle of both sides supporting free elections but each side demanding control of the process by which those elections will occur. This is hardly an ennobling debate, but it is one which thus has eluded resolution. The administration asserts that it can be resolved, but it presents no evidence to that effect and proposes no real hope of breaking the logjam.

FIGURE 19.1 A page from the *Congressional Record*, August 23, 1978, page S14225. **(1)** Date of issue. **(2)** Subject being commented on. **(3)** Speaker. **(4)** Text of remarks. (*Source:* U.S. Congress, *Congressional Record*, U.S. Government Printing Office, 1978.)

5. CONGRESSIONAL INDEX

a. Published weekly by Commerce Clearing House, the *Congressional Index* gives all the legislation covered by Congress during that week.

b. (See Fig. 19.2, p. 173).

6. DIGEST OF PUBLIC GENERAL BILLS AND RESOLUTIONS

a. Contains a digest of the main points in each bill of general and public nature; gives an introduction to the bill, the committee remarks, and the last reported action on the bill.

b. See Fig. 19.3, p. 174.

c. Cite *Digest of Public General Bills and Resolutions* as:

Digest of Public General Bills and Resolutions, No. 1, Part 1 (Washington, D.C.: Government Printing Office, 1978), H.R. 11718.

---

88   9-13-78   **House of Representatives (H) Bills**   **28,947**
For status see House Status Table Division.

INTRODUCTIONS FOR AUGUST 17, 1978—
continued

(1) [**H 13,948—Criminal law—state and local**
    governments—assistance
(2) —[By Conyers.
(3) [To amend the Omnibus Crime Control and
    Safe Streets Act of 1968 to improve the
    federal system of assistance to the criminal
    justice system. (To Judiciary.)

H 13,949—Judicial procedure—public
utilities—declaratory judgment
By Danielson.
To amend Title 28, United States Code, to provide for a declaratory judgment in certain cases involving public utilities. (To Judiciary.)

H 13,950—Judicial procedure—Puerto
Rico—Spanish
By Edwards (Calif.), Seiberling, Drinan, Volkmer, Beilenson, Butler, McClory and Corrada.
To amend Title 28 of the United States Code to provide that certain judicial pleadings and proceedings in the Commonwealth of Puerto Rico may be conducted in the Spanish language. (To Judiciary.)

H 13,951—Income tax—libraries—public
charities
By Gephardt.
To amend the Internal Revenue Code of 1954 to treat as public charities certain institutions which operate libraries. (To Ways and Means.)

INTRODUCTIONS FOR AUGUST 17, 1978—
continued

information, and materials concerning lotteries conducted by nonprofit organizations in accordance with state law. (To Judiciary, and Post Office and Civil Service.)

H 13,957—Government procurement—
domestic goods and services
By Luken, Benjamin, Applegate, Fithian, Guyer, Fary, Nowak, Derwinski, Eilberg, Bevill, Jenrette, Buchanan, Flowers, Cornwell, Murphy (Ill.), Lloyd (Tenn.), Gaydos, Lederer, Walker, Carney, Mikulski, Goodling and Wilson (Bob-Calif.).
To establish a reasonable and fair preference for domestic products and materials in government procurement and in procurement with federal funds, and to promote free and fair trade in government procurement of foreign products and materials. (To Government Operations.)

H 13,958—Communications—television—
high frequency station
By Maguire, Rinaldo, Rodino, Roe, Simon, Spellman, Thompson, Tsongas, Walgren and Waxman.
To amend Section 307 of the Communications Act of 1934 to provide that each state shall have at least one very high frequency commercial television station located within the state. (To Interstate and Foreign

5

FIGURE 19.2   Excerpt from a page of the *Congressional Index, 1977–1978,* September 13, 1978, page 28,947.   **(1)** House of Representatives bill number and subject of bill.   **(2)** Bill sponsor.   **(3)** Brief description of the bill.   (*Source:* CCH, *Congressional Index,* Commerce Clearing House, 1978. Reproduced with permission from *Congressional Index,* published and copyrighted by Commerce Clearing House, Inc., Chicago, Ill.)

(1) ⌐**H.R. 11718** Mr. Burgener. et al.; 3/22/78. Ways and Means
(2) *See* digest of H.R. 8452
(3)

H.R. 11719   Mr. Byron; 3/22/78. Interstate and Foreign Commerce

Amends the Clean Air Act to provide that a revision of an implementation plan concerning standards of air quality control in an air quality control region will have met the requirements of the Act where ambient air monitoring for four consecutive quarters (prior to the publication of proposed rulemaking on the revision) of operat'on at emission levels contemplated by the revision has recorded no violation of primary or secondary ambient air quality standards for the pollutants affected by the revision within the area significantly affected by the revision, unless demonstrated that such monitoring was substantially inadequate to measure compliance with such standards.

(4)

H.R. 11720   Mr. Conable, et al.; 3/22/78 House Administration

Amends the Federal Election Campaign Act of 1971 to add *Title V: Financing of General Election Campaigns for the House of Representatives* - Directs the Secretary of the Treasury to maintain in the Presidential Election Campaign Fund, the House of Representatives Election Campaign Account. Sets forth eligibility requirements to be met by candidates for election to the House of Representatives seeking payments from such Account. Limits expenditures from personal funds which may be made by candidates meeting such eligibility requirements.
Entitles eligible candidates to specified matching payments. Limits to $150,000 the aggregate payments which may be made to all candidates in an election.
Provides for the participation of the Commission in judicial proceedings arising under this Act.
Authorizes appropriations necessary to carry out the purposes of this Act.

H.R. 11721   Mr. Corrada, et al.; 3/22/78. Education and Labor
(5) ⌐*See* digest of H.R. 11371

H.R. 11722   Mr. Dornan; 3/22/78. Judiciary

(6) ⌐Grants Federal courts exclusive jurisdiction of actions between a United States citizen and a foreign citizen involving the enforcement of a foreign decree awarding custody of a person who a is under 16 year of age and is in the United States.

FIGURE 19.3 Excerpt from *Digest of Public General Bills and Resolutions*, page H.R. 11725.   **(1)** House of Representatives bill number.   **(2)** Bill sponsor.   **(3)** Date bill was introduced.   **(4)** Committee acting on bill.   **(5)** Reference to House of Representatives bill number 11371.   **(6)** Description of bill. (*Source:* U.S. Congress, *Digest of Public General Bills and Resolutions,* U.S. Government Printing Office, 1978.)

7. *CONGRESSIONAL QUARTERLY ALMANAC*

a. Gives a summary of previous congressional sessions and contains voting records of congressmen and detailed reports on legislation approved or rejected.

b. Cite *Congressional Quarterly Almanac* as:

"Major Legislation of 95th Congress, First Session," in Congressional Quarterly Almanac 1977, ed. Carolyn Mathiasen (Washington, D.C.: Congressional Quarterly, Inc., 1977), p. 2.

8. *CONGRESSIONAL INFORMATION SERVICE INDEX TO PUBLICATIONS (CIS/INDEX)*

a. Monthly index to congressional publications. Index is by subject, witness names, popular law names, report numbers, document numbers, and bill and public law numbers.

b. *Congressional Record* is not included, as it has its own index.

c. See Fig. 19.4, p. 176.

d. Cite CIS/INDEX as:

Congressional Information Service Index to Publications, Vol. 9, No. 2, ed. by James Adler (Washington, D.C.: Congressional Information Service, 1977), p. 71.

9. *UNITED STATES CODE*

a. In general, a code is a compilation of all the laws of a jurisdiction and is usually arranged in a classified order.

b. Most codes also contain the U.S. Constitution, the text of public laws, court abstracts, historical references, and a popular common name index to acts.

c. The *United States Code* is the official compilation of all federal laws. It is updated by supplements or pocket parts.

d. The *United States Code Annotated* and the *United States Code Service* are unofficial compilations of the laws. They are often useful because each annotates the statutory law with judicial decisions relating to the *United States Code*.

e. Fig. 19.5 (p. 177) shows Title 29, Section 151 of the *United States Code*.

f. Cite *United States Code* as:

29 U.S.C. §151.

(Title 29) (*United States Code*) (Section 151).

10. *UNITED STATES REVISED STATUES*

a. This is the official compilation of all federal laws.

b. The *United States Revised Statutes* are arranged under titles, chapters, and sections and give the text of all federal laws.

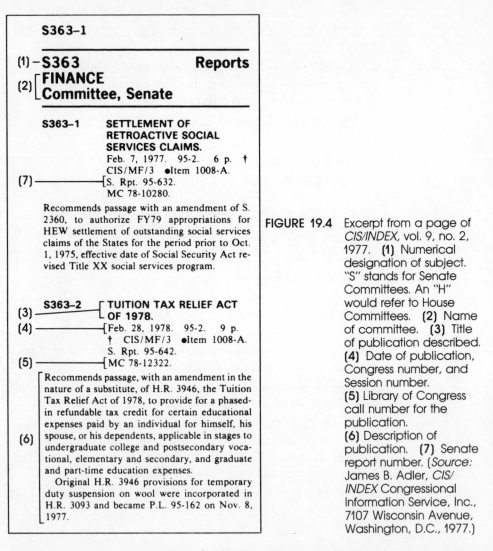

FIGURE 19.4 Excerpt from a page of *CIS/INDEX,* vol. 9, no. 2, 1977. **(1)** Numerical designation of subject. "S" stands for Senate Committees. An "H" would refer to House Committees. **(2)** Name of committee. **(3)** Title of publication described. **(4)** Date of publication, Congress number, and Session number. **(5)** Library of Congress call number for the publication. **(6)** Description of publication. **(7)** Senate report number. (*Source:* James B. Adler, *CIS/ INDEX* Congressional Information Service, Inc., 7107 Wisconsin Avenue, Washington, D.C., 1977.)

quitting of his labor by an individual employee an illegal act; nor shall any court issue any process to compel the performance by an individual employee of such labor or service, without his consent; nor shall the quitting of labor by an employee or employees in good faith because of abnormally dangerous conditions for work at the place of employment of such employee or employees be deemed a strike under this chapter.

(June 23, 1947, ch. 120, title V, § 502, 61 Stat. 162.)

§ 144. Separability of provisions

If any provision of this chapter, or the application of such provision to any person or circumstance, shall be held invalid, the remainder of this chapter, or the application of such provision to persons or circumstances other than those as to which it is held invalid, shall not be affected thereby.

(June 23, 1947, ch. 120, title V, § 503, 61 Stat. 162.)

SUBCHAPTER II—NATIONAL LABOR RELATIONS

SUBCHAPTER REFERRED TO IN OTHER SECTIONS

This subchapter is referred to in sections 142, 186, 402 of this title; title 15 section 1014; title 18 section 1951; title 39 section 1209; title 42 section 2000e; title 43 section 1333; title 47 section 222; title 50 sections 784, 792a.

§ 151. Findings and declaration of policy

The denial by some employers of the right of employees to organize and the refusal by some employers to accept the procedure of collective bargaining lead to strikes and other forms of industrial strife or unrest, which have the intent or the necessary effect of burdening or obstructing commerce by (a) impairing the efficiency, safety, or operation of the instrumentalities of commerce; (b) occurring in the current of commerce; (c) materially affecting, restraining, or controlling the flow of raw materials or manufactured or processed goods from or into the channels of commerce, or the prices of such materials or goods in commerce; or (d) causing diminution of employment and wages in such volume as substantially to impair or disrupt the market for goods flowing from or into the channels of commerce.

The inequality of bargaining power between employees who do not possess full freedom of association or actual liberty of contract, and employers who are organized in the corporate or other forms of ownership association substantially burdens and affects the flow of commerce, and tends to aggravate recurrent business depressions, by depressing wage rates and the purchasing power of wage earners in industry and by preventing the stabilization of com-

to the friendly adjustment of industrial disputes arising out of differences as to wages, hours, or other working conditions, and by restoring equality of bargaining power between employers and employees.

Experience has further demonstrated that certain practices by some labor organizations, their officers, and members have the intent or the necessary effect of burdening or obstructing commerce by preventing the free flow of goods in such commerce through strikes and other forms of industrial unrest or through concerted activities which impair the interest of the public in the free flow of such commerce. The elimination of such practices is a necessary condition to the assurance of the rights herein guaranteed.

It is declared to be the policy of the United States to eliminate the causes of certain substantial obstructions to the free flow of commerce and to mitigate and eliminate these obstructions when they have occurred by encouraging the practice and procedure of collective bargaining and by protecting the exercise by workers of full freedom of association, self-organization, and designation of representatives of their own choosing, for the purpose of negotiating the terms and conditions of their employment or other mutual aid or protection.

(July 5, 1935, ch. 372, § 1, 49 Stat. 449; June 23, 1947, ch. 120, title I, § 101, 61 Stat. 136.)

AMENDMENTS

1947—Act June 23, 1947, amended section generally to restate the declaration of policy and to make the finding and policy of this subchapter "two-sided".

EFFECTIVE DATE OF 1947 AMENDMENT

Section 104 of act June 23, 1947, provided: "The amendments made by this title [this subchapter] shall take effect sixty days after the date of the enactment of this Act [June 23, 1947], except that the authority of the President to appoint certain officers conferred upon him by section 3 of the National Labor Relations Act as amended by this title [section 153 of this title] may be exercised forthwith."

§ 152. Definitions

When used in this subchapter—

(1) The term "person" includes one or more individuals, labor organizations, partnerships, associations, corporations, legal representatives, trustees, trustees in bankruptcy, or receivers.

(2) The term "employer" includes any person acting as an agent of an employer, directly or indirectly, but shall not include the United States or any wholly owned Government corporation, or any Federal Reserve Bank, or any State or political subdivision thereof, or any person subject to the Railway Labor Act [45 U.S.C. 151 et seq.], as amended from time to time, or any labor organization (other than when acting as an employer), or

FIGURE 19.5 Page of the *United States Code*, vol. 7, page 713. **(1)** Title number and topic. **(2)** Subchapter title. **(3)** Section number and heading. **(4)** Text of Section 151 of Title 29, *United States Code*. (*Source: United States Code*, U.S. Government Printing Office, 1948.)

11. *STATUTES AT LARGE*

a.   Arranged chronologically, this reference contains the laws passed by Congress and is compiled at the end of each congressional session.

b.   The appropriate "H.R." and "S." numbers are provided, along with the date and the public law number.

c.   Each volume has an index by dates, a numerical list index of the laws, and a subject index.

d.   Cite each statute by the appropriate title:

> Labor Management Relations Act, 29 U.S.C. §151 (1964).

e.   If no statute title is given, cite by giving full date:

> Act of Sept. 8, 1950, Ch. 924, §2, 64 Stat. 798.
>
> (Date of Act) (Chapter 924) (Section 2) (Volume 64) (*Statutes at Large*) (page 798)

f.   After 1959 (contrary to the above citation) chapter numbers are not used. Instead, only the public law number is used. Cite as:

> National Labor Relations Act, Pub. L. No. 101, 49 Stat. 449.

g.   Fig. 19.6 (p. 179) shows a part of the Labor Management Relations Act taken from Volume 49 of *Statutes at Large*.

19.3   JUDICIAL BRANCH

1.   *Federal Courts*

a.   There are three divisions of the federal court system. The Supreme Court is the highest court of the United States. Cite cases from the U.S. Supreme Court as:

> Supreme Court of the United States, District No. 56, October Term, 1977.

When the cases are published in official form, cite as (see also Chapter Thirty):

(1)

(2)

[CHAPTER 120]

AN ACT

To amend the National Labor Relations Act, to provide additional facilities for the mediation of labor disputes affecting commerce, to equalize legal responsibilities of labor organizations and employers, and for other purposes.

Be it enacted by the Senate and House of Representatives of the United States of America in Congress assembled,

SHORT TITLE AND DECLARATION OF POLICY

(3)

SECTION 1. (a) This Act may be cited as the "Labor Management Relations Act, 1947".

(b) Industrial strife which interferes with the normal flow of commerce and with the full production of articles and commodities for commerce, can be avoided or substantially minimized if employers, employees, and labor organizations each recognize under law one another's legitimate rights in their relations with each other, and above all recognize under law that neither party has any right in its relations with any other to engage in acts or practices which jeopardize the public health, safety, or interest.

It is the purpose and policy of this Act, in order to promote the full flow of commerce, to prescribe the legitimate rights of both employees and employers in their relations affecting commerce, to provide orderly and peaceful procedures for preventing the interference by either with the legitimate rights of the other, to protect the rights of individual employees in their relations with labor organizations whose activities affect commerce, to define and proscribe practices on the part of labor and management which affect commerce and are inimical to the general welfare, and to protect the rights of the public in connection with labor disputes affecting commerce.

TITLE I—AMENDMENT OF NATIONAL LABOR RELATIONS ACT

(4) 49 Stat. 449. 29 U. S. C. §§ 151–166.

SEC. 101. The National Labor Relations Act is hereby amended to read as follows:

"FINDINGS AND POLICIES

(5)

"SECTION 1. The denial by some employers of the right of employees to organize and the refusal by some employers to accept the procedure of collective bargaining lead to strikes and other forms of industrial strife or unrest, which have the intent or the necessary effect of burdening or obstructing commerce by (a) impairing the efficiency, safety, or operation of the instrumentalities of commerce; (b) occurring in the

5

FIGURE 19.6 Page from the *United States Statutes at Large*, vol. 61, page 136. **(1)** Approval date, bill number, and Public Law number. **(2)** Preamble to Act. **(3)** Popular title of Act. **(4)** Citation to Statutes and *United States Code*. **(5)** Text of Amendment. (*Source:* U.S. Congress, *United States Statutes at Large,* U.S. Government Printing Office, 1947.)

346 U.S. 486 (1977)

(Volume 346) (United States Reporter) (page 486) (Year 1977)

b. The second highest federal court is the U.S. Court of Appeals. Cite as:

United States Court of Appeals, Ninth Circuit, No. 76-5496, July 9, 1976 (or as CA-9, 1976).

c. The appellate and district court decisions are reported in complete text. Those cases from the federal district courts are reported in the *Federal Reporter* series. District court decisions are also reported in the *Federal Supplement* (see also Chapter Thirty).
Cite as:

25 F. 196

(Volume 25) (*Federal Reporter*) (page 196)
Or as:

540 F. 2d 975

(Volume 540) (*Federal Reporter* 2d Series) (page 975)
Or as:

120 F. Supp. 219

(Volume 120) (*Federal Supplement*) (page 219)

d. Cases from the courts may also be cited with the names of the parties. Cite as:

NLRB v. Operating Engineers, Local 25, 400 U.S. 297 (1977).

(Plaintiff name versus defendant name) (Volume 400) (United States Reports) (page 297) (year 1977)

2. *The National Labor Relations Board*

a. The National Labor Relations Board (NLRB) was established by the National Labor Relations Act (NLRA) in 1935.

b. The primary function of the Board is to hear complaints filed by employers or employees who believe one of the parties has violated the NLRA and has committed an unfair labor practice. The Board is also charged with conducting union elections and decertifications.

c. Transcripts of hearings before the Board are published in the NLRB Reports. The hearings are cited as:

40 NLRB 295.

(Volume 40) (*National Labor Relations Board Reports*) (page 295)

d. The NLRB also publishes a variety of reports and bulletins covering various topics. Cite as:

National Labor Relations Board, Forty-third Annual Report for the the Fiscal Year Ended September 30, 1978 (Washington, D.C.: U.S. Government Printing Office, 1978).

5

CHAPTER TWENTY

State Government References

All state governments have their statutes and all laws regulating activity within the state put in written form for public use.

20.1 STATUTES

1. State statutes are published in much the same manner as the federal statutes.

2. Each state has its public laws published into bound volumes.

3. Updates are made by annual pocket supplements or by current annual bound volumes.

4. Fig. 20.1 (p. 183) shows page 326 of Volume 9 of the Colorado Revised Statutes giving Section 23-31-101.

5. Cite statutes as:

Colo. Rev. Stat. 9, §23-31-101 (1973).

(*Colorado Revised Statutes*) (Volume 9) (Section 23-31-101) (Year 1973).

20.2 REGULATORY AGENCIES

1. Each state generally publishes the rules promulgated by its regulatory agencies.

ARTICLE 31

(2)

(2) [**Colorado State University**

(4) **23-31-101. College established - objects.** A school is established and shall be known by the name and title of "Colorado state university". The design of the institution is to afford thorough instruction in agriculture and the natural sciences connected therewith. To effect that object most completely, the institution shall combine physical with intellectual education and shall be a high seminary of learning in which the graduates of the common school of both sexes can commence, pursue, and finish a course of study, terminating in thorough theoretical and practical instruction in those sciences and arts which bear directly upon agriculture and kindred industrial pursuits.

(5) **Source:** G. L. § 54; G. S. § 34; R. S. 08, § 88; C. L. § 8069; CSA, C. 38, § § 2(1), 13; L. 51, p. 767, § 1; CRS 53, § 124-10-1; C.R.S. 1963, § 124-10-1.

(6) **Law review.** For note, "The Problem of the Local Improvement District in Colorado", see 12 Rocky Mt. L. Rev. 45 (1939).
The name of this institution was changed to Colorado state university by an act adopted in 1957. Lewis v. State Bd. of Agriculture, 138 Colo. 540, 335 P.2d 546 (1959).

FIGURE 20.1 Page from the *Colorado Revised Statutes,* vol. 9, page 326. **(1)** Name of Title 23. **(2)** Name of Article 31. **(3)** Index of Title 23, Article 31 contents. **(4)** Text of Section 23-31-101. **(5)** List of sources for Section 23-31-101. **(6)** Reference to law review pertaining to Section 23-31-101. (*Source:* State of Colorado, *Colorado Revised Statutes,* Secretary of State, Denver, Colo., 1974. Copyright 1974 by the Secretary of State of Colorado for the State of Colorado.)

2. Such regulatory agencies include public taxation, workmen's compensation, public utilities, land use, and the like.

3. Cite as:

> Colorado, Department of Health, Air Pollution Control Division, <u>Air Quality Implementation Plan for State of Colorado</u> (Denver: Colorado Department of Health, 1972).

5

CHAPTER TWENTY-ONE

Other Government References

In addition to those publications issued by the executive, legislative, and judicial branches of the government, other government departments and agencies prepare and distribute publications. Those illustrated here are representative of federal, state, county, and city governments.

A. Federal

1. Federal agencies, bureaus, and departments publish a variety of documents for use by the public.

2. These publications may take the form of bulletins, reports, regulations, or may be revisions of earlier publications.

3. Cite as:

> U.S. Department of Labor, Bureau of Labor Statistics, Producer Prices and Price Indexes, Data for January, 1979 (Washington, D.C.: U.S. Government Printing Office, 1979).

> Homer J. Calkin, Women in American Foreign Affairs (Washington, D.C.: Department of State, August 1977).

> U.S. Department of Commerce, 1st Annual Progress Report, Footwear Industry Vitalization Program (Washington, D.C.: U.S. Government Printing Office, 1978).

B. State

1. State governments compile a variety of documents which are also designed for use by the public.

185

2. State documents present kinds of information similar to those presented by the federal government.

3. Cite as:

> Colorado, Department of Labor and Employment, Division of Employment and Training, Colorado Employers Handbook (Denver, 1976).
>
> Colorado, Department of Health, Air Pollution Control Division, Colorado Motor Vehicle Emissions Test Center, Annual Report 1975/76 (Denver, 1976).
>
> Colorado, Office of the Attorney General, Report of the Attorney General Concerning the Nursing Home Industry in the State of Colorado (Denver, 1977).

C. Counties

1. The publications from a county agency or commission may be informational or regulatory reports and bulletins.

2. These documents may be for general use by the public or may take the form of reports on agency activity.

3. Cite as:

> Larimer County, Planning Commission, Larimer County Land Use Plan (Fort Collins, Colo., 1977).
>
> Larimer County, Crisis and Information Center, Larimer County Human Services Directory (Fort Collins, Colo., 1979).
>
> Larimer County, Board of Commissioners, Larimer County Water and Sewer Standards and Procedures Manual (Fort Collins, Colo., 1972).

D. Cities

1. City governments issue many kinds of reports, regulations, and bulletins from their agencies, boards, and commissions.

2. These may be information of general interest to residents, reports on agency activities, or regulatory in nature.

3. Cite as:

> Fort Collins, City Council, Code of Ordinances of the City of Fort Collins, Colorado, 1958 as Amended (Fort Collins, Colo., 1976).
>
> Fort Collins, Planning and Zoning Board, Research and Survey Report (Fort Collins, Colo., 1966).
>
> Poudre School District R-1, Catalog of Instructional Media, 1970 (Fort Collins, Colo., 1970).

CHAPTER TWENTY-TWO

United Nations Reference Books

The United Nations has several publications regarding its documents, treaties, and miscellaneous papers. The most important and more commonly used for students and others in business are as follows.

1. YEARBOOK OF THE UNITED NATIONS. New York, United Nations, Office of Public Information, 1947–date.

    a. This annual yearbook is a synopsis of the activities of various bodies of the United Nations.

    b. Both a name index and a subject index are given.

    c. Cite as:

> "Third United Nations Conference on the Law of the Sea," Yearbook of the United Nations, 1974 (New York: Office of Public Information, United Nations, 1977), p. 71.

2. UNITED NATIONS. UNDEX: UNITED NATIONS DOCUMENT INDEX, SERIES A, B, AND C. New York. 1950–date.

    a. Gives a listing of bibliographic information of all U.N. documents and publications.

    b. Gives list of all printed material of International Court of Justice.

    c. Items are listed in English and French languages.

    d. There are four indexes: subject, country, proceedings, and resolutions.

5

e. Cite the index as:

> United Nations, UNDEX: United Nations Document Index, Series C, January 1978 (New York: United Nations, 1978), p. 49.

3. STATISTICAL YEARBOOK. New York, United Nations, Statistical Office, 1949–date.

a. Gives statistical information on a large number of topics: education, agriculture, labor, and other general subjects.

b. The yearbook is arranged by country.

c. Cite the yearbook as:

> Statistical Yearbook 1977 (New York: United Nations, 1978), p. 284.

4. DEMOGRAPHIC YEARBOOK. New York, United Nations, Statistical Office, 1948–date.

a. An annual publication of statistics on each member country of the United Nations.

b. Labor conditions, housing, income, products, and the like are detailed.

c. Cite the yearbook as:

> Demographic Yearbook 1976 (New York: United Nations, 1977), p. 105.

22.1 UNITED NATIONS DOCUMENTS: CITATION FORMS

1. Citations for United Nations materials vary. In citing official records, the citation order is: volume, material, name, supplement, page, date. Cite as:

> 13 U.N. ECOSOL 325
>
> (Volume or Session 13) (U.N. publication from the Economic and Social Council) (page 325)

2. U.N. documents are cited by document number:

> U.N. Doc. ST/ESA/SERA/60 (1977 document of the Population Division of the Secretariat of the Regional Commission)

Symbols of U.N. documents are made from letters and numbers, each indicating the authority which issued the document. Each separate element or letter separated from another by diagonal lines is an internal reference designated by the United Nations. A more thorough explanation of the symbols used by the United Nations can be found in *A List of United Nations Document Series Symbols*, published by the United Nations.

United Nations official records are published by four main United Nations bodies. These are the General Assembly, the Economic and Social Council, the Trusteeship Council, and the Security Council. Subdivisions of these bodies also publish various documents.

5

PART SIX

Selected Sources of Business Information

Business research requires information from numerous, widely utilized sources of valuable data. Part Six identifies the most useful sources of business information and provides a working knowledge of their contents.

CHAPTER TWENTY-THREE

Indexes to Books and Periodicals

Books and periodicals play an important part in the research process. Chapter Twenty-three lists and briefly explains some of the most widely used book and periodical indexes relative to the business field.

1. CUMULATIVE BOOK INDEX. New York, H. W. Wilson, 1928–date.

An annual publication, the *Cumulative Book Index* is an extension of the *United States Catalog* and lists most of the books published in the United States from 1928 to date. Also included are many English-language books published in foreign countries. Entered under one alphabetical listing, the books are arranged by author, title, and subject.

2. BUSINESS BOOKS AND SERIALS IN PRINT. New York, R. R. Bowker, 1977–date.

A continuation of *Business Books in Print,* this annual publication has both author and title indexes and over 6,000 subject categories in the book section. The serials are classified into 170 subject categories and have title access. Full bibliographic information and ordering information are given for each entry.

3. N. W. AYER AND SON'S DIRECTORY OF NEWSPAPERS AND PERIODICALS. Philadelphia, Ayer, 1869–date.

Over 22,000 newspapers and periodicals published in the United States are listed in *Ayer's.* There is both a geographical and an alphabetical listing. It includes extensive information, such as name, place of publication, frequency of issue, circulation, price, and editor's name.

4. BALACHANDRAN, M. A GUIDE TO TRADE AND SECURITIES STATISTICS. Ann Arbor, Mich., The Pierian Press, 1977.

Alphabetically arranged by subject, this book provides an analysis of the "most-used securities statistics." The Best insurance reports, S&P publications, and the Moody items are among those serials analyzed.

5. CURRENT CONTENTS: BEHAVIORAL, SOCIAL, AND EDUCATIONAL SCIENCE. Philadelphia, Institute for Scientific Information, 1969–date.

Current Contents is an up-to-date series of publications listing many periodicals in the behavioral, social, and educational fields. The title pages of selected periodicals are reproduced in the index.

6. ULRICH'S INTERNATIONAL PERIODICALS DIRECTORY. New York, Bowker, 1932–date.

Ulrich's is an extensive list of periodicals in nearly all subject areas. Arrangement is according to titles and subjects indexed at the end of each volume.

7. THE STANDARD PERIODICAL DIRECTORY. New York, Oxbridge, 1964–date.

Generally used as a supplement to *Ayer's* and *Ulrich's*, this directory also covers government publications, yearbooks, and house organs in both the United States and Canada. Arrangement is by specific subject with a title index.

6

CHAPTER
TWENTY-FOUR

Indexes to Articles

Periodical articles are of value to the researcher because they provide current information. The following presents six categories of indexes to journals and periodicals of interest to business-oriented research.

24.1 INDEXES TO GENERAL ARTICLES

1. NEW YORK TIMES INDEX. New York, New York Times, 1913–date.
Published semimonthly, this subject index is valuable to researchers in many fields of study. Brief abstracts of articles found in the *New York Times* newspaper are given, along with the date, column number, and page where the full article can be found.

2. PUBLIC AFFAIRS INFORMATION SERVICE BULLETIN. New York, Public Affairs Information Service, 1915–date.
The *PAIS Bulletin* is a useful research tool in business because it not only cites periodicals, but also lists—by subject—selected pamphlets, yearbooks, society publications, government documents, and a record of new legislation. The *Bulletin* is published weekly and cumulated into bound annual volumes.

3. READERS' GUIDE TO PERIODICAL LITERATURE. New York, H. W. Wilson, 1900–date.
Published twice a month and accumulated into annual volumes, the *Reader's Guide* is a subject and author index to several hundred well-known popular, nontechnical magazines.

6

4. WALL STREET JOURNAL INDEX. New York, Dow Jones, 1955–date.

Similar to the *New York Times Index* in format, the index to *The Wall Street Journal* is useful to the business world. It enables a researcher to find every news item published in *The Wall Street Journal*.

5. U.S. SUPERINTENDENT OF DOCUMENTS. MONTHLY CATALOG OF UNITED STATES GOVERNMENT PUBLICATIONS. Washington, D.C., 1895–date.

The *Monthly Catalog* is the subject, author, and title list to all government publications. Published each month, the issues are bound into volumes annually and have a cumulative yearly index.

24.2 INDEXES TO BUSINESS ARTICLES

1. BUSINESS EDUCATION INDEX. New York, McGraw-Hill Book Company, 1939–date.

Issued annually, *Business Education Index* is a subject and author approach to articles in the business education field. It is compiled by Delta Pi Epsilon, the national honor graduate fraternity in business education.

2. BUSINESS PERIODICALS INDEX. New York, H. W. Wilson, 1958–date.

BPI is a subject index to over 200 periodicals in finance, insurance, banking, accounting, marketing, data processing, taxation, labor, and other business-related subjects. Issued monthly, it is cumulated quarterly and then bound into annual volumes.

3. DANIELLS, LORNA M. BUSINESS INFORMATION SOURCES. Berkeley, University of California Press, 1976.

This guide is a complete annotated list of selected business books and reference sources. The subject coverage is extensive, including all areas of business and areas such as computer science and statistics. Loose-leaf services, microforms, and computerized literature searches are also provided.

4. F & S INDEX OF CORPORATIONS AND INDUSTRIES. Cleveland, Predicasts, Inc., 1960–date.

Periodical and newspaper articles about many corporations and industries are indexed by this service. *F & S* is divided into two sections: I—Industries, in which articles are listed by SIC numbers, and II—Corporations, in which articles are listed alphabetically by corporate name. The SIC number (Standard Industrial Classification number) is a four-digit code prepared by the Technical Committee on Standard Industrial Classification, under the Office of Statistical Standards of the Bureau of Budget. The first two digits show the major industrial group in which the product line is classified. The last two digits further classify the product more specifically in this industrial group. For example:

> The SIC number 3574 is composed of *35*, for the major group designating machinery except electrical; *7*, for the group number for office, computing, and accounting machines; and *4*, for the industry number referring to calculating and accounting machines except electronic computing equipment. Therefore, the SIC number *3574* stands for calculating and accounting machines except electronic computing equipment.

24.3 INDEXES TO ACCOUNTING ARTICLES

1. ACCOUNTANTS' INDEX. New York, American Institute of Accountants, 1921–date.

An annual publication with quarterly supplements, this index is a bibliography of pamphlets, articles, and books in the accounting field and covers a broad scope of information for accountants. Subject and author indexes are included.

2. ACCOUNTING ARTICLES. Chicago, Commerce Clearing House, 1970–date.

Issued monthly, *Accounting Articles* is an annotated loose-leaf service of accounting and business books, pamphlets, and articles. It has two cumulative indexes, one by author, the other by subject.

24.4 INDEXES TO ECONOMICS ARTICLES

1. INDEX OF ECONOMIC ARTICLES IN JOURNALS AND COLLECTIVE VOLUMES. Sponsored by the American Economic Association. Homewood, Ill., Irwin, 1961–date.

A multivolume set, this index is a survey of economic articles from 1886 to 1974. Beginning in 1977, with 1972 articles (there is a five-year lag in publishing time), Congressional committee hearings are given. A subject and an author index are included.

2. JOURNAL OF ECONOMIC LITERATURE. Nashville, American Economic Association, 1963–date.

This is a very practical bibliography of economic items. Issued quarterly, it covers books and periodical articles. All articles are abstracted, and the books are annotated. Access to information is alphabetical by specific subject area.

24.5 INDEXES TO INSURANCE ARTICLES

1. INSURANCE LITERATURE. New York, Special Libraries Association, Insurance Division, 1951–date.
This source references insurance exclusively. It gives current material in the insurance area. Included within are pamphlets, annuals, books, and association proceedings. Information may be found by both subject and title approach.

2. BEST'S INSURANCE REPORTS: LIFE—HEALTH. Oldwick, N.J., Best, 1906–date.
BEST'S INSURANCE REPORTS: PROPERTY—LIABILITY. Oldwick, N.J., Best, 1899–date.
Issued annually, with monthly and weekly supplements, these two reports give extensive information about United States and Canadian insurance companies. In addition to biographical information, each company's financial position and operating data are provided. The listing is alphabetical with a separate geographical section.

24.6 INDEXES TO SCIENCE ARTICLES

1. APPLIED SCIENCE AND TECHNOLOGY INDEX. New York, H. W. Wilson, 1958–date.
Published monthly, with quarterly and annual cumulations, this index is a subject listing of over 200 periodicals in science-related areas. It is useful for research in computer science areas and other process technologies affecting business decisions.

2. ENGINEERING INDEX. New York, American Society of Mechanical Engineers, 1920–date.
Listing includes several hundred technical journals of both United States and foreign publications; this index is particularly useful for literature searching in the data processing and information systems areas. Issued monthly, the index also gives abstracts of the articles cited.

6

CHAPTER
TWENTY-FIVE

Directories

Directories provide classified listings of businesses and individuals. These listings are complete with appropriate addresses and financial information.

1. DUN AND BRADSTREET'S MILLION DOLLAR DIRECTORY. New York, Dun and Bradstreet, 1959–date.
This is an annual listing of businesses with a net worth of $1 million or more, indicating type of product and gross sales. To provide information for businesses with a net worth between $500,000 and $1 million, Dun and Bradstreet also publishes *Middle Market Directory*.

2. ENCYCLOPEDIA OF NATIONAL ASSOCIATIONS. Detroit, Gale Research, 1956–date.
Canadian and United States national associations are listed in this publication. The address, names of officers, number of members, and purpose are given for each association. The associations are listed alphabetically.

3. KELLY'S DIRECTORY OF MANUFACTURERS AND MERCHANTS. London, Kelly's Directories, Ltd., 1887–date.
Published yearly, *Kelly's* is a listing of many of the major import and export companies of the world.

4. S & P REGISTER OF CORPORATIONS, DIRECTORS, AND EXECUTIVES, UNITED STATES AND CANADA. New York, Standard and Poor's, 1928–date.
S & P Register is a listing of directors and executives of nearly 35,000 corporations. Full biographical information is given for all corpo-

6

rations and their executives. Such information includes corporation name, address, telephone, board members' names, officers' names, type of product manufactured, SIC number, and usually the number of employees and annual dollar sales. All executives' names, home addresses, all corporations with which they are principally involved, where and when they attended college, and birthdates are given. The index is alphabetically arranged by corporate name and by each executive's name. Also included is a geographic index.

5. THOMAS' REGISTER OF AMERICAN MANUFACTURERS. 12 vols. New York, Thomas Publication Company, 1905–date.

Thomas' Register is a listing of over 100,000 manufacturers, giving their product lines and address. Information is listed by manufacturer's name and product(s), and serves as a buyer's guide.

6. U.S. BUREAU OF LABOR STATISTICS. DIRECTORY OF NATIONAL UNIONS AND EMPLOYEE ASSOCIATIONS. Washington, Government Printing Office, 1971, with later supplements.

This directory provides thorough coverage of national and international labor unions. It lists names of officers, affiliated organizations, publications, convention information, and membership data.

CHAPTER TWENTY-SIX

Dictionaries

Dictionaries are a necessity in any research project. They aid in obtaining correct spelling, abbreviations, acronyms, synonyms, and definitions of all words.

1. KOHLER, ERIC L. A DICTIONARY FOR ACCOUNTANTS. 5th ed. Englewood Cliffs, N.J., Prentice-Hall, 1975.
This dictionary is concise yet thorough. It gives explanations and definitions of terms commonly used in the accounting field.

2. DICTIONARY OF BUSINESS AND MANAGEMENT. New York, Wiley-Interscience, 1978.
All areas of business and information of general interest to business are presented in this dictionary. It is actually more than an ordinary dictionary, for it includes acronyms, abbreviations, and tables of interest, income, and exchange.

3. MUNN, C. G. ENCYCLOPEDIA OF BANKING AND FINANCE. Boston, Bankers Publishing Company, 1973.
Munn's Encyclopedia contains concise explanations of terms relating to credit, accounting, trusts, insurance, and other finance-related terms.

4. PRENTICE-HALL, INC. ENCYCLOPEDIC DICTIONARY OF BUSINESS LAW. Englewood Cliffs, N.J., Prentice-Hall, 1961.
This dictionary thoroughly covers business law. It defines terms within the legal context of business.

5. MCGRAW-HILL DICTIONARY OF MODERN ECONOMICS, A HANDBOOK OF TERMS AND ORGANIZATIONS. Compiled by

6

Douglas Greenwald. New York, McGraw-Hill Book Company, 1973. The McGraw-Hill Dictionary is similar to the Sloan-Zurcher dictionary, listed next, except that it is designed for the scholar of economic principles. In addition, Greenwald also describes several European and American government organizations important in the field of economic research.

6. SLOAN, H. S., AND ZURCHER, A. J. DICTIONARY OF ECONOMICS. New York, Barnes, 1971.
Sloan and Zurcher's dictionary is definitive in the field of economics. Brief definitions or explanations of several thousand terms, court decisions, economic statistics, agencies, and legislative acts are presented.

7. ROBERT, HAROLD S. ROBERT'S DICTIONARY OF INDUSTRIAL RELATIONS. Washington, Bureau of National Affairs, 1971.
Robert's Dictionary is a complete work giving definitions of labor terms, information regarding important industrial relations cases, and related agencies.

8. BLACK, H. C. BLACK'S LAW DICTIONARY. 4th ed. St. Paul, West Publishing Company, 1968.
Perhaps the best-known dictionary of legal terms, *Black's Law Dictionary* not only defines legal words but also often cites important decisions as they relate to specific legal terms.

6

CHAPTER TWENTY-SEVEN

Services and Newsletters

Various kinds of information can be found in publications identified as "services." These cover a wide variety of business functions and activities, typical of which are following.

27.1 FINANCIAL

1. CORPORATION RECORDS. New York, Standard and Poor's Corporation, 1940–date. Title varies.
This publication is a loose-leaf service that gives a description of a corporation's background, stocks, bonds, and financial reports, and is periodically updated.

2. MOODY'S BANK AND FINANCE MANUAL. New York, Moody's Investors Service, Inc., 1929–date. Title varies.
Issuing biweekly news reports, this service presents broad coverage of banking institutions, insurance, investment, mortgage, real estate, and finance companies.

3. MOODY'S BOND RECORD. New York, Moody's Investors Service, Inc., 1931–date. Title varies.
Published monthly, this publication covers over 15,000 bond issues and gives the user an easy reference to the pertinent facts regarding market position and statistical background.

4. MOODY'S BOND SURVEY. New York, Moody's Investors Service, Inc., 1936–date.
Published weekly, this publication reports on the entire bond market and presents comments and recommendations on individual issues.

6

5. MOODY'S DIVIDEND RECORD. New York, Moody's Investors Service, Inc., 1930–date.

Published biweekly, this publication covers 9,500 issues, showing payments, declarations, income bond interest payments, and tax rulings. Moody's also publishes the *Annual Dividend Record* each January, which covers the previous year's dividend information.

6. MOODY'S HANDBOOK OF WIDELY HELD COMMON STOCKS. New York, Moody's Investors Service, 1957–date. Title varies.

This quarterly publication contains summary reports on selected common stocks, including dividends and earnings.

7. MOODY'S INDUSTRIAL MANUAL. New York, Moody's Investors Service, Inc., 1920–date. Title varies.

Issuing reports biweekly, this service provides background and financial information on industrial firms in the United States and abroad which are listed on the New York or American Stock Exchange.

8. MOODY'S MUNICIPAL AND GOVERNMENT MANUAL. New York, Moody's Investors Service, Inc., 1929–date. Title varies.

Publishing biweekly reports, this service provides background information and financial data on obligations of federal, state, county, and city governments, as well as their agencies. It also includes tax and school districts and port authorities.

9. MOODY'S PUBLIC UTILITY MANUAL. New York, Moody's Investors Service, Inc., 1914–date. Title varies.

Issued biweekly, this service reports vital statistics on water, power and light, gas, and transit companies. Also included are public utility maps.

10. MOODY'S OTC INDUSTRIAL MANUAL. New York, Moody's Investors Service, Inc., 1970–date.

Issued weekly, this publication reports on the over-the-counter market transactions involving the most actively traded issues.

11. MOODY'S STOCK SURVEY. New York, Moody's Investors Service, Inc., 1936–date.

Published weekly, *Moody's Stock Survey* reports on individual groups as well as industry groups, giving recommendations for buying, selling, or holding.

12. MOODY'S TRANSPORTATION MANUAL. New York, Moody's Investors Service, Inc., 1909–date. Title varies.

Issuing weekly reports, this basic source book covers various aspects of conventional transportation agencies: tunnel, bridge, and canal companies; oil pipelines; and traction lines.

13. STANDARD AND POOR'S FIXED INCOME INVESTOR. New York, Standard & Poor's Corporation, 1972–date. Supersedes BOND OUTLOOK.

Published weekly, this service gives ratings on corporate and municipal bonds with respect to the obligor's credit-worthiness. Indicated ratings are based on possibility of default, provisions of the obligation, and protection available.

14. STANDARD AND POOR'S INDUSTRY SURVEYS. New York, Standard & Poor's Corporation, 1973–date.

Published quarterly, this publication performs a current and basic analysis of 69 major domestic companies. It also includes a statistical supplement that updates corporate data in the analysis, including background information, current position, and projected trends.

15. STANDARD AND POOR'S STOCK REPORTS, AMERICAN STOCK EXCHANGE. New York, Standard & Poor's Corporation, 1973–date.

Published quarterly, this service reports on over 1,200 companies, appraising the stock of those companies listed on the American Stock Exchange. The report also includes listing of significant income statement and balance sheet items with an analysis of their earnings reports.

16. STANDARD AND POOR'S STOCK REPORTS, N.Y. STOCK EXCHANGE. New York, Standard & Poor's Corporation, 1973–date.

Published quarterly, this service reports on over 1,400 companies listed on the New York Stock Exchange. Information on sales, earnings, and potential dividends is included, as well as projections on the overall long-term outlook.

17. STANDARD AND POOR'S STOCK REPORTS. OVER THE COUNTER. New York, Standard & Poor's Corporation, 1973–date.

Published quarterly, this service reports on companies' OTC transactions and those listed on regional stock exchanges. The report includes income statement, balance sheet items, earnings reports and information on dividends, price ranges and capitalization.

18. THE HOLT INVESTMENT ADVISORY. New York, T. J. Holt & Co., Inc., 1967–date.

Published bimonthly, this publication contains comprehensive information and advice on the stock market, money trends, bonds, and warrants.

19. MCGRAW-HILL'S PERSONAL FINANCE NEWSLETTER. New York, McGraw-Hill Book Company. P. H. Gross, editor. 1969–date.

Published biweekly, this newsletter provides information on various kinds of personal investment opportunities as well as notes on retirement plans.

20. LANSTON LETTER. New York, Aubrey G. Lanston & Co., Inc. David M. Jones, editor. 1949–date.

This weekly publication presents an analysis of the financial market and the factors that influence it.

21. DAILY COMMODITY COMPUTER TREND ANALYZER. New York, Commodity Research Bureau, Inc., 1969–date.

This report is issued daily to report the trends of futures in a wide variety of commodity markets.

22. C & P WARRANT ANALYSIS. Fort Lee, N.J., C & P Research, Inc. W. G. Caroll, editor. 1970–date.

Stock warrants that have been actively traded are presented in this biweekly publication.

23. UNITED BUSINESS AND INVESTMENT REPORT. Boston, United Business Service. Sidney McNath, managing editor. 1919–date.

This weekly publication presents a comprehensive report on current developments in investments and business. Commodity price trends and forecasts for the stock market are also included.

24. THE ALLEN REPORT. Placentia, Calif., R. C. Allen, publisher and editor. 1968–date.

Articles and charts regarding commodity and futures trading appear in this weekly publication.

25. INVESTOR RELATIONS NEWSLETTER. Chicago, Enterprise Publications. R. G. Gulian, editor. 1965–date.

Published monthly, this newsletter contains information covering all facets of investor relations. Practical information is also presented for use by corporate financial officers and top management.

26. THE PREDICTOR. Windsor, Conn., The Predictor, Inc. John F. Ferraro, editor. 1965–date.

A computerized analysis, this weekly publication covers market trends, presents buy-hold-sell advice, and recommends specific stocks.

27.2 ECONOMIC

1. BUREAU OF NATIONAL AFFAIRS SERVICE. Washington, Bureau of National Affairs, Inc., 1935–date.

This service issues several publications covering many aspects of government, industry, and labor.

2. U.S. MASTER TAX GUIDE. Chicago, Commerce Clearing House, Inc., 1933–date.

This service presents tax control information to assist in tax management.

3. UNITED STATES BUSINESS SERVICE AND INVESTMENT REPORT. Boston, United Business Service, 1919–date. Title varies.

This service presents a weekly forecast based on the combined opinion of recognized business and economic authorities. Included are maps, tables, and charts.

4. ECONOMIC ALMANAC. New York, National Industrial Conference Board, 1940–date.

This biennial publication provides comprehensive information on government and business in both the United States and Canada.

5. DUN'S REVIEW AND MODERN INDUSTRY. New York, Dun and Bradstreet, Inc., 1893–date. Title varies.

This monthly publication presents reports on industrial development statistics.

6. STANDARD AND POOR'S REGISTER OF CORPORATIONS, DIRECTORS AND EXECUTIVES, United States and Canada. New York, Standard & Poor's Corporation, 1927–date.

This annual publication contains names of executives in every industrial area throughout the United States and Canada. The volume is arranged by Standard Industrial Classification codes and indices as well as alphabetically according to corporation title.

7. VALUE-LINE INVESTMENT SURVEY. New York, Arnold Bernhard Co., 1943–date.

Published weekly, this service gives ratings and reports of selected stocks.

8. NEWSLETTER OF THE TWENTIETH CENTURY FUND. New York, Twentieth Century Fund, Inc. M. J. Rossant, editor. 1967–date.

Published three or four times a year, this newsletter presents specialized information on research and public education, emphasizing economic and social questions and international issues.

9. THE KIPLINGER WASHINGTON LETTER. Washington, Kiplinger Washington Editors, Inc. A. H. Kiplinger, editor. 1923–date.

Published weekly, this newsletter presents data of interest to businessmen and covers such topics as business forecasts, economics, finance, labor, as well as others.

10. ANDREWS MARKET CYCLE INVESTING. Valencia, Calif. R. E. Andrews, owner and editor. 1972–date.

This monthly analysis illustrates economic trends in terms of the effect economic cycles have on investments.

11. C E P NEWSLETTER. New York, Council on Economic Priorities. W. C. Schwartz, editor. 1975–date.

Issued semiannually, this publication presents information on the social obligations of businesses. Topics included are energy use, employment practices, environmental hazards, and many others.

12. FSUC NEWSLETTER. Washington, Federal Statistics Users Conference. John H. Aiken, editor. 1959–date.

This is a monthly publication containing information on federal statistical programs. Also included are statistics on such areas as labor, social security, industrial crime, energy, and other topics of interest to those involved with business and economics.

27.3 BUSINESS AND INDUSTRY

1. FAIR EMPLOYMENT REPORT. Silver Spring, Md., Business Publications, Inc. Leonard A. Eisner, publisher and editor. 1964–date.
This biweekly publication is directed toward consultants, unions, government agencies, and business executives. It presents information on current developments in the areas of discrimination in employment practices.

2. SECURITIES REGULATION AND LAW REPORT. Washington, Bureau of National Affairs, Inc. Don Blatt, editor. 1969–date.
This weekly publication reports on current regulations in the areas of securities law, accounting practices, commodity law, and judicial and administrative procedures.

3. SECURITY LETTER. New York, Security Letter, Inc. Robert McCrie, publisher and editor. 1970–date.
Published semimonthly, this newsletter is directed toward solving problems of internal control, fraud, embezzlement, and personnel practices.

4. NATIONAL SERVICE NEWSLETTER. Washington, National Service Secretariat. D. J. Eberly, editor. 1966–date.
This newsletter is not published on a regular basis. It concerns such topics as youth unemployment, training programs, community service, and manpower needs.

5. OCCUPATIONAL HEALTH & SAFETY LETTER. Washington, Environews, Inc. Gershon Fishbein, publisher and editor. 1971–date.
Published semimonthly, it reports on current activities of the Occupational Health and Safety Administration as they affect organizational administration.

6. PUBLIC RELATIONS NEWS. New York. Denny Griswold, publisher and editor. 1944–date.

Each weekly issue contains a case study on a public relations issue in various kinds of organizations. Also included are current events with which executives are concerned in the field of public relations.

7. RICKENBACKER REPORT. Briarcliff Manor, Rickenbacker Report Corporation. W. E. Rickenbacker, editor. 1968–date.

A semimonthly publication summarizing domestic and foreign events of a general economics, politics, financial, or business nature.

8. INVENTORIES MANAGEMENT NEWSLETTER. Cambridge, Mass. Arthur D. Little, Inc. A. P. Lagace, editor. 1973–date.

Issued three times each year, it describes new inventions available for licensing. Information on patent status is also presented.

9. NATIONAL COUNCIL FOR SMALL BUSINESS MANAGEMENT DEVELOPMENT NEWSLETTER. Milwaukee, University of Wisconsin Extension. W. O. Metcalf, editor. 1960–date.

This quarterly publication is directed toward the management levels of small business, providing them with information on programs as well as articles on innovations in the field.

10. CUSTOMER SERVICE NEWSLETTER. Washington, Marketing Publications, Inc. W. Blanding, editor. 1973–date.

A monthly publication dealing with the customer services provided by firms, it reports on activities such as telephone use, order processing costs, trends, and training.

11. E D P INDUSTRY REPORT. Waltham, Mass, International Data Corp. J. Peacock, editor. 1964–date.

Published 24 times each year, this publication reports on all segments of the electronic data processing industry and its subsidiaries.

12. HOUSING AND URBAN AFFAIRS DAILY. Washington, National Housing Publications, Inc. H. L. Mauir, editor. 1961–date.

This daily issue from Washington reports administrative, legislative, and industry developments in the fields of housing and urban affairs.

13. AFL-CIO NEWS. Washington, American Federation of Labor and the Congress of Industrial Organizations. 1955–date.

This is a weekly report on labor affairs as well as a schedule of events open to member involvement. Foreign language versions are also available.

14. BANK PERSONNEL NEWS. Washington, American Bankers Association. D. C. Flynn, editor. 1972–date.

This monthly publication, directed toward bank personnel administrators, provides information on new developments in Congress, public and private agencies, and the courts.

15. NEW CAREER WAYS NEWSLETTER. Haverhill, Mass., Career Publishing Company. W. J. Bond, editor and publisher. 1975–date.
This monthly publication provides data on a wide variety of subjects of interest to business. Included are pension reform highlights, advertising, cost cutting, OSHA, hiring procedures, work loads, computer use, and other business practices.

16. THE RETAIL MANAGEMENT LETTER. Plymouth, Mass., Management Facts Company. J. W. Moon, editor and publisher. 1975–date.
A monthly report for executives, this newsletter summarizes consumer and government developments. It also gives sources for additional information and a report on the economic outlook.

17. BUSINESS OPPORTUNITIES DIGEST. Clarksville, Tenn. J. F. Straw, editor and publisher. 1963–date.
Issued monthly, this publication reports on over 100 business opportunities. Also included is information on businesses for sale and/or wanted, financing available, facilities, etc.

18. IDEA: EXECUTIVE NEWSLETTER. Roanoke, Va., International Downtown Executive Association. W. R. Hill, editor. 1973–date.
This monthly report covers all aspects of "downtown" activity including planning and development, promotional marketing, and legislative enactments.

19. PUBLIC RELATIONS NEWS. New York. Denny Griswold, editor and publisher. 1944–date.
Published weekly, it contains reports of new techniques, trends, case studies, new firms or branches, and changes in names of firms.

20. THE BOARD ROOM REPORT. New York, Boardroom Reports, Inc. Martin Buhagiar, editor. 1971–date.
Published twice monthly, this is a useful source for new information and reference sources pertaining to all areas of business and industry.

CHAPTER
TWENTY-EIGHT

Handbooks

Handbooks are generally known as "ready reference" materials. The following are some of the more popular handbooks relevant to business research.

1. PURCHASING HANDBOOK. New York, McGraw-Hill Book Company. George W. Aljian, editor. 1973.
This is a standard reference book covering purchasing policies, practices, procedures, contracts, and forms.

2. CREDIT MANAGEMENT HANDBOOK. Homewood, Ill., Richard D. Irwin, Inc. 1965.
This handbook was prepared and edited by the Credit Research Foundation, New York, and explains the organization of a credit department as well as how to use credit ratings or reporting services.

3. THE DOW JONES INVESTORS HANDBOOK. New York, Dow Jones, Inc. Maurice L. Farrell, editor. 1978.
This publication is a reference to stock and bond market indicators, giving complete Dow Jones Averages through 1977 as well as 1977 records of common and preferred stocks and bonds listed on both exchanges. It also shows yearly highs and lows as well as the year's most active stocks.

4. HANDBOOK OF LABOR UNIONS. Washington, American Council on Public Affairs. Florence Peterson, editor. 1944.
This handbook contains factual information about many of the national and international unions within the American labor movement.

5. MARKETING HANDBOOK. New York, Ronald Press Company, A. W. Frey, editor. 1965.
This handbook deals with principles and practices for effective distribution of goods and services.

6. PRODUCTION HANDBOOK. New York, Ronald Press Company. Gordon B. Carson, editor. 1972.
This reference provides information on the production aspects of industrial and factory management and also includes an extensive bibliography.

7. BUSINESS SYSTEMS HANDBOOK. New York, McGraw-Hill Book Company. J. W. Haslett, editor. 1979.
Strategies are presented and developed for establishing and maintaining administrative control.

8. J. K. LASSER'S BUSINESS MANAGEMENT HANDBOOK. 3d ed. New York, McGraw-Hill Book Company. Bernard Griesman, editor. 1968.
In this handbook, business managers are provided with advice and expertise on problems encountered in the administration of an organization.

9. HANDBOOK OF ORGANIZATIONS. Chicago, Rand McNally & Co. James G. Marck, editor. 1965.
This is a collection of contributions made by authorities in the field of organization theory, presenting current attitudes and developments in the discipline.

10. MANAGEMENT SERVICES HANDBOOK. New York, AICPA. Henry de Vos, editor. 1954.
The accountants' contribution to management services and controls are given in this publication.

11. LABOR RELATIONS PRIMER. Homewood, Ill., Dow Jones-Irwin. Wesley M. Wilson, editor. 1973.
A comprehensive guide, it offers a basic understanding of labor law presented in layman's terms with practical applications illustrated.

12. HANDBOOK OF INTERNATIONAL MARKETING. New York, McGraw-Hill Book Company. Alexander O. Stanley, editor. 1963.
Designed to give an insight into market structure, financial resources, and legal restrictions necessary for the successful transaction of a business abroad, this is a useful tool.

13. THE DARTNELL TRADE HANDBOOK. 2nd ed. Chicago, published in cooperation with the American Institute for Foreign Trade by Dartnell Corporation. Leslie L. Lewis, editor. 1965.
Contents consist of a variety of information pertinent for exporting and operating a business abroad.

14. LIFE AND HEALTH INSURANCE HANDBOOK. Homewood, Ill., Richard D. Irwin. Davis Wienert Gregg, editor. 1964

This handbook is primarily concerned with pension and profit-sharing plans. It also contains information on government life and health benefit plans.

15. THE DARTNELL SALES MANAGERS' HANDBOOK. 10th ed. Chicago, Dartnell Corporation. John C. Aspley and John C. Harkness, editors. 1973.

This publication contains bibliographical and statistical data and covers practical aspects regarding the administration of a sales organization.

16. INTERNATIONAL HANDBOOK OF ADVERTISING. New York, McGraw-Hill Book Company. S. Watson Donn, editor. 1964.

In addition to supplying useful information on international advertising in general, this handbook deals with the problems of advertising in several individual countries.

17. QUALITY CONTROL HANDBOOK. 2nd ed. New York, McGraw-Hill Book Company. Joseph M. Juran et al., editors. 1962.

This handbook treats the administration and management of the total quality control function as well as that for specific products.

18. PURCHASING HANDBOOK. 2nd ed. New York, McGraw-Hill Book Company. George W. Aljian, editor. 1966.

All aspects of the purchasing function are delineated in this handbook.

19. FINANCIAL ANALYST'S HANDBOOK. Homewood, Ill., Dow Jones-Irwin. Sumner N. Levine, editor. 1975.

Contained within is information on methods, theory, and portfolio management, with analyses made by industry.

20. DARTNELL PUBLIC RELATIONS HANDBOOK. Chicago, Dartnell Corporation. 1967.

Internal communications, external public relations, and available media are some of the topics treated in this publication.

21. ACCOUNTANT'S HANDBOOK. 5th ed. New York, Ronald Press Company. Rufus Wixon, Walter G. Kell, and Norton H. Bedford, editorial consultants. 1970.

Developed by recognized authorities in the field, this volume presents the principles, rules, and procedures necessary for commercial and financial accounting.

22. BUSINESS GAMES HANDBOOK. New York, American Management Association. Robert G. Graham and Clifford T. Gray, editors. 1969.

The text was developed to show how firms can utilize business games for training, and it also includes samples of games in use and their purpose.

23. LABOR RELATIONS HANDBOOK. Part I. Princeton, N.J., Auerbach. Vivian Wilson, editor. 1972.
Basic information covering the fundamentals of labor law and arbitration, as well as the day-to-day contacts between management and labor representatives, is included.

24. HANDBOOK OF BUSINESS ADMINISTRATION. New York, McGraw-Hill Book Company. Harold B. Maynard, editor. 1967.
This handbook contains a comprehensive collection of data on the total process of management. Authorities present chapters on all management functions including organization; research and development; management of materials, manufacturing, marketing, and finances; systems, data processing, accounting, and control; and many others.

CHAPTER
TWENTY-NINE

General References

This chapter includes all areas too general or too specific to be in a separate category. The areas covered are government, census and statistics, international business, miscellaneous directories, handbooks and catalogs, and factbooks of statistics and ratios.

29.1 GOVERNMENT

Government publications can be found on almost every topic of concern to business and industry. They can take the form of reports, requirements, general information, forecasts, or directives. Each month the Superintendent of Documents prepares a *Monthly Catalog of United States Government Publications*. This publication provides an index to all documents issued during that period, arranged alphabetically by the agency from which they were issued. A yearly cumulative index is also available.

1. GOVERNMENT REFERENCE BOOKS. Littleton, Colo., Libraries Unlimited, Inc. Alan Edward Schnorr, editor. 1978.
This is a biennial guide to United States government publications.

2. NEW GUIDE TO POPULAR GOVERNMENT PUBLICATIONS. Littleton, Colo., Libraries Unlimited, Inc. Walter L. Newsome. 1978. Appearing in this annotated reference book are entries grouped by subject matter and also bibliographic citations.

3. GENERAL SERVICES ADMINISTRATION, NATIONAL ARCHIVES AND RECORD SERVICE. Washington, USGPO, 1969.

6

This volume lists all publications from this agency. Information is included on their contents, availability, and price.

4. DECISIONS AND ORDERS. Washington, National Labor Relations Board, 1975.
A listing of the board's decisions and the orders issued by the board for that period is published and updated periodically.

5. COMPUTER LITERATURE BIBLIOGRAPHY. Washington, National Bureau of Standards. W. W. Youden, editor. 1967.
This is a two-volume publication with references to 5,200 items from books, journals, and conference proceedings.

6. PUBLICATIONS OF THE BUREAU OF LABOR STATISTICS JANUARY–DECEMBER. Washington, Bureau of Labor Statistics, 1974.
Contained herein is a compilation of all publications of the bureau for the stated period, with references to their availability.

7. STATISTICS OF INCOME 1972 INDIVIDUAL INCOME TAX RETURNS. Washington, Internal Revenue Service, 1973.
Information is presented here on all sources of income, taxes, dividends, and other selected items based on returns.

8. GUIDE TO U.S. GOVERNMENT PUBLICATIONS. McLean, Va., Documents Index. John L. Andriot, editor. 1973–date.
This is an annotated guide to current publications from U.S. government agencies. It also contains a complete listing of classification numbers used by the Superintendent of Documents. Issued at 18-month intervals, 1973–date.

9. FEDERAL RESERVE BULLETIN. Washington, Board of Governors of the Federal Reserve System, 1915–date.
Issued monthly, this publication contains current and new developments in the areas of banking, industrial production, law, and business. Also contains comprehensive reporting of domestic financial statistics.

10. FEDERAL REGISTER. Washington, Office of the Federal Register, National Archives and Records Service, General Services Administration, 1935–date.
Issued daily, Monday through Friday, this document presents all regulations and notices issued by federal agencies, including Presidential Proclamations and Executive Orders.

11. MONTHLY CATALOG OF UNITED STATES GOVERNMENT PUBLICATIONS. Washington, USGPO Superintendent of Documents, 1895–date.

Lists of all publications from the Superintendent of Documents, and from all agencies, departments, and branches of the United States government are contained in this publication.

12. U.S. DEPARTMENT OF LABOR NEW PUBLICATIONS. Washington, Office of Information, Department of Labor, USGPO, 1948–date.
This is an annual publication with monthly supplements of new publications.

13. THE MONTHLY LABOR REVIEW. Washington, USGPO, 1915–date.
Published monthly, this periodical contains a comprehensive compilation of current statistics on labor and industrial relations.

14. A SURVEY OF FEDERAL GOVERNMENT PUBLICATIONS OF INTEREST TO SMALL BUSINESS. Washington, Small Business Administration, USGPO, 1965.
Contained in this publication is an extensive list of booklets and pamphlets identified by industry or subject that are available from government agencies.

15. U.S. INDUSTRIAL OUTLOOK. Washington, U.S. Bureau of Domestic Commerce, USGPO, 1977.
Major industry trends and projections are contained in this publication.

16. SURVEY OF CURRENT BUSINESS. Washington, U.S. Department of Commerce, USGPO, 1920–date.
This monthly publication contains statistics, projections, and forecasts of business and economic conditions.

17. SOCIAL SECURITY BULLETIN. Washington, U.S. Social Security Administration, USGPO, 1938–date.
Published monthly, each issue of the bulletin contains data on payments, benefits, and changes therein.

18. STANDARD INDUSTRIAL CLASSIFICATION MANUAL. Washington, U.S. Executive Office of the President, Office of Management and Budget, USGPO, 1972. Supplement issued in 1978.
Published on an irregular schedule (previous edition—1967), this manual was prepared for use in classifying organizations according to activity, thereby providing uniformity and comparability in statistical data collected by public and private sources.

19. U.S. GOVERNMENT RESEARCH AND TECHNICAL REPORTS. Springfield, Va., Clearinghouse for Federal Scientific Information, 1946–date.

Published semimonthly, these volumes give an abstract and an-
nouncement service of the current scientific and technical reports
available in 22 fields including the behavioral and social sciences.

20. GOVERNMENT PUBLICATIONS, A GUIDE TO BIBLIO-
GRAPHIC TOOLS. New York, Pergamon Press. Vladimir M. Palic.
1976.

This publication identifies public documents of a general nature as
well as international government organizations and publications by
foreign countries.

21. UNITED STATES GOVERNMENT MANUAL. Washington,
USGPO, 1935–date.

This is an annual publication listing names and addresses of federal
agencies and the names of their top officials. Also described are the
functions of these agencies.

29.2 U.S. BUREAU OF THE CENSUS STATISTICS AND RATIOS

1. CENSUS OF POPULATION. Washington, U.S. Bureau of the
Census, 1790–date.

The census of population is taken every ten years and contains statistics on the number of inhabitants, characteristics of the population, the labor force, and characteristics by age.

2. CENSUS OF BUSINESS. Washington, U.S. Bureau of the Census, 1929–date.

This multivolume set covering every type of business operation is
published quinquennially.

3. CENSUS OF MANUFACTURERS. Washington, U.S. Bureau of
the Census, 1810–date.

The *Census of Manufacturers* provides detailed data on manufacturing activity for geographic areas and is published quinquennially.
Data include products shipped and materials consumed.

4. CENSUS OF TRANSPORTATION. Washington, U.S. Bureau of
the Census, 1963–date.

Statistical information covering commodities transport, passenger
transportation, truck inventory and use, and bus and truck carriers
is published quinquennially in this collection.

5. STATISTICAL ABSTRACT OF THE UNITED STATES. Washington, U.S. Bureau of the Census, 1878–date.

The annual publication provides a summary of statistics on social,
political, and economic organizations in the United States. This vol-

6

ume also contains a recent trends section and a statistics in brief, which are available separately.

6. COUNTY AND CITY DATA BOOK. Washington, U.S. Bureau of the Census, 1949–date.
Published irregularly, this supplement to the statistical abstract presents statistical information on population characteristics by region, division, state, county, metropolitan areas, and cities. Selected items are taken from the latest censuses of agriculture, business, and manufacturers.

7. BUREAU OF THE CENSUS CATALOG. Washington, U.S. Bureau of the Census, 1878–date. Title varies.
Each quarter these data are cumulated into an annual volume. Monthly supplements are also issued. All publications of the Bureau are listed, and it also contains selected papers by staff members, data files, and tables.

8. CENSUS OF AGRICULTURE. Washington, U.S. Bureau of the Census, 1840–date.
This census is taken as of October on a quinquennial basis. Also included with the agricultural data every ten years is a census of irrigation and drainage.

9. CENSUS OF RETAIL TRADE: AREA STATISTICS. Washington, U.S. Bureau of the Census, Business Division, 1972–date.
This series is published on an irregular basis and contains data by kind of business, by states. Included are the numbers of establishments, receipts, employees, and payrolls in cities with 500 or more establishments and 2,500 or more inhabitants.

10. CENSUS OF WHOLESALE TRADE: AREA STATISTICS. Washington, U.S. Bureau of the Census, Business Division, 1972–date.
This series is published on an irregular basis and contains data on kinds of businesses by states. Also included are the numbers of establishments, receipts, employees, and payrolls for cities with over 300 establishments and with 2,500 or more inhabitants.

11. BUSINESS CONDITIONS DIGEST. Washington, U.S. Bureau of the Census, 1961–date.
Published monthly, this digest provides economic time series and indicators for business forecasting and analysis.

12. HISTORICAL STATISTICS OF THE UNITED STATES: COLONIAL TIMES TO 1970. Washington, U.S. Bureau of the Census, 1975.
This edition presents over 8,000 statistical time series accompanied by text notes and other reference sources dealing with business, economics, and government.

6

1. INTERNATIONAL DIRECTORY OF MARKETING RESEARCH HOUSES AND SERVICES. New York, American Marketing Association, 1962.

This is a sourcebook to public and private international organizations and programs.

2. TRADE LISTS. Washington, U.S. Bureau of International Commerce, 1975–date.

A compilation of listings by country, which also contains names of suppliers, dealers, agents, distributors, manufacturers, importers, and exporters for various commodities and services, *Trade Lists* is published irregularly.

3. FOREIGN COMMERCE HANDBOOK—BASIC INFORMATION AND A GUIDE TO SOURCES. Washington, U.S. Chamber of Commerce, 1967–date.

A listing of foreign trade services, business organizations, and embassies that is compiled every four or five years.

4. GUIDE TO FOREIGN TRADE STATISTICS. Washington, U.S. Bureau of the Census, 1975.

This periodical covers import and export trade to and from the United States.

5. FOREIGN PRIVATE MANUFACTURING INVESTMENT AND MULTINATIONAL CORPORATIONS. New York, Prager Publishers, Inc. Sanjaya Lall, editor. 1975.

A comprehensive bibliography, with annotations for each listing, this publication covers investments, labor relations, and research.

6. BUSINESS INTERNATIONAL. New York, Haynes Publishing Co., Inc., 1974–date.

This weekly publication concerns business and international trade and investment.

7. DIRECTORY OF AMERICAN FIRMS OPERATING IN FOREIGN COUNTRIES. New York, World Trade Academy Press, Inc. Juvenal L. Angel, compiler. 1979.

This directory presents a list of American corporations operating outside the United States.

8. YEARBOOK OF LABOR STATISTICS. Geneva, International Labor Office, 1930–date.

An annual publication containing international labor statistics, it is arranged by subject matter and includes employment, hours of work, social security, as well as others.

9. NETWORK RATES AND DATA. Skokie, Ill., Standard Rate and Data Service, 1919–date.

A monthly publication, this service collects United States and Canadian advertising rates and data for newspapers, radio, and television, as well as magazines of various kinds.

10. WORLD ECONOMIC SURVEY. New York, United Nations, Department of Economics and Social Affairs, 1948–date.

Published annually, the survey provides a comprehensive review of world economic conditions in text form with supporting charts and tables.

11. PRINCIPAL INTERNATIONAL BUSINESSES. New York, Dun & Bradstreet, 1974–date.

Cited as being the "world marketing directory," this annual publication lists over 44,000 companies alphabetically by name of country. Included is such information as name of head officer, line of business, SIC number, sales and number of employees. SIC numbers and name of country are indexed.

12. WILLINGS PRESS GUIDE, 1979, 105th ANNUAL EDITION. Sussex, England, Thomas Skinner Directories, 1979.

This directory is a guide to the press of the United Kingdom and to the principal publications of Europe and the United States.

29.4 OTHER

1. BUSINESS REFERENCE SOURCES: AN ANNOTATED GUIDE FOR HARVARD BUSINESS SCHOOL STUDENTS. Boston, Harvard University Graduate School of Business Administration. Lorna M. Daniells, compiler, 1971.

This guide contains references to a wide variety of books and journals in business administration.

2. ENCYCLOPEDIA OF BUSINESS INFORMATION SOURCES. 3d ed. Detroit, Gale Research Company. Paul Wasserman, managing editor. 1976.

A detailed listing of subjects of interest to managerial personnel, the encyclopedia contains references to source tools, periodicals, organizations, directories, handbooks, bibliographies, as well as other sources of information.

3. LABOR FACT BOOK. New York, Labor Research Association, 1931–date.

Published biennially, this fact book presents developments and recent events in the labor field.

4. GUIDEBOOK TO LABOR RELATIONS. New York, Commerce Clearing House, 1960–date.
Published annually, the guidebook reports major rules and decisions handed down during the year on various topics. It also provides easy references for locating official texts or other authorities if needed.

5. THE BUSINESSMAN'S GUIDE TO WASHINGTON. Englewood Cliffs, N.J., Prentice-Hall. William Ruder and Raymond Nathan, editors. 1964.
This volume contains a complete listing of federal agencies that assist and control private industries.

6. EMPLOYMENT RELATIONS ABSTRACTS name changed in 1973 to WORK RELATED ABSTRACTS. Detroit, Information Coordinators, Inc., 1950–date.
A loose-leaf publication with monthly supplements, the abstract lists over 200 current publications dealing with research and developments in areas of labor, management, government, and employee relations.

7. LEGAL ASPECTS OF MARKETING. New York, McGraw-Hill Book Company. Howard C. Marshall, editor. 1964.
This volume contains descriptive information with regard to the legal restrictions that affect the marketing of goods and services.

8. AMA BOOKSHELF. New York, American Management Association, 1968–date.
Published annually, this annotated catalog lists all publications of the AMA that are still in print. A monthly supplement contains new studies.

9. LABOR RELATIONS YEARBOOK. Washington, Bureau of National Affairs, 1967–date.
This annual publication reports significant issues in collective bargaining, labor organizations, labor conferences, the role of the government, and economic data.

10. LABOR RELATIONS REFERENCE MANUAL. Washington, Bureau of National Affairs, 1935–date.
Published biennially, this manual gives summary reports with respect to rulings, court opinions, and decisions of the NLRB.

11. LABOR ARBITRATION REPORTS. Washington, Bureau of National Affairs, 1946–date.
Reports of awards made by arbitrators, recommendations of fact-finding boards, laws, and court decisions regarding arbitration issues and decisions of the National Wage Stablization Board are published annually.

12. EXECUTIVE GUIDE TO INFORMATION SOURCES. Detroit, Business Guides Company, 3 volumes. 1965.
These volumes provide a detailed listing of 2,300 business and business related subjects with a record of periodicals, organizations, directories, and other sources pertinent to each topic.

13. THE STANDARD PERIODICAL DIRECTORY. New York, Oxbridge Communications, Inc., 6th edition, 1979–1980.
This comprehensive guide to U.S. and Canadian periodicals lists information on more than 60,000 publications.

14. PUBLIC AFFAIRS INFORMATION SERVICE BULLETIN. New York, PAIS, Inc., 1915–date.
Published weekly September through July, bimonthly in August, with annual cumulations, the bulletin lists current books, pamphlets, government publications and public as well as private agency reports. It also contains articles on economic and social conditions and international relations.

15. MANAGEMENT ABSTRACTS. London, Kraus Reprint Nendeln, Liechtenstein, British Institute of Management, 1969.
Information on all aspects of general management, as well as personnel, financial, production, and office management, is presented.

16. WASHINGTON INFORMATION DIRECTORY 1979–1980. Washington, Congressional Quarterly, Inc., 1975–date.
Published annually, it covers a wide variety of subjects including business, economics, government, science, space, housing, urban affairs, and gives names and addresses of sources that may be contacted for information on these subjects. Included are both public and private agencies.

29.5 FACTBOOKS: STATISTICS AND RATIOS

1. AMERICAN STATISTICS INDEX. Washington, D.C., Congressional Information Service, 1972–date.
Published monthly, *ASI* is a comprehensive indexing service for statistics gathered by the United States government. It is a guide to all statistical publications of the government. *ASI* identifies the statistical data by a subject, title, and agency report number index; it catalogs these data, giving full bibliographic information, and describes briefly the content of each publication. The annual compilation is generally a two-volume set; one volume is the index, and the other is the abstracting service.

2. BAROMETER OF SMALL BUSINESS. San Diego, Accounting Corporation of America, 1950–date.

A semiannual publication, the *Barometer* is a principal reference book of operating statistics for small business. It is alphabetically indexed by type of business, and each is thoroughly analyzed. The data presented are taken from IBM cards containing the entries to the books of clients served by the Accounting Corporation of America's computer processing service.

3. BUSINESS CONDITIONS DIGEST. Washington, D.C., USGPO, 1961–date.

Issued monthly, *BCD* provides a look at the economic factors useful to financial analysts and forecasters. It includes several graphs and tables indicating economic conditions and measures.

4. DUN AND BRADSTREET. KEY BUSINESS RATIOS. New York, Dun and Bradstreet, various dates.

Key Business Ratios provides financial ratios for 125 retailing, wholesaling, manufacturing, and construction businesses, arranged alphabetically by industry or product line.

5. EDITOR & PUBLISHER. MARKET GUIDE. New York, Editor & Publisher Company, 1924–date.

The *Market Guide* gives current data on over 1,500 newspaper markets in both the United States and Canada. Arranged alphabetically by state, then city, such information as number of banks, population, principal industries, shopping centers, newspapers, types of transportation, and retail stores is provided for each city.

6. PREDICASTS. Cleveland, Predicasts, Inc., 1960–date.

Published quarterly with annual cumulations, *Predicasts* lists articles containing predictions and forecasts which have appeared in periodicals, trade journals, and newspapers. The information is indexed by subject and by SIC number.

7. RAND MCNALLY, CO. COMMERCIAL ATLAS AND MARKETING GUIDE. New York, Rand McNally, 1911–date.

Published annually, this commercial atlas is quite thorough, giving geographic, economic, industrial, and government data on cities and states in the United States. Large maps indicating county seats, ZIP codes, trading areas, and manufacturing cities are included. Some similar information about Canada and other parts of the world is also given.

8. ROBERT MORRIS ASSOCIATES. ANNUAL STATEMENT STUDIES. Philadelphia, Robert Morris Associates, 1923–date.

Issued annually, this guide is quite similar in content to Leo Troy's financial ratio book, listed later. The statement studies are useful to anyone doing a financial analysis of a particular product line or industry.

9. SALES AND MARKETING MANAGEMENT. SURVEY OF BUY-ING POWER. New York, Bill Publications, 1978.

This annual publication appears each summer as a supplement to an issue of *Sales and Marketing Management*. Useful for the marketing researcher, it contains data on changes in regional markets, population, number of households in each state, total dollar amount of retail, food, general merchandise, auto, drug, home furnishings sales, and so on. Each state is alphabetically indexed. Some Canadian data are given.

10. STATISTICAL SOURCES. Detroit, Gales Research Company. Paul Wasserman, editor. 1962–date.

Arranged alphabetically by subject, *Statistical Sources* is a comprehensive guide to sources of data about the United States and foreign countries. United States documents and United Nations documents are indexed. Full bibliographic information is given for all sources cited.

11. SURVEY OF CURRENT BUSINESS. Washington, D.C., U.S. Department of Commerce, 1920–date.

This monthly periodical contains in-depth articles on various economic and business topics. Included are business and economic statistics, projections-trends, and national income and product tables.

12. TROY, LEO. ALMANAC OF BUSINESS AND INDUSTRIAL FINANCIAL RATIOS. Englewood Cliffs, N.J., Prentice-Hall, 1978.

Arranged by industry, *Troy's* provides financial ratios for both industry and product types. The 1978 edition has two tables for each industry: Table I reports the operating and financial information for corporations regardless of net profit; Table II gives this same information only for those corporations which operated with a profit.

13. VALUE LINE INVESTMENT SURVEY. New York, Arnold Bernhard Company, 1943–date.

Published weekly, *Value Line* gives both text materials and graphic-chart display of various products and industries. It has four parts: I, Summary and Index; II, Selection and Opinion; III, Ratings and Reports; and IV, Explanation of Terms. The industries represented are indexed alphabetically.

6

CHAPTER THIRTY

Compiled Sources of Legal Information

Legal questions are technical areas requiring specialized methods of research. The following is a basic introduction to research sources of legal information.

30.1 LAW: ENCYCLOPEDIAS

1. CORPUS JURIS SECUNDUM. American Law Book Company, 1936–date.
Corpus Juris Secundum (C.J.S.) restates the text of case law from the first reported case to present cases. It is a revision and update of the earlier *Corpus Juris*. In general, C.J.S. functions in a way similar to an encyclopedia; that is, it gives an overview of the law and contains pertinent citations to cases, form-books, treatises, and journal articles. There is a five-volume topic and subject index. Replacement volumes and pocket supplements are issued to keep the set current.

2. AMERICAN JURISPRUDENCE 2d. Rochester, N.Y., Lawyers Cooperative Publishing Company, 1936–date.
American Jurisprudence 2d (Am. Jur. 2d) is similar to C.J.S. The scope and the subject index approach are the same as C.J.S. One of these encyclopedias is typically used in the first stage of the research process. Both encyclopedias give an overview of the law of a particular topic, and also indicate pertinent court cases.

3. AMERICAN LAW REPORTS. San Francisco, Bancroft-Whitney, 1919–date.

American Law Reports (A.L.R.) is a reporter series in four parts. The first, A.L.R., consists of 175 volumes and contains appellate level court cases from 1919 to 1948. A.L.R. 2d is a 100-volume set with court cases from 1948 to 1965. The third series, A.L.R. 3d, was first published in 1965 and is the current court case reporter. The fourth series is A.L.R. Fed and contains federal court cases from 1969 to the present. The A.L.R. series presents legal topics in annotation or essay form and supports these annotations by citing leading cases and current court decisions.

30.2 INDEXES TO PERIODICALS

1. INDEX TO LEGAL PERIODICALS. New York, H. W. Wilson, 1908–date.
A monthly publication, this index directs the researcher to articles on various topics of law and law-related matters. Most of the journals included are law school reviews. Both subject and specific case name indexes to articles are given.

2. COMMERCE CLEARING HOUSE. BUSINESS LAW ARTICLES. Chicago, Commerce Clearing House, 1965–date.
A continuation of the *Legal Periodical Digest,* this service indexes and digests legal periodical articles. The topics are exclusively related to business law; subjects include labor relations, antitrust contracts, partnerships, corporations, and the like. Arrangement of topics is alphabetical with subject and author indexes.

30.3 DIGESTS

1. AMERICAN DIGEST SYSTEM. St. Paul, West Publishing Company, 1897–date.
The *American Digest System* is a master index consisting of nine separate units. The units cover all reported federal and state court cases from 1658 to the present.

Century Digest	1658–1896
First Decennial	1897–1906
Second Decennial	1907–1916
Third Decennial	1916–1926
Fourth Decennial	1926–1936
Fifth Decennial	1936–1946

6

Sixth Decennial	1946–1956
Seventh Decennial	1956–1966
General Digest	1966–date

The digests are alphabetically indexed by subject. Text arrangement is first by subject; then significant court cases are used to illustrate that subject, alphabetically arranged by state.

2. FEDERAL DIGEST. St. Paul, West Publishing Company, 1940–date.

The *Federal Digest* gives a historical overview of federal court case law. Indexed are Supreme Court decisions and cases found in the *Federal Reporter* and the *Federal Supplement*. The indexing is done by descriptive word, but there also is a Table of Cases in Volumes 66 through 68.

3. U.S. SUPREME COURT DIGEST. St. Paul, West Publishing Company, 1943–date.

This digest is a duplicate of the *American Digest System*, listed previously. Arranged by descriptive words, the digest also has a Table of Cases index. Pocket supplements are published annually to update the service.

4. REGIONAL DIGESTS. St. Paul, West Publishing Company, various dates.

As part of the West Publishing Company's *National Reporter System*, each geographic region of the United States (see section 30.6) has a separate digest. The digests report the cases cited in the regional reporters; therefore, they are useful in providing cases from a given state and surrounding jurisdictions. A Table of Cases and a Descriptive-Word Index are included to aid in finding pertinent cases. (See Fig. 30.1, p. 229.)

30.4 Supreme Court Reports

1. UNITED STATES REPORTS. Washington, D.C., U.S. Government Printing Office, 1817–date.

Cited as "U.S.," this reporter is the official edition of the five reporters giving U.S. Supreme Court decisions. It contains the text of all Supreme Court cases. (See Fig. 30.2, p. 230.)

2. UNITED STATES SUPREME COURT REPORTS. Rochester, N.Y., Lawyers Co-operative Publishing Company, 1882–date.

This is an unofficial or lawyers' edition of the Supreme Court reporters. The texts of all Supreme Court decisions are given, along erally small policies and industrial insurance, the accounts of which policyholders are debited to the agent.—Garrison v. California Employment Stabilization Commission, 149 P.2d 711, 64 C.A.2d 820.

(2) **Colo.App.** Gen.St. c. 55, § 16, making it an offense for the agent of an unlicensed foreign insurance company to adjust any loss on a policy issued by such company, does not authorize the punishment, as an "accessory," of an adjuster employed by such company to advise a committee lawfully acting in the adjustment of a loss.—French v. People, 40 P. 463, 6 Colo. App. 311.

Gen.St. c. 55, § 16, making it an offense for the agent of an unlicensed foreign insurance company to adjust in Colorado a loss, does not prohibit such a company from sending into the state a professional adjuster to ascertain the amount of the loss preparatory to an adjustment in a foreign state.—Id.

(3) **Kan.** To solicit an insurance company not authorized to do business in Kansas to consent to the assignment of an insurance policy issued by it at a time when it was so authorized, is not a violation of Gen.St. par. 3331, making it an offense to forward applications for a company not authorized to do business in the state.—First Nat. Bank of Ottawa v. Renn,
(4) 65 P. 698, 63 Kan. 334.

Mont. Division by a fire insurance agent of his commission personally with an officer of an insurance corporation was an illegal and criminal "rebate," within the meaning of Rev. Codes, §§ 4026, 4027, 4028.—Smith v. Kleinschmidt, 187 P. 894, 57 Mont. 237.

Okl.Cr. Comp.Laws 1909, § 3750, held intended to penalize only persons who act as insurance solicitors without a license, and, while acting as such, negotiate and conclude insurance contracts for compensation.—Bolen v. State, 149 P. 1074, 11 Okl.Cr. 594.

An information based on Comp.Laws 1909, § 3750, must allege that the insurance contracts solicited were negotiated for compensation.—Id.

Or. The statute penalizing "twisting" by persons engaged in insurance business does not purport to infringe upon the right of free speech by prohibiting fair comment and criticism, but manifests intent to protect legitimate business against false and malicious statements. Code 1930, § 46–142.—Woolley v. Hiner, 100 P.2d 608, 164 Or. 161.

Wash. In action against insurance agent for violating Rem.Comp.Stat. §§ 7243, 7244, penalizing disposing of premium notes before delivery of policy, where accused was found guilty, held, that it was proper for the trial court in its judgment to both fix the fine and revoke the license of accused, even though, if the court did not do so, it possibly would become the duty of the insurance commissioner to revoke the license of one so convicted.—State v. Cannon, 217 P. 18, 125 Wash. 515.

(5) &—**31. Offenses by persons dealing with insurers.**

Library references

C.J.S. Insurance § 90.

Cal.App. Statute providing that it is unlawful to present or cause to be presented any false or fraudulent claim for the payment of loss under a contract of insurance, does not proscribe only the filing of a false written proof of loss, but proscribes the presentment of any false demand under a policy of insurance irrespective of the form of that demand. West's Ann.Insurance Code, §§ 554, 556(b). —People v. Teitelbaum, 329 P.2d 157, 163 C.A.2d 184, appeal dismissed, certiorari denied 79 S.Ct. 738, 359 U.S. 206, 3 L.Ed.2d 759.

Cal.App. Under section of Insurance Code rendering it unlawful to prepare any writing with intent to use it in support of any fraudulent claim for payment of loss under contract of insurance, writing required need not be false or fraudulent as long as it is intended to be presented or used in support of any false or fraudulent claim. Insurance Code, § 556 (a, b).—People v. Zelver, 287 P.2d 183, 135 C.A.2d 226.

Cal.App. In prosecution for crime of filing false claim of fire loss, evidence was sufficient to sustain finding that furniture listed on the itemized statement of loss filed by defendant with insurer was not present on the premises at the time of the fire. Insurance Code, § 556.—People v. Turley, 259 P.2d 724, 119 C. A.2d 632.

Evidence on issue of whether defendant, when submitting inventory of fire loss to insurer, knew that items appearing on inventory were not on premises at time that fire occurred and had guilty intent was sufficient to sustain conviction for filing false claim of loss. Insurance Code, § 556.—Id.

In prosecution based on statute making it unlawful to present false claim for payment of loss under insurance contract, the basis of the offense alleged is accused's intent to defraud which intent does not depend solely upon the legal obligation arising out of the insurance contract. Pen.Code, § 950; Insurance Code, § 556.—Id.

Cal.App. Evidence on issue of whether defendants, who had not signed preliminary claim of loss on which draft for payment under burglary policy was issued, but who had subscribed proof of loss when draft was delivered, had guilty intent, was sufficient to sustain convictions for fraudulently subscribing false proof of loss.—People v. Ross, 233 P.2d 68, 105 C.A.2d 235.

Cal.App. Evidence sustained conviction for preparing a computation of nonexisting stock loss from fire sustained by insured shoe store owner, with intent to allow computation to be presented to insurer in support of false claim for loss. Insurance Code, § 556.—People v. Burton, 205 P.2d 1065, 91 C.A.2d 695, certiorari denied Sugarman v. People of State of Cal., 70 S.Ct. 187, 338 U.S. 886, 94 L.Ed. 544.

Cal.App. Evidence sustained conviction of one owning partnership interest in tavern, for violation of the insurance code by presenting a false claim for insurance on a quantity of liquor allegedly stolen from the tavern.—People v. Engelhart, 176 P.2d 789, 78 C.A.2d 6.

Cal.App. Evidence as to whether accused actually lost, in robbery of his restaurant,

6

FIGURE 30.1 Page from West's *Pacific Digest*, vol. 21, page 435. **(1)** General subject. **(2)** State of case described and if case was in Appeals Court. **(3)** Synopsis of case. **(4)** Case name and cite. **(5)** West publication "key" number and specific subject. (*Source: Pacific Digest*, West Publishing Company, 1971. © West Publishing Company.)

(1) 42 [OCTOBER TERM, 1969

Syllabus 399 U.S.

(2) [CHAMBERS *v.* MARONEY, CORRECTIONAL SUPERINTENDENT

(3) [CERTIORARI TO THE UNITED STATES COURT OF APPEALS FOR THE THIRD CIRCUIT

No. 830. Argued April 27, 1970—Decided June 22, 1970

(4) [Petitioner was one of four men arrested after the auto in which they were riding was stopped by police shortly after an armed robbery of a service station. The arrests resulted from information supplied by the service station attendant and bystanders. The car was driven to a police station, where a search disclosed two revolvers, one loaded with dumdum bullets, and cards bearing the name of an attendant at another service station who had been robbed at gunpoint a week earlier. In a warrant-authorized search of petitioner's home the next day police found and seized ammunition, including dumdum bullets similar to those found in one of the guns in the car. At his first trial, which ended in a mistrial, petitioner was represented by a Legal Aid Society attorney. Another Legal Aid Society attorney, who represented him at the second trial, did not confer with petitioner until a few minutes before that trial began. The materials taken from the car and the bullets seized from petitioner's home were introduced in evidence and petitioner was convicted of robbery of both service stations. Petitioner did not take a direct appeal, but sought, unsuccessfully, a writ of habeas corpus in the Pennsylvania courts and in the federal courts, challenging the admissibility of the materials taken from the car and the ammunition seized in his home, and claiming that he was denied the effective assistance of counsel. The Court of Appeals dealt with the claim that the attorney's lack of preparation resulted in the failure to exclude the guns and ammunition by finding harmless error in the admission of the bullets and ruling that the materials seized from the car were admissible in evidence, and concluded that the claim of prejudice from substitution of counsel was without substantial basis. *Held:*

(5) [1. The warrantless search of the automobile was valid and the materials seized therefrom were properly introduced in evidence. Pp. 46–52.

FIGURE 30.2 Page from *U.S. Reports,* vol. 399, page 42. **(1)** Date of Supreme Court term. **(2)** Case name. **(3)** Description of type of appeal. **(4)** Synopsis of case. **(5)** What the Supreme Court held. (*Source:* U.S. Supreme Court, *United States Reports,* U.S. Government Printing Office, 1970.)

with explanatory material prepared by the editors. Also included are cross-references from the official editions (see **1,** above) to the lawyers' edition.

3. SUPREME COURT REPORTER. St. Paul, West Publishing Company, 1882–date.

This set is an unofficial edition which is part of the West Publishing Company *National Reporter System.* As with the reporter above, this gives the text of U.S. Supreme Court cases. There are cross references from this edition to the official reporter. It duplicates the *United States Reports* beginning with Vol. 106 page 1 of *United States Reports.*

4. UNITED STATES LAW WEEK. Washington, D.C., Bureau of National Affairs, 1933–date.

Published weekly, this service is divided into two main parts: a Supreme Court section and a General Law section. The text of Supreme Court cases is given in the Supreme Court section, while the General Law section contains topics such as agency rulings, statutes, and trends. There is a subject index to both sections, and a case name approach can be used for the Supreme Court section.

30.5 Federal Court Reporters

1. FEDERAL REPORTER. St. Paul, West Publishing Company, 1879–date.

The *Federal Reporter* contains all federal appellate level court cases, decisions from the Court of Claims, and those of the U.S. Court of Customs and Patent Appeals. There are two sets of the *Federal Reporter.* The first is simply titled *Federal Reporter* and consists of 300 volumes. The second set, *Federal Reporter 2d,* starts anew with Volume 1.

2. FEDERAL SUPPLEMENT. St. Paul, West Publishing Company, 1932–date.

The *Federal Supplement* is an extension of the *Federal Reporter* in that it also includes selected District Court cases, cases of the Customs Court, and Court of Claims cases from 1932–1960. The Court of Claims cases from 1960 to the present are in the *Federal Reporter.*

30.6 State Court Reporters

Most states publish their own judicial decisions. The state publications are considered the official reports. The West Publishing Company issues an unofficial series of state reporters as a part of the *National Reporter System*. The states are divided into seven regions with each region represented by a reporter. The seven regions are Pacific, North Western, South Western, North Eastern, South Eastern, Atlantic, Pacific, and Southern. Each contains the judicial decisions of the states comprising that region.

30.7 Citation of Cases

All cases are cited in the same manner. Order of citation is volume, reference source, page.

> For example, a case found on page 209 of volume 301 of the *United States Reports* is cited as:
>
> 301 U.S. 209.
>
> Similarly, one found on page 10 of volume 293 of the *Pacific Reporter, 2d Series* is cited:
>
> 293 P.2d 10.
>
> A case on page 112 of the *Federal Supplement*, Volume 2 is cited:
>
> 2 F.Supp. 112

In general, all legal citations follow this order. When the case name is referred to, along with the source, the same order is used. Cite as:

> Pressman v. Termin, 60 Cal.2d 208, 359 P.2d 35, 50 Cal. Rptr. 47 (1960).
>
> (*Pressman v. Termin* is found in) (Volume 60) (*California Second Series*) (page 208); (Volume 359) (*Pacific Reporter, Second Series*) (page 35); (Volume 50) (*California Reporter*) (page 47) (year 1960).

Citation is to the official reporter first, then to the unofficial. In the final example, the official or government (here it is the state government) issued reporter is the *California Second Series*. A handy pocket-size guide to legal citations is *A Uniform System of Citation*, 12th edition (Cambridge, Mass.: Harvard Law Review Association, 1976). It is considered the most definitive guide to legal citations by lawyers, law students, tax specialists, and professionals in those fields.

30.8 Citators

A citator is another research tool used in locating the law and cases illustrating a point of law. Rather than being arranged by subject as the encyclopedias, index sources, and digests are, the citators are arranged by court case citation. Cases may be cited in the whole or a particular significant headnote or syllabus within the case text may be presented. For example, most court reports have a short summary of the facts and laws covering the case being cited. These summaries are called *syllabi* (plural form).

30.9 Citator Sources

SHEPARD'S CITATIONS. Colorado Springs, Shepard's Citations, Inc., 1873–date.

Shepard's Citations is a well-known citation service. It enables the researcher to trace the judicial history of every reported decision and to determine which, if any, reported decisions and legislative enactments apply to or affect the statutes of a certain jurisdiction. *Shephard's Citations* covers all facets of the legal areas, such as the U.S. Constitution, the U.S. Code, state codes and constitutions, court rules, federal and state court cases, acts of legislative bodies, articles in legal periodicals, and the like.

The process of using one of *Shepard's Citations* is commonly called "Shepardizing." To "Shepardize" a case, a headnote, a legal periodical, or other material, a researcher must first find the correct cite. For example:

> A significant case is found in Volume 81 of the *Colorado Reports*, page 25 (81 Col. 25).

Knowing where the case may be found, one is able to select the proper Shepard's citator to use.

> For the above court case, the *Colorado Reports Citations* should be consulted (see Fig. 30.3, p. 234).

> The citator arrangement is numerical by volume, so the citator page with Vol. 81 shown at the top is found. One then goes down the columns of numbers until number (page) 25 is reached. Here will be presented all the citations to other materials and court cases which relate to the case found in Volume 81, page 25 of the *Colorado Reports*.

	Vol. 81]						
$-18-$ c181Col^{3}42	**Vol. 81]**	$-535-$ 514P2d^{2}336 419FS^{2}169 419FS^{3}169	$-478-$ f475P2d^{2}711	$-242-$ 513P2d^{6}463	$-480-$ 485P2d^{1}513	$-342-$ 183Col^{5}95	$-202-$ 51DJ536
$-68-$ 50DJ288	$-10-$ 537P2d751		$-491-$ 169Col^{2}292 187Col^{2}429 48DJ491	$-262-$ 33CoA289	$-494-$ 509P2d^{1}1288 50DJ140	$-353-$ 5/74CoL16	$-218-$ 36CoA^{8}378
$-72-$ 28CoA^{2}309 28CoA^{4}309	$-25-$] 413US^{2}191] 37L$\mathbb{E}^2$553] 93SC^{2}2689]	**Vol. 82**		$-272-$ c174Col^{3}103 186Col432 188Col316 35CoA^{3}170	$-518-$ d29CoA^{3}128	$-376-$ 166Col^{4}38 f176Col^{1}260	$-232-$ 168Col^{8}50 52DJ499
$-158-$ 33CoA300 500P2d^{1}373	$-73-$ 170Col^{12}423 170Col^{18}424	$-1-$ 536P2d^{1}324 536P2d^{1}850 425FS^{1}1099	$-497-$ o175Col^{6}542 o175Col^{7}542 26A3317s	$-280-$ f185Col^{1}248 f185Col^{2}248	$-540-$ 37A334n 37A372n	$-409-$ 172Col^{1}354 31CoA529 f34CoA^{7}418	$-237-$ 168Col^{3}370
$-183-$ 167Col^{1}493 167Col^{1}495 39A3650n 39A3665n 54A3424n	$-92-$ 492P2d^{1}861 $-113-$ 173Col^{1}311	$-13-$ 167Col^{10}103 28CoA^{10}445 32CoA^{13}425 534P2d^{15}328	$-589-$ 167Col^{6}120 q171Col^{5}360 181Col^{5}200	$-289-$ 166Col^{4}530 168Col^{4}258	$-556-$ 479P2d^{1}985 $-582-$ 176Col^{1}171	$-429-$ j471P2d^{5}426 $-456-$ 5CoL1474	$-255-$ 541P2d^{2}120 543P2d^{2}93 543P2d^{3}93 $-262-$ 28CoA^{1}336 29CoA173
$-220-$ 176Col^{1}360 40A3173n 40A3185n 40A3190n	$-125-$ 166Col^{4}255 170Col^{1}174 d482P2d^{1}396	$-77-$ d31CoA199 73A3601n	**Vol. 83** $-1-$ q166Col^{1}166	$-295-$ 184Col^{3}102	$-587-$ 499P2d^{1}621	$-481-$ 166Col^{5}505	30CoA^{1}346
$-239-$ 32A3809n	$-144-$ 31CoA^{2}36	$-81-$ 52A3827n $-98-$ 28CoA^{6}140	$-4-$ 166Col^{9}425 167Col^{15}118 168Col86 181Col^{9}244 5CoL166	$-300-$ 74McL1146 $-315-$ 168Col^{3}370	**Vol. 84** $-19-$ 169Col^{4}18 30CoA152 34CoA^{2}374	$-502-$ 167Col^{1}10 $-544-$ 526P2d1352	$-289-$ 177Col^{1}228 36CoA^{1}126 $-304-$ 168Col^{8}355 33CoA267 24StnL657
$-258-$ 5CoL1474	$-168-$ 34CoA^{4}45 $-181-$ 171Col^{1}503 31CoA^{1}447	$-115-$ 168Col^{1}549 $-150-$ 169Col^{4}228 496P2d^{3}1068	$-72-$ 170Col^{5}221	$-329-$ 339FS^{8}724 $-335-$ 6/73CoL9	$-22-$ 34A3290n	$-596-$ 181Col^{5}192	$-327-$ 541P2d^{3}125
$-276-$ 39A3460n $-279-$ d168Col462	$-233-$ f29CoA^{1}379 f34CoA^{1}375	$-156-$ 489P2d^{1}341	$-89-$ 32CoA^{5}141 $-118-$	$-341-$ 173Col^{1}314 175Col^{1}568	$-41-$ 171Col^{9}515 $-57-$	**Vol. 85** $-1-$ 28CoA^{3}520	$-346-$ d528P2d^{12}979

(2) (3) (4)

FIGURE 30.3 Page from *Shepard's Citations, Colorado Reports*, vol. 71, no. 2, August 1978, page 23. **(1)** Title of reports being "Shepardized." **(2)** Designation of volume of *Colorado Reports* being "Shepardized." **(3)** Page number of case being "Shepardized." **(4)** Citation to cases related to a case on page 25. (*Source: Shepard's Colorado Citations*, Shepard's Citations, 1978.)

In addition to material relevant to the case in question, there are coded abbreviations before each case cite to indicate the history of the case. The abbreviations will show that the case may have been affirmed (a), dismissed (D), reversed (r), superseded (S), is a connected case (CC), or is the same case (s) but in another reporter. The disposition of the case also is indicated by abbreviations. At the beginning of each citation, there is an explanation and a guide to its use.

CHAPTER
THIRTY-ONE

Compiled Sources of Tax Information

Tax questions require specialized research sources. The following briefly describes the tax research procedure and the aids necessary for tax research.

31.1 Primary Authority

There are three areas of primary authority: statutory, administrative, and judicial.

31.2 Statutory Authority

In the area of statutory law, the four main sources of information are as follows:

INTERNAL REVENUE CODE

Internal Revenue Code of 1954 (various publishers). The *Internal Revenue Code of 1954* (I.R.C.) is the tax law as passed by Congress. First issued in 1913, the I.R.C. was codified in 1939, then again in 1954. Since then, many court decisions have modified and interpreted the tax law in the 1954 Code. Congress has often amended the 1954 Code in legislation called Revenue Acts. Examples of such acts are the Tax Reform Act of 1976 and the Revenue Act of 1978. The *Internal Revenue Code* is the starting point to research any tax

6

question. The I.R.C. is organized into subtitles, chapters, subchapters, parts, subparts, and sections. The sections are the most useful reference and appear in sequential numerical order. Each section is further divided into subsections.

> For example, a general reference might be to I.R.C. Sec. 355, whereas a specific reference might be I.R.C. Sec. 355 (a)(1)(A)(ii). (See Fig. 31.1, below.)

HOUSE REPORTS

House Reports (previously detailed in Part Five, section 19.2), are the reports of the House of Representatives on bills of Congress. All major revenue bills are originated in the House of Representatives. Hearings are conducted by the House Ways and Means Committee; following these hearings, the Committee sends the bill, along with a report, back to the House. It then is given a number prefixed by "H.R." If the House of Representatives passes the bill, it then is referred to the Senate Finance Committee.

CH. 1—NORMAL TAXES AND SURTAXES   113

section 356 as relates to this section) shall apply with respect to a plan of reorganization (whether or not a reorganization within the meaning of section 368 (a)) for a railroad approved by the Interstate Commerce Commission under section 77 of the Bankruptcy Act, or under section 20b of the Interstate Commerce Act, as being in the public interest.

(1) SEC. 355. DISTRIBUTION OF STOCK AND SECURITIES OF A CONTROLLED CORPORATION.

(2)   (a) EFFECT ON DISTRIBUTEES.—
            (1) GENERAL RULE.—If—
                (A) a corporation (referred to in this section as the "distributing corporation")—
                    (i) distributes to a shareholder, with respect to its stock, or
(3)   (ii) distributes to a security holder, in exchange for its securities,
            solely stock or securities of a corporation (referred to in this section as "controlled corporation") which it controls immediately before the distribution,

---

FIGURE 31.1   A page from the *U.S. Statutes at Large,* 83rd Congress 1954, vol. 68A.   **(1)** Section number and title.   **(2)** Subsection (a).   **(3)** General rule and explanation.   (*Source:* U.S. Congress, *United States Statutes at Large,* U.S. Government Printing Office, 1954.)

SENATE REPORTS

Senate Reports (previously discussed in Part Five, section 19.2), are significant in the adoption of tax acts. The Senate Finance Committee is the counterpart of the House Ways and Means Committee. The Senate Finance Committee reviews all the "H.R." bills and reports to the Senate on each bill. If the Senate passes a bill, the bill then returns to the House where, if no major differences exist, it is then referred to the President for signature.

COMMITTEE REPORTS

Committee reports from the House Ways and Means Committee and the Senate Finance Committee are useful in determining what Congress intended in the legislation. Even though the committees have no legislative power per se, they are influential in tax proposals. Committee reports are published in the *Internal Revenue Bulletin*. They are later accumulated in the *Cumulative Bulletin*.

31.3 ADMINISTRATIVE AUTHORITY

The administrative agency with authority in the tax area is the Internal Revenue Service. The IRS consists of seven districts and performs such duties as aiding taxpayers in interpreting tax laws, auditing taxpayers, and issuing administrative laws called Regulations.

INCOME TAX REGULATIONS

Generally, with each change in the *Internal Revenue Code* that is passed by Congress, the Commissioner of the Internal Revenue Service issues new Regulations, known as *Income Tax Regulations*. The Income Tax Regulations are reproduced as a three-volume set which is also an integral part of the *Code of Federal Regulations*.

6

> For example, Reg. Sec. 1.355 deals with Section (§) 355 of the *Internal Revenue Code* from part 1 of the *Code of Federal Regulations*.

TREASURY DECISIONS

Amendments to the Regulations are called Treasury Decisions, or T.D.'s. These are issued by the Commissioner of the Internal Revenue Service and approved by the Secretary of the Treasury. T.D.'s are issued to the public in the *Federal Register* and the *Internal Revenue Bulletin* (I.R.B.); then they are accumulated in the *Cumulative Bulletin*.

INTERNAL REVENUE BULLETIN

The *Internal Revenue Bulletin* (I.R.B.) is a weekly publication of the U.S. Government Printing Office. In addition to the Treasury Decisions, the I.R.B. also contains:

1. Copies of Internal Revenue Acts
2. Supreme Court decisions which affect the Internal Revenue Code
3. Revenue Rulings
4. Lists of the Commissioner's confirmations
5. Ways and Means Committee reports, Senate Finance reports, and Joint Conference Committee reports.

CUMULATIVE BULLETIN

The *Cumulative Bulletin* (C.B.) is the accumulative edition of six months of the I.R.B.'s. Published twice a year, the C.B. is published by the Government Printing Office.

REVENUE RULINGS

Revenue rulings are public information releases issued by the Commissioner of the Internal Revenue Service. They clarify the IRS position regarding tax issues which are substantive in nature, and are used as precedent in many tax cases. The Commissioner publishes rulings deemed to be of general application in each issue of the *Internal Revenue Bulletin*.

REVENUE PROCEDURES

Another type of public release issued by the Internal Revenue Service is *Revenue Procedures*. Revenue procedures are concerned with the internal management of the IRS such as techniques and operations of the various departments. Each revenue procedure is clarified and numbered by year, as are revenue rulings.

In citing a revenue procedure or a revenue ruling, the following form should be used:

> Rev. Proc. 71-390, 1971-2 C.B. 1101.
>
> (Revenue procedure 71-390) (Volume 2 of *Cumulative Bulletin* in 1971) (page 1101).
>
> Rev. Rul. 74-21, 1974-2 C.B. 972
>
> (Revenue ruling 74-21) (Volume 2 of *Cumulative Bulletin* in 1974) (page 972).

If the ruling had not yet been accumulated, the citation would have been:

> Rev. Rul. 74-21, I.R.B. 1974-(week).
>
> (Revenue ruling 74-21) (*Internal Revenue Bulletin* in 1974) (week in 1974).

TECHNICAL INFORMATION RELEASE

A Technical Information Release ("T.I.R., (date)"), filed by the IRS, gives technical information of interest to taxpayers. Information such as procedures and requirements of the IRS and filing dates would constitute a T.I.R.

31.4 JUDICIAL AUTHORITY

Judicial primary authority is concerned with the interpretation of the statutes and the evaluation of the rulings and regulations as applied to a given situation which is the subject of litigation.

DISTRICT COURTS

Before the Board of Tax Appeals was created in 1924, taxpayers who sought relief from a particular tax liability were required to pay the tax and then sue for a refund in the Federal District court.

The Federal District Courts have jurisdiction over:

1. Enforcement of summons, the compelling of attendance, testimony, or production of books, papers, and other data

2. Issuance of processes, judgments, and orders of revenue law

3. Actions for damage to the United States officers or employees
4. Action to enforce liens, or subject property to payment of tax
5. Action of bonds

The Prentice-Hall *American Federal Tax Reports* (AFTR) and the *United States Tax Cases* (USTC), published by Commerce Clearing House, both provide District Court decisions in tax matters. The *Federal Supplement* (F. Supp.), discussed in section 30.5, also gives District Court decisions.

COURT OF CLAIMS

The Court of Claims also has the power to hear Federal tax matters. It has jurisdiction over any claim filed against the United States which is: (1) founded by an Act of Congress, (2) founded upon the Constitution, or (3) founded upon any regulation of an executive department.
Court of Claims decisions are also published in AFTR and USTC.

TAX COURT

The Tax Court (formerly the Board of Tax Appeals) has limited jurisdiction over tax litigation. It is an administrative body, not a judicial court in the technical sense. It does have jurisdiction over statutory tax matters, such as income and estate and gift taxes. To satisfy the administrative rule of "exhaustion of remedies," the taxpayer must have had the case reviewed by the Commissioner of the IRS and have received therefrom a notice of deficiency of tax before the taxpayer may appeal the issue to the Tax Court.

The headquarters of the Tax Court is in Washington, D.C., but the Court can sit at any place in the United States. It is structured to provide easy access to taxpayers.

The decisions of the Tax Court are reported as memoranda decisions. These memoranda decisions are published in four separate volumes:

1. *United States Board of Tax Appeals Reports*, Washington, Government Printing Office, for years to 1942.

Cite as:

4 B.T.A. 293.

(Volume 4) (*Board of Tax Appeals Report*) (page 293)

2. *The Tax Court of the United States Reports,* Washington, Government Printing Office, for years after 1942.

Cite as:

> 10 T.C. 491.
> (Volume 10) *(Tax Court Reports)* (page 491).

3. *Board of Tax Appeals Memorandum Decisions,* Englewood Cliffs, N.J., Prentice-Hall, for years before 1942.

Cite as:

> 2493 P-H Memo BTA.
> (paragraph number 2493) *(Prentice-Hall Memorandum)*
> *(Decisions of the Board of Tax Appeals).*

4. *Tax Court Memorandum Decisions,* New York, Commerce Clearing House, for years after 1942.

Cite as:

> 30 T.C.M. 59.
> (Volume 30) *(Tax Court Memorandum)* (page 59).

COURT OF APPEALS

Decisions appealed from the District Courts and the Tax Court can be heard by any one of ten Circuit Courts of Appeals. These ten circuits divide the United States into ten geographical regions, with each region being designated a "circuit." (The District of Columbia has its own circuit.) Decisions from the Courts of Appeals are published in the *Federal Reporter* series (Fed. or F.2d). They are also reported in the AFTR and the USTC. The Circuit Court memorandum decisions, also known as *per curiam* decisions, are often found in the *Internal Revenue Bulletin* under "Court Decisions."

SUPREME COURT

The U.S. Supreme Court is the highest level of authority, and its decisions are "the law of the land." Although the U.S. Supreme Court is technically a court of limited jurisdiction, it has authority over tax matters and a broad range of legal issues.

U.S. Supreme Court decisions are found in several publications (see Part Five). These include:

1. *The Internal Revenue Bulletin,* under "Court Decisions" and cited as Ct.D.

2. The *United States Reporter Series,* cited (Volume) U.S. (page).

3. The *Supreme Court Reporter Series,* cited (Volume) S.Ct. (page).

4. The *United States Reports, Lawyer's Edition,* cited (Volume) L.Ed. (page).

5. *The American Federal Tax Report Series,* cited (Volume) AFTR (page) or (Volume) AFTR 2d (page).

6. The *United States Tax Cases,* cited (Volume) USTC (paragraph).

31.5 SECONDARY AUTHORITY

Secondary authority materials often provide some guidance to the researcher of tax questions and aid in furnishing previous cases of similar facts upon which evidence is gathered. Any source of tax information not considered a primary authority is a secondary authority.

CITATOR

A citator is a valuable source for evaluating primary tax materials. Two tax citators are published. They are similar to the legal citators discussed in sections 30.7 and 30.8.

Commerce Clearing House (CCH) publishes the *CCH Citator.* It is a loose-leaf service providing the judicial history of each cited case. It identifies each court which has deliberated upon this case and indicates the Commissioner's acquiescence or nonacquiescence, which is the Commissioner's endorsement or disagreement with the Court's decision. The *CCH Citator* is a compact service and details the basic information regarding a case.

Prentice-Hall also publishes a tax citator. The *Federal Tax Citator* is a four-volume set with a loose-leaf supplement. Volume 1 contains decisions and rulings reported to the year 1943; Volume 2 continues the decisions until the year 1949; Volume 3 contains the decisions and rulings from 1949 through 1955; Volume 4 covers years 1956 through 1967. A separate loose-leaf supplement presents the latest decisions on current matters (see Fig. 31.2, p. 243).

COURT AND TC DECISIONS
Treasury Decisions & Rulings Start on Page 13,301

—A—

AAA CYCLES v U.S., 41 AFTR2d 78-1072, 447 F Supp 929 (DC Ill) (See Richman, R. R. v U.S.)

AARON, A. A., INC., 1978 P-H TC Memo ¶ 78,028

AARON RENTS INC. v U.S., 42 AFTR2d 78-5940 (DC Ga, 9-20-78)

(1) A. & A. TOOL & SUPPLY CO. THE v COMM., 182 F2d
(2) 300, 39 AFTR 517 (USCA 10)
(3) q-13—Williams, C. F. & Jeanne V., 1978 P-H TC Memo 78-1262

ABATTI, BEN & MARGARET L., 1978 P-H TC Memo ¶ 78,392 (See Abatti, Tony & Sheila Gruis)

ABATTI, SHEILA, 1978 P-H TC Memo ¶ 78,392 (See Abatti, Tony & Sheila Gruis)

ABATTI, TONY, 1978 P-H TC Memo ¶ 78,392 (See Abatti, Tony & Sheila Gruis)

ABATTI, TONY & NINFA, 1978 P-H TC Memo ¶ 78,392 (See Abatti, Tony & Sheila Gruis)

ABATTI, TONY & SHEILA GRUIS, 1978 P-H TC Memo ¶ 78,392

ABDALLA, JACOB & MARY T., 69 TC 697, ¶ 69.58 P-H TC
App (T) 8-18-78 (USCA 5)
App (G) 8-21-78 (USCA 5)

ABEGG v COMM., 26 AFTR2d 70-5154, 429 F2d 1209 (USCA 2)
g—Malmstedt, Margaret E. Johnson v Comm., 42 AFTR2d 78-5295, 578 F2d 526 (USCA 4) [See 26 AFTR2d 70-5156, 429 F2d 1211, n. 1]

ABEGG, WERNER, 50 TC 145, ¶ 50.17 P-H TC
g-1—Malmstedt, Margaret E. Johnson v Comm., 42 AFTR2d 78-5295, 578 F2d 526 (USCA 4)

ABEL INVEST. CO. v U.S., 29 AFTR2d 72-894 (DC Neb)
e-1—Bank of America v U.S., 42 AFTR2d 78-5226 (DC Calif)

ABERNATHY, RUSSELL & BETTY, 1978 P-H TC Memo ¶ 78,370

ABERSON; U.S. v, 25 AFTR2d 70-411, 419 F2d 820 (USCA 2)
e-2—Lane, Robert J.; U.S. v, 42 AFTR2d 78-5107, 561 F2d 1078 (USCA 2)

ABINGDON POTTERIES INC., 19 TC 23, ¶ 19.4 P-H TC 1952
e-1—I.S.C., Inc., 1978 P-H TC Memo 78-1197, 78-1198 [See 19 TC 26-27]

ABRAMS—contd
e—Taubman, Lester v U.S., 42 AFTR2d 78-5120, 449 F Supp 523 (DC Mich) [See 28 AFTR2d 71-6130, 333 F Supp 1148, n. 11]

ABRAMSON; COMM. v, 124 F2d 416, 28 AFTR 779 (USCA 2)
e-2—Rev Rul 78-164, 1978 P-H 54,908

ABRUZZINO, ROBERT, EST. OF, 61 TC 306, ¶ 61.32 P-H TC
e-1—Letter Ruling 7810001, 1978 P-H 142,099

ACACIA MUT. LIFE INS. CO. v U.S., 20 AFTR2d 5291, 272 F Supp 188 (DC Md)
e-1—Central Ill. Public Service Co. v U.S., 41 AFTR2d 78-722, 435 US 31, 98 S Ct 922

ACH v COMM., 17 AFTR2d 700, 358 F2d 342 (USCA 6)
e—Schering Corp. & Subsidiaries, 69 TC 599, 69 P-H TC 334

ACH, PAULINE W., 42 TC 114, ¶ 42.8 P-H TC
e—Schering Corp. & Subsidiaries, 69 TC 599, 69 P-H TC 334 [See 42 TC 125-126]

ACKER; COMM. v, 4 AFTR2d 5778, 361 US 87
e—Fulman, Arthur, Trustee v U.S., 41 AFTR2d 78-700, 434 US 533, 98 S Ct 845 [See 4 AFTR2d 5780, 361 US 91]
e—Bates, Alfred O. v U.S., 42 AFTR2d 78-5483 (USCA 6)
Central Motor Co. v U.S., 42 AFTR2d 78-5585 (USCA 10) [See 4 AFTR2d 5780, 361 US 91]
f-1—Johnson, Bobby K. v Artru, Thomas, 41 AFTR2d 78-315 (DC Tex)
f-1—Southard, Clifford C. v Comm., 42 AFTR2d 78-5503 (DC Okla)

ACKER v COMM., 1 AFTR2d 1998, 258 F2d 568 (USCA 6)
f-1—Johnson, Bobby K. v Artru, Thomas, 41 AFTR2d 78-315 (DC Tex)
e-5—Bates, Alfred O. v U.S., 42 AFTR2d 78-5483 (USCA 6)
f-6—Southard, Clifford C. v Comm., 42 AFTR2d 78-5503 (DC Okla)

ACKER, FRED N., 26 TC 107, ¶ 26.10 P-H TC 856
f-1—Pohlman, Berentje C. M., 1978 P-H TC Memo 78-715
f-1—Dunn, Alton G., Jr. & Nancy C., 1978 P-H TC Memo 78-865
e-1—Jedinak, Edward J. & Lucille M., 1978 P-H TC Memo 78-964 [See 26 TC 112-113]
f-1—White, Marvin C., 1978 P-H TC Memo 78-1139 [See 26 TC 112-113]
f-1—Bolden, Gladys E., 1978 P-H TC Memo 78-1220 [See

6

FIGURE 31.2 Excerpt from Prentice-Hall's *Federal Tax Citator,* November 27, 1978, page 13001. **(1)** Case name. **(2)** Citation of case. The case can be found on page 300 of volume 182 of the *Federal Reporter, Second Series* and on page 517, Volume 39 of the Prentice-Hall *American Federal Tax Reporter.* **(2)** Citation to corresponding case. (*Source: Federal Taxes Citator,* Prentice-Hall, 1979. Prentice-Hall Federal Taxes Citator. Copyright 1979 by Prentice-Hall, Inc., Englewood Cliffs, N.J. 07632.)

based on sales. *Harry W. Bockhoff,* 3 BTA 560.

(15) Prospective earnings capitalized; Hoskold's formula.—Most accurate way to value patents by capitalizing prospective earnings is Hoskold's formula. *Heberlein Patent Corp. v U.S.* (DC NY;1938), 23 AFTR

1132, aff'd without discussing this point (2 Cir), 105 F2d 965, 23 AFTR 282.

(40) Following ruling not determinative as to future transactions: ARR 520, CB Dec. 1921, p. 156; ARM 35, CB June 1920, p. 142. *RevRul* 67-123, 1967-1 CB 383.

(2) [**Jigs, Dies, Patterns, Special Tools—Drawings, Tracings, Models**

[¶15,381] **Basic rules.**—Special tools (jigs, dies, patterns, etc.), used on or with production equipment, may be depreciated or charged to expense, usually depending on useful life. Items with a useful life of 1 year or less are properly expensed; but they have been held depreciable in a composite group. ¶15,383(15). Assets with an over-one-year life have been expensed in such a group. ¶15,383(20). Useful life, cost and other factors must be proved. ¶15,383(30). Obsolescence (e.g., changing styles) may be a factor. ¶15,383(5); **(3)** and ¶15,429. Guidelines, ¶15,196, may apply to taxable years ending before 1971 (e.g., ¶45,354(5); cf. ¶43,355, Footnote (1)). Under the class life asset depreciation system explained at ¶15,466 et seq., subsidiary assets are included in the asset classes. However, they could be excluded under certain circumstances during the period beginning on 1-1-71 and ending 12-31-73. See *RevProc 72-10,* Footnote 2, at ¶45,301, and Reg. §1.167(a)—11(b)(5)(vii), ¶15,466.5.

Drawings, tracings, blueprints, models etc. are subject to the same rules. ¶15,383(10); (25).

Costs of depreciable research and experimental property, including drawings and models, may be deductible expense. Sec. 174, ¶16,207; Reg. §1.174-2(b), ¶16,208.5. And see ¶16,209(10); ¶15,373(30). For patent drawings and models, see ¶15,371 et seq.

[¶15,383] **Special tools; drawings, etc.—**

(5) Shoe manufacturer.—Cost of lasts, dies and patterns with average useful life of **(4)** 1 year or less was deductible expense. *Inter. Shoe Co.,* 38 BTA 81.

Lasts, dies and patterns for "standard-style" shoes were correctly depreciated in 2 years. Same items for "style" shoes had short life (often 10 days) and were expense. *Conrad Shoe Co.,* 1 BTA 798.

Useful life of 90% of lasts, etc. for extreme style novelty shoes ended in tax year; cost was expense. Other 10%, used in next fiscal year, depreciable in 2 years. Conrad Shoe, above, distinguished. *Milford Shoe Co.,* ¶37,361 P-H MemoBTA.

(10) Machinery manufacturer proved cost of over 10,000 insured drawings and patterns (models); average life was 20 years. Expensing in some years didn't bar connected treatment as capital items. *R. S. Newbold & Son Co.,* 7 BTA 471.

(20) Glass maker.—Cost of molds and patterns (made and bought), with lives from 1 day to 5 years, were properly expensed; no depreciation on estimated cost. *Sneath Glass Co.,* 1 BTA 736.

(25) Drawings, tracings, blueprints, etc.—Deduction allowed for drawings, etc. destroyed when co. began making tractor of new design. Value of those acquired with patents determined. *Wallis Tractor Co. et al.,* 3 BTA 981.

See also "Drawings", ¶15,268; "Jigs and dies", ¶15,273; "Tools", ¶15,369, "Woodcuts and electros", ¶15,284.

Drawings and models as part of patent's cost—Reg. §1.167(a)-6; ¶15,118.

Obsolescence of drawings and blueprints. ¶15,445; 15,448(10).

Intangibles, generally. ¶15,338.

(30) Proof.—Sheet-metal manufacturer

FIGURE 31.3 Page from Prentice-Hall's *Federal Taxes,* 1979, vol. 3, page 15,140. **(1)** Topic being discussed. **(2)** Further breakdown of main topic. **(3)** Text giving basic rules of depreciation of jigs, dies, and so on. **(4)** Synopsis of a case illustrating a point concerning depreciation of a glass maker's business. Gives citation of case (Volume 1 of *Board of Tax Appeals Memorandum Decisions,* page 736). (*Source: Federal Taxes,* Prentice-Hall, 1979. Prentice-Hall Federal Taxes. Copyright 1979 by Prentice-Hall, Inc., Englewood Cliffs, N.J. 07632.)

Tax services are loose-leaf publications updated weekly with current tax information which directs a tax researcher to primary authorities and sources. One loose-leaf tax service is *Prentice-Hall Federal Taxes*, Englewood Cliffs, N.J., Prentice-Hall, 1945–date. The Prentice-Hall tax service consists of ten volumes:

Volume 1	Index, Table of cases
Volumes 2–4	Income Tax Compilation. Volumes contain editorial interpretation of the law and annotated digests of how the law has been applied previously (see Fig. 31.3, p. 244).
Volume 5	Procedure and Administrative Volume.
Volume 6	Current matter, current I.R.B. rulings, court proceedings, and new legislation.
Volume 7	Proposed Regulations and AFTR 2d Advance Sheets Volume.
Volume 8	Estate and Gift Tax Volume.
Volume 9	Excise Tax Volume.
Volume 10	Internal Revenue Code Volume.

Another similar loose-leaf tax service is *CCH Federal Tax Reports*, St. Paul, Commerce Clearing House, 1913–date. A major difference between the Prentice-Hall service and the CCH service is that the CCH service contains advance sheets to USTC, a Commerce Clearing House publication, while the Prentice-Hall service contains the advance sheets to AFTR, a Prentice-Hall publication.

31.6 TAX ENCYCLOPEDIAS

While there is no traditional encyclopedia in the tax research field, Merten's *Law of Federal Income Taxation* is used as a tax encyclopedia. It traces the general principles, background, and concepts of tax law. General explanations on various tax matters and concepts are given.

CHAPTER
THIRTY-TWO

Computer Literature

Computer literature searching is becoming a popular and efficient method of doing research. Several types of data bases are available for the researcher to choose from. Lockheed Aircraft Corporation's Lockheed Information Service and On-Line Bibliographic Search Service, owned by System Development Corporation, are two of the primary on-line searches available to the business world.

Lockheed provides the business-oriented person with *Predicasts Terminal System*. This system covers all of the Predicast publications including *F & S Index to Corporations and Industries*, Predicasts' *Source Directory* and *Predicasts*, the forecasting service. The terminal system offers instant access to these publications to aid the researcher in finding statistics and articles regarding a particular company or an industry.

Both Lockheed and System Development Corporation provide access to *INFORM*, a data base by Abstracted Business Information of Louisville, Kentucky. Over 200 business periodicals are indexed by *INFORM*. Information is distributed on a subscription basis; each week abstracts are sent to the subscribers. From these abstracts the subscriber can choose those articles of value to him and request a copy of the article. The periodicals abstracted cover business subjects such as finance, statistics, marketing, management, accounting, labor, personnel, and business law.

The area of computerized searching is growing rapidly. More data bases and more on-line interactive stock accesses are being made available to the public. In addition to the use of computers in gathering periodical articles, there are many other sources of direc-

6

tory information. The U.S. Department of Commerce and Dun and Bradstreet are just two of several publishers of computerized directories. The directories range from those of federal agencies (*Directory of Computerized Data Files and Related Software from Government Agencies,* Department of Commerce) to a directory on financial information (*Compustat* by Investor Management Sciences).

To aid the researcher in finding various data bases, there are directories for identifying computer services:

1. INTERNATIONAL DIRECTORY OF COMPUTER AND INFORMATION SYSTEM SERVICES. London, Europa Publications, 1974. Representing over 100 countries and 3,000 institutions, this directory gives information on the computer services offered by government agencies, research centers, and educational institutions.

2. ENCYCLOPEDIA OF INFORMATION SYSTEMS AND SERVICES. Ann Arbor, Mich., A. T. Kruzas Associates. A. T. Kruzas, editor. 1974.

This directory, or encyclopedia directory, is similar to the one named above, but the scope is broader. It covers over 1,700 organizations, including libraries, colleges, universities, research centers, and other consulting/research institutes.

PART SEVEN

Style Guide

This style guide is a quick reference to rules and illustrations for abbreviation, capitalization, number, and punctuation usages. A business writer must be aware of these rules and apply them consistently. In addition, the writer must be aware of any variations preferred by an educational institution or employing organization and use them when applicable.

CHAPTER THIRTY-THREE

Abbreviated Forms

Shortened forms are used to save space in business and technical communications. To make a report more readable, follow these guidelines for the use of abbreviated forms:

1. Use an abbreviated form only when the reader can be expected to comprehend it as easily as the word it represents.

2. Use the same abbreviated form to represent a word or term throughout the report.

3. Spell the word or term the first time it is used and follow it with the abbreviated form in parentheses.

> Bureau of Labor Statistics (BLS)

4. Consider presenting a glossary of abbreviated forms in the appendix if a report includes many such forms.

5. Do not use lowercase abbreviations in the text of a formal report; for example, *amt.* for *amount.* (Exceptions are shown in applicable sections.)

6. Shorten an abbreviated form, if necessary, to save space in a graphic aid or in a financial report. If the reader might not recognize the form, follow it with an asterisk and place another asterisk below the graphic aid where the form is identified or explained.

7. Use a current vocabulary, acronyms and initialisms, or technical dictionary to locate the standard abbreviated form for a word.

7

33.1 Types

Abbreviated forms consist of abbreviations, acronyms, and initialisms.

ABBREVIATIONS

An abbreviation, the shortened form of a word, is created by omitting letters (Mr. = Mister). Most abbreviations are shown in lowercase letters followed by a period (acct. for account).

ACRONYMS AND INITIALISMS

Acronyms and initialisms are constructed from the initial letter(s) of each successive major part of a compound term. These abbreviated forms are usually shown in capital letters without spaces or periods. An acronym forms a word (COBOL: Common Business Oriented Language); an initialism does not form a word (NLRB: National Labor Relations Board). An acronym that through usage has become a common noun is written in lowercase letters (laser: light amplification by simulated electron radiation).

33.2 Common Terms

Acronyms and initialisms have been developed for many frequently used business terms; traditional abbreviations are used for terms common to research and documentation.

BUSINESS TERMS

Abbreviated forms for common business terms are usually shown in capital letters without period or spaces:

LIFO	Last In, First Out
GNP	Gross National Product
LCL	Less than Carload Lot
PERT	Program Evaluation and Review Technique
R&D	Research and Development
CRT	Cathode Ray Tube
FORTRAN	Formula Translation System
FOB (or f.o.b.)	Free On Board
COD (or c.o.d.)	Collect on Delivery

7

Abbreviations for terms common to research and documentation are usually written in lower case with periods and spaces. The only Latin word underscored in the content or in a content footnote is *sic*.

app.	appendix
ca., circa.	about (in reference to time period)
cf.	compare
ed.	edited by or editor
eds.	editors
e.g.	for example
et al.	and others
f. (ff.)	and the following page or pages
fol.	folio
ibid.	in the same place (as the previous citation)
i.e.	that is
MS/ms, MSS/mss	manuscript (manuscripts)
n.	note
n.d.	no date
n.n.	no name
no. (nos.)	number (numbers)
n.p.	no publisher or no place
n. pag.	no page number
p. (pp.)	page (pages)
rev.	revised
sic	as it originally appeared
supp.	supplement
tr., trans.	translated by
viz.	namely
vol. (vols.)	volume (volumes)

33.3 GEOGRAPHIC LOCATIONS

Spell out the official name of a geographic location included in the body of a report or letter. However, a geographic location may be shown in abbreviated form if (1) it occurs within a graphic aid, (2)

7

company policy permits, (3) the term is commonly abbreviated in the mass media or in the industry.

ADDRESSES

Do not abbreviate "street" or any word used in lieu of "street."

Avenue	Road
Boulevard	Route
Lane	

The identifying direction that precedes a street number or street name is spelled out:

620 South Eighth Street

A direction or section of a city following the street name is shown in capital letters with periods and without spaces.

1225 Pennsylvania Avenue, N.W.

CANADIAN PROVINCES

Use the standard abbreviation for Canadian provinces in footnotes and bibliographic entries. The postal abbreviation is used only in the inside address and on the envelope of a letter.

Province	Standard	Two-letter
Alberta	Alta.	AB
British Columbia	B.C.	BC
Labrador	Lab.	LB
Manitoba	Man.	MB
New Brunswick	N.B.	NB
Newfoundland	Nfld.	NF
Northwest Territories	N.W.T.	NT
Nova Scotia	N.S.	NS
Ontario	Ont.	ON
Prince Edward Island	P.E.I.	PE
Quebec	Que. or P.Q.	PQ
Saskatchewan	Sask.	SK
Yukon Territory	Y.T.	YT

7

With the exception of the word "Saint" (St. Louis), the names of cities are not abbreviated.

> Mount Ivy
> North Acton

COUNTRIES

Do not abbreviate the name of the country on the inside address or on the envelope. Show it on a separate line in capital letters.

> Senorita Maria Espinosa
> Calle de Estrelita
> Madrid 14
> SPAIN

STATES

Use the standard abbreviation in footnotes and bibliographic entries. The two-letter abbreviation is used with the ZIP code on the inside address and on the envelope, following the comma after the city. The numerical ZIP code is shown one space after the two-letter abbreviation (Denver, CO 80200).

States, Districts, and Territories	Standard Abbreviation	ZIP Code Abbreviation
Alabama	Ala.	AL
Alaska	Alaska	AK
Arizona	Ariz.	AZ
Arkansas	Ark.	AR
California	Calif.	CA
Colorado	Colo.	CO
Connecticut	Conn.	CT
Delaware	Del.	DE
District of Columbia	D.C.	DC
Florida	Fla.	FL
Georgia	Ga.	GA
Guam	Guam	GU
Hawaii	Hawaii	HI
Idaho	Idaho	ID
Illinois	Ill.	IL

7

Indiana	Ind.	IN
Iowa	Iowa	IA
Kansas	Kans.	KS
Kentucky	Ky.	KY
Louisiana	La.	LA
Maine	Maine	ME
Maryland	Md.	MD
Massachusetts	Mass.	MA
Michigan	Mich.	MI
Minnesota	Minn.	MN
Mississippi	Miss.	MS
Missouri	Mo.	MO
Montana	Mont.	MT
Nebraska	Nebr.	NB
Nevada	Nev.	NV
New Hampshire	N.H.	NH
New Jersey	N.J.	NJ
New Mexico	N.M.	NM
New York	N.Y.	NY
North Carolina	N.C.	NC
North Dakota	N.D.	ND
Ohio	Ohio	OH
Oklahoma	Okla.	OK
Oregon	Ore.	OR
Pennsylvania	Penn.	PA
Puerto Rico	P.R.	PR
Rhode Island	R.I.	RI
Samoa	A.S.	AS
South Carolina	S.C.	SC
South Dakota	S.D.	SD
Tennessee	Tenn.	TN
Texas	Tex.	TX
Utah	Utah	UT
Vermont	Vt.	VT
Virgin Islands	V.I.	VI
Virginia	Va.	VA
Washington	Wash.	WA
West Virginia	W.V.	WV
Wisconsin	Wis.	WI
Wyoming	Wyo.	WY

7

33.4 MEASUREMENTS

Spell out a unit of measurement (mile, degree, pound, foot) included in the body of a report. However, if many units of measurement, each preceded by a number, occur in a technical report, they may be abbreviated.* Use a period after one-word abbreviations (gallon—gal.) but not after a multiple-word abbreviation (revolutions per minute—rpm). The singular form and the plural form of most abbreviations are the same:

bbl.	barrel
cal.	calorie
doz. or dz.	dozen
ft.	foot (feet)
gal.	gallon
in.	inch (inches)
lb.	pound
mm.	millimeter
wpm	words per minute

33.5 ORGANIZATIONS

The names of organizations—such as associations, communications systems, corporations, and government agencies—may be shown in abbreviated form.

ASSOCIATIONS

The names of many professional, civic, academic, and business associations are shown in capital letters without periods or spaces. To assure that an association name is shown correctly, follow the practice of the specific association.

ABA	American Bankers Association or American Bar Association
AFL-CIO	American Federation of Labor–Congress of Industrial Organizations

7

*In graphic aids and in technical material, symbols may be used in lieu of abbreviations.

AIB	American Institute of Banking
AMA	American Medical Association or American Management Association
AMS	Administrative Management Society
AICPA	American Institute of Certified Public Accountants
BBB	Better Business Bureau
NAM	National Association of Manufacturers
NEA	National Education Association

COMMUNICATIONS SYSTEMS

Call letters of radio and television stations are shown in capital letters without periods or spaces. The designations TV, FM, AM, and Channel are usually separated from the call letters by a hyphen.

KOA-TV	FM-97
WOW-Channel 6	WABC-AM/FM

CORPORATIONS

The words Company (Co.), Corporation (Corp.), Incorporated (Inc.), and Limited (Ltd.) are frequently abbreviated in the official names of business organizations. Two abbreviations (Inc. and Ltd.) are separated from the company name by a comma (Brown, Inc.). Used within a sentence, these abbreviated forms are preceded and followed by a comma.

The president of Heritage Inns, Ltd., has announced a 4 percent dividend.

The abbreviated forms of well-known corporations are written in capital letters without periods or spaces.

IBM	International Business Machines
GM	General Motors

The names of federal and state agencies may be shown in capital letters without periods or spaces:

CBI	Colorado Bureau of Investigation
FDIC	Federal Deposit Insurance Corporation
FRB	Federal Reserve Board (Bank)
GAO	Government Accounting Office
SBA	Small Business Administration
SEC	Securities and Exchange Commission
UTEP	University of Texas at El Paso

33.6 Titles

Degrees, certifications, courtesy, and family titles are abbreviated.

ACADEMIC DEGREES

Various reference sources show academic titles in different abbreviated forms, sometimes with and sometimes without periods. Some abbreviated forms have the same meaning and should not be used together—Dr. and M.D.; Dr. and Ph.D. (or any other abbreviated form meaning Dr.). However, professor and Ph.D. do not mean the same and may be used together. Use the abbreviated form after the name:

James Allan, Ph.D., has been hired.

B.B.A.	Bachelor of Business Administration
B.S.B.A.	Bachelor of Science in Business Administration
D.B.A.	Doctor of Business Administration
J.D.	Doctor of Jurisprudence
M.B.A.	Master of Business Administration
Ph.D.	Doctor of Philosophy

7

CERTIFICATIONS

Some professional associations certify practitioners who have the proper amount of experience and pass a rigid examination. The certification designation follows the comma after the surname and is written in capital letters without periods or spaces.

Mr. Steve Rice, CPA, spoke at the meeting.

CPA	Certified Public Accountant
CAM	Certified Administrative Manager
CPS	Certified Professional Secretary
CLU	Certified Life Underwriter

COURTESY TITLES

The courtesy titles (Mr., Mrs., Messrs., Miss, Ms.) precede a name. The title *Ms.* may be used to represent a woman, regardless of her marital status. Courtesy titles are not generally used in internal communications.

FAMILY TITLES

The abbreviations Jr. and Sr. follow the surname. In a sentence, the abbreviation is set off by commas:

Joseph Cross, Jr., spoke at the meeting.

Roman numeral designations are not set off by commas:

John F. Allen III

33.7 Time

Days of the week and months of the year are represented by standard abbreviations in graphic aids and financial reports.

Sun.	Jan.	July
Mon.	Feb.	Aug.
Tues.	Mar.	Sept.

Wed.	Apr.	Oct.
Thur.	May	Nov.
Fri.	June	Dec.
Sat.		

When space is at a premium, the abbreviation may be shortened even more, and the period may be omitted.

33.8 PLURALS

The plural of an abbreviated form is made by the addition of a lowercase *s*:

Two CLUs were interviewed.

33.9 POSSESSIVE FORMS

An apostrophe is used to show the possessive of an abbreviated form. The singular possessive is made by the addition of an apostrophe and *s*.

We need a CPA's advice.

The plural possessive of an abbreviated form is made by the addition of an *s* and an apostrophe to the plural.

Three CPAs' evaluations were sought.

CHAPTER THIRTY-FOUR

Capitalization

These rules apply to most business communications. Certain types of specialized communications, however, may contain additional capitalization for visual effect, emphasis, or clarification.

When in doubt about the capitalization of a specific word, consult a current dictionary.

34.1 BASIC RULE

Capitalize proper nouns—the names of specific persons, places, and things.

John Adams   New York   Ford

34.2 COMPASS POINTS

Capitalize compass points used as proper nouns and proper adjectives identifying specific geographical areas of cities, states, countries, and the world.

the South Side (Chicago)

Southern California

West Texas

United States: the East, the West, the North, the South, the West Coast, the Midwest, the Southwest, the Pacific Northwest, the Eastern Seaboard

World: the Far East, the Middle East, Western Europe

Do not capitalize compass points that indicate direction; they are usually adverbs, not nouns.

> Salt Lake City is 500 miles west of Denver.

34.3 COURSES

Capitalize a course only when it is specifically named or when it includes a proper noun.

> John took English Composition I.
> Mr. Hanson teaches Spanish.

Do not capitalize a field of study or a course that is not specifically named.

> I plan to take an accounting course.

34.4 DERIVATIVES

Capitalize the names of nations, races, and religions when they are used as proper nouns and proper adjectives.

> China   Chinese people

Do not capitalize a proper adjective or a proper noun that has become a common term.

> chinaware   manila folder

34.5 FIRST WORDS

Capitalize important words in a list, outline, quotation, or sentence.

LIST

Capitalize the first letter of each first word in a tabulated list, whether or not the words are identified by numbers or letters.

> Three types of investments were recommended by the financial analyst:

1. Bonds
2. Preferred stocks
3. Real estate investment trusts

OUTLINE

Capitalize all words except prepositions, conjunctions, and articles in the major division and first subdivision of an outline. Capitalize only the first word in lesser subdivisions.

I. Higher Wages in Dallas
    A. More Professional People Employed
        1. In the medical and related professions
        2. In business and related professions
        3. In the technical professions
            a. Engineers
            b. Scientists

QUOTATION

Capitalize the first letter of the first word in a quotation consisting of a complete sentence.

Ms. Bartrand said, "Most of the periodicals you requested are now being bound."

34.6 GEOGRAPHIC NAMES

Capitalize the names of continents, countries, regions, states, towns, mountains, bodies of water, and so on.

Asia	Boston
Argentina	Rocky Mountains
Appalachia	Sahara
Wyoming	Otoe County
Missouri River	

Capitalize the nicknames of states

Cornhusker State	Lone Star State

Do not capitalize a geographic term when it is used as a common noun.

The Big Antlers River is now navigable. The *river* channel was changed by the Corps of Engineers.

34.7 GOVERNMENT TERMS

Capitalize the titles of government agencies, political assemblies, and high-ranking officials.

AGENCIES

Capitalize the important words in names of governmental agencies (administrations, bureaus, authorities, boards, departments, commissions, and so on).

> Bureau of Land Management
> Housing and Urban Development

In communications prepared by state and federal government offices, the organizational unit is usually capitalized even when it is used without the complete title.

> The Environmental Protection Agency establishes guidelines to decrease the pollution of the air and water. This Agency has now established state and regional offices.

ASSEMBLIES

Capitalize the names of these specific governmental assemblies.

> Senate (U.S. and state)
> House of Representatives
> Congress

OFFICIALS

Capitalize the title of a high-ranking government official when it precedes the individual's name or is used in place of the name.

> President   Chief Justice
> Vice-president   Chief of Staff
> Governor

> The Governor vetoed the bill.

7

Do not capitalize these titles when they refer to a certain category or class of individuals.

> The governors will meet in Houston next year.
> Many of the presidents of this country have been lawyers.

34.8 HYPHENATED WORDS

Capitalize the part(s) of a hyphenated noun that is a proper adjective or proper noun.

> mid-July sales
> Spanish-American

34.9 IDENTIFYING ELEMENTS

Capitalize names that identify an item or a place.

1. Capitalize the noun preceding a number or letter.

Flight 173	Column 1	Schedule B
Room 22	Table 5	Check 1099
Chapter IV	Exhibit B	Invoice 123456
Chart 3	Form 1040	

The words *page*, *line*, *paragraph*, and *size* are not capitalized.

2. Capitalize the names of buildings and rooms.

> Prudential Plaza   Columbine Room

34.10 LETTER PARTS

Capitalize special parts of a letter.

CLOSING

Capitalize the first letter of the first word in the complimentary closing.

> Sincerely yours   Very truly yours
> Yours truly

Capitalize the first word as well as the courtesy title and surname in the salutation.

Gentlemen	Dear Abby
Dear Ms. Finch	My dear Mr. Carne
Dear Member	Dear Sir

SUBJECT

Capitalize all words but articles, conjunctions, and short prepositions in the subject line of a letter or memo. For emphasis, the entire subject line may be shown in capital letters.

SUBJECT: How the Sales Department Can Save $40,000 by Changing to Radio Advertising

34.11   PUBLICATIONS

Capitalize the important words in titles of books, periodicals, newspapers, articles, pamphlets, brochures, speeches, and so on. Do not capitalize (1) prepositions having fewer than four letters (unless these words begin a sentence or are capitalized by the using organization), (2) articles (a, an, the) or (3) conjunctions. The first word and last word of a title are always capitalized.

The Organization Man (book)
U.S. News & World Report (magazine)
"And the Energy Crisis Goes On" (article)

In direct-mail advertising, the title of a publication may be written in capital letters.

34.12   TIME

With the exception of seasons, time designations are capitalized.

DAYS/MONTHS

Capitalize the days of the week and the months of the year.

The meeting will be held on Wednesday, January 14.

7

Do not capitalize a word representing the seasons unless it is specifically identified or is personified.

> fall weather
> winter coat
> He was graduated Fall Semester, 1978.
> Old Man Winter damaged the apple crop.

SPECIAL DAYS/ERAS

Capitalize holidays, historic events, and descriptive expressions referring to eras.

> the Fourth of July   the Great Depression

34.13 TITLES

Titles of organizations, internal units, and positions are capitalized.

ORGANIZATIONS

Capitalize the titles of business, professional, philanthropic, educational, and religious organizations, associations, institutions, and societies.

> Ford Motor Company   Rockefeller Foundation
> Academy of Management   University of Missouri
> National Association of
>   Manufacturers

POSITIONS

Capitalize a job or position title when it precedes the name of the individual and when it appears in the address or closing lines of a letter or memo.

> Professor Adams
> Captain Henry
> President Alexander Duprey

Do not capitalize a job or position title when it is used without a name or when it is an apposition with a name.

7

The professor answered my question.

Henry Delaney, president of Amalgamated Company, resigned in June.

UNITS

Capitalize the titles of departments, divisions, sections, committees, boards, and other subdivisions of the employing organization.

Training Department	Board of Directors
Manufacturing and Design Division	Employee Benefits Committee
Payroll Section	

Do not capitalize these subdivision titles when:

1. They refer to another organization's subdivisions.

Will your organization's marketing department handle the details of this campaign?

or

2. They do not refer to a subdivision of a specific organization.

Recruitment and training are functions of a personnel department.

34.14 TRADE NAMES

Capitalize brand names, trade names, and trademarks. In advertising material, the entire name may be capitalized.

Coca-Cola   Xerox

Do not capitalize a name that through usage has become common and refers to the generic term. Consult a current dictionary to determine if a trade name should be capitalized.

nylon   mimeograph

CHAPTER THIRTY-FIVE

Number Usage

Legal documents, technical reports, and statistical presentations do not comply with all the listed rules.

Numbers in legal documents are often written in figures and in words to assure accuracy and to clarify the content. In technical reports, all numbers are usually written in figures to facilitate rapid reading and also to coincide with equipment, experiment, or project data. To save space in technical reports and statistical presentations, symbols ($, %, #, and so on) are often used to represent certain words.

35.1   BASIC RULE

This basic rule is used to express numbers in business writing.

UNDER TEN

Express numbers one through ten in words.

This department hired *nine* employees.

OVER TEN

Express numbers over ten in figures.

The insurance company has *250* agents.

Express related numbers in figures. Related numbers may consist of either construction:
Series of three or more numbers.

> We need to purchase 8 desks, 24 chairs, and 10 porcelain tables. (Related: series—one number above ten.)

Two or more numbers joined by one of these connecting words: *and, or, to.*

> Benson & Benson employs 42 staff accountants and 4 auditors. (Related: connecting word—*and*; one number above ten.)

Express unrelated numbers according to the basic rule. Unrelated numbers do not have either of these constructions:
Series of three or more numbers.
Two or more numbers joined by *and, or, to.*

> Each of the *ten* books contains more than *500* pages. (Unrelated: not in a series; no connecting words.)

Express a number in words at the beginning of a sentence.

> Thirty-five students attended the seminar.

If the number cannot be written in one or two words, revise the sentence.

> Nine hundred fifty-one people were included in the class-action suit.
> Revised: The class-action suit included 951 people.

35.2 AGES

Express ages of individual persons, places, and things in words.

> Mr. Woodward retired from his civil service job at the age of fifty-five.

Two exceptions to this rule exist:
Express ages in figures when they have a contractual or statistical significance.

> The minimum age for enlistment is 18. (contractual significance)

Express exact ages in figures.

> A trust was established for the child when he was 2 years 7 months and 12 days old.

35.3 CLOCK TIME

Express clock time in figures when it is followed by an abbreviation (a.m., p.m., A.M., P.M., CST, EST, MST, PST) or by the word *o'clock*.

> Train 27 leaves New York at 11:30 a.m. (or 11:30 A.M.)
>
> The Personnel Department will take applications until 4 o'clock on Friday.

Express clock time in words when it is not followed by an abbreviation or the word *o'clock*.

> The switchboard is open from eight until five.

35.4 COMBINATION NUMBERS

Express the first number of a consecutive combination as a word and the second in figures.

> One 70-page procedure manual has been prepared by our management analyst.

If the second number is significantly shorter than the first, express the second number in words and the first in figures.

> One box containing 75 ten-page instruction booklets was damaged in shipment.

35.5 DATES

Express dates in figures.

> Your first payment will be due on February 15.

1. When the day precedes the month and when it is used without the month, use *st, nd, rd,* or *th* or ordinal numbers spelled out.

Please let us have your remittal before the tenth of January.

Ms. Smith will be out of town until the 20th.

2. In the heading of a business communication, the month, day, and year are used (July 6, 19—).

3. The date in the heading of an informal memo may be expressed in numbers (7/6/81) if company policy permits.

4. This form is used by many government agencies:

20 August 19—.

5. The usage selected depends upon the policy of the organization.

35.6 DECIMALS

Express a decimal in figures.

Estimated snowfall in Ute Ski Basin is 18.5 inches greater than last year's.

If a whole number does not precede the decimal point, write zero (0) before the decimal point unless the decimal amount begins with a zero.

The cost of living index rose 1.2 last month, compared with .09 for the same period last year.

Precipitation for the entire month of November measured 0.5 (not .5) inches.

35.7 FRACTIONS

Express a fraction in words with a hyphen between the parts.

Two-thirds of the records were destroyed in the fire.

1. Express a mixed number (whole number and a fraction) as a figure. In typewritten format the whole number and fraction are separated by a space.

Supervisory employees will be granted 1½ days' compensatory time for overtime work during the move.

7

2. Write a fraction as a figure if it cannot be expressed in one or two words. Such fractions are not followed by *th*, *nd*, or *rd*, even though the syllable is pronounced in speaking.

> The shutter speed on the X-Bar camera is 1/1000 of a minute.
>
> While on suspension, the officer was paid one-third of his salary.

35.8 IDENTIFICATION NUMBERS

With few exceptions, identification numbers are expressed in figures.

SERIAL

Express serial numbers in figures without commas, using spaces or hyphens where appropriate.

> Invoice No. 4571   Check No. 4071
>
> page 1402   Policy No. 123 47 826
>
> Social Security No. 508-76-2144

HOUSE AND BUILDING

Express house and building numbers in figures with the exception of *one*.

> 3548 Dominion Street   9 Paxton Building
>
> One Park Lane

STREET

Express streets named with numbers through ten in words; express streets named with numbers above ten in figures, using *st*, *nd*, *rd*, or *th*.

> 2101 Seventh Street   3859 20th Street

Streets named with numbers above ten may be expressed without *st*, *nd*, *rd*, or *th* when another word separates the house number from the street number.

> 1478 East 34 Street.

35.9 MEASUREMENTS

Express numbers preceding units of measurement in figures. In technical writing and graphic aids, abbreviations and symbols may be used to express units of measurement.

> 5 feet 3 inches
> 9-volt batteries
> 3,380 miles

35.10 MONEY

Amounts of money are usually expressed in figures.

$1 OR MORE

Express amounts of $1 or more in figures preceded by a dollar sign. Express even dollar amounts without a decimal point and zeros.

> $10.25 $1,000

UNDER $1

Express amounts under a dollar in figures followed by the word *cents*. When amounts over a dollar and under a dollar appear in series, write each in figures preceded by a dollar sign.

> Please enclose 50 cents to cover the mailing costs.
>
> The sales tax on the three nonfood grocery items amounted to $.85, $1.24, and $.75, respectively.

EVEN AMOUNTS

Express even amounts of $1 million or more by writing the dollar sign and number plus the word *million, billion,* or *trillion*. This rule also applies to numbers of a million or more (other than money) which would normally be expressed in figures.

> The new athletic facility cost over $7 million.
>
> More than 3 million tax returns are stored by the National Archives and Records Service in this division.

7

35.11 ORDINALS

Express an ordinal number in words if it can be written in one or two words. Express it in figures if it cannot be written in one or two words; the ending *st*, *nd*, *rd*, or *th* follows the figures.

tenth year   twenty-fifth anniversary
125th item

Express ordinal dates in figures.

Please return the questionnaire before the 10th of March.

35.12 PERCENTAGES

Express percentages in figures followed by the word *percent*.

By paying before April 1, you can take advantage of the 10 percent discount.

35.13 PERIODS OF TIME

Express a period of time in words.

fifteen days   twenty-two   ten years
                      seconds
six months   fifteen minutes

TWO OR MORE WORDS

Express a period of time in figures if it involves more than two words.

365 days (not: three hundred sixty-five days)

CREDIT TERMS

Express a period of time in figures if it refers to credit terms, discount periods, or interest rates.

Please sign this 6 percent, 90-day note to cover the balance of your payment.

CHAPTER THIRTY-SIX

Punctuation

Punctuation is a tool used to clarify the meaning of written communications. It can also change the emphasis or give more than one meaning to the same sequence of words.

36.1 APOSTROPHE

Use the apostrophe to form a contraction and to show the possessive form of a noun and an indefinite pronoun.

CONTRACTIONS

An apostrophe is inserted at a point where a letter (or letters) has been omitted when two words are combined. The use of contractions is not recommended in formal reports.

do not	don't
there is	there's
you are	you're
it is	it's

POSSESSIVES

When a noun does not end in "s," add an apostrophe and "s" to form the possessive.

277

year	one year's salary
children	children's
man	man's
men	men's
company	company's
attorney	attorney's

When a noun ends in "s," add only an apostrophe to form the possessive.

years	eight years' experience
companies	companies'
attorneys	attorneys'

If a new syllable is formed in the pronunciation of the possessive form of a singular noun ending in an "s" or an "s" sound, add an apostrophe and "s."

boss	boss's

Exception: Add only an apostrophe if (1) the addition of the extra syllable makes the word difficult to pronounce or (2) the word contains more than one syllable.

Cornelius	Cornelius'

A few words end in "s" but are neither possessive nor plural. They are merely descriptive words that become a part of the noun they precede and do not require an apostrophe.

sales department	sports coat

A noun preceding a gerund (a verb form ending in -*ing* and used as a noun) is always in the possessive case.

Jane's working is necessary to supplement the family income.

The possessive case of an indefinite pronoun is formed by the addition of an apostrophe and an "s."

someone's	anyone's	anybody's

This rule does not apply to personal pronouns. The possessive is formed by a change in the spelling of the pronoun rather than by

7

the addition of an apostrophe: my, mine, our, ours, your, yours, his, her, their, theirs, its.

36.2 ASTERISK

Use an asterisk to identify an item that is explained in a different position on the page.

GRAPHIC AIDS

In a graphic aid (table, chart, diagram, illustration) containing figures, use an asterisk to indicate that a word, figure, or symbol is explained below the aid.

Recent Federal Pay Hikes	Raise
October, 1977	5.0%
October, 1978	5.2%
October, 1979	7.1%
October, 1980*	5.5%

*Proposed by the President.
Source: U.S. Civil Service Commission.

CONTENT

In the body of a report, an asterisk is used to indicate that a word or concept is explained at the bottom of the page.

This acreage is listed in the U.S. General Property Index.*

*This index identifies property according to owner and location: section, precinct, township, county, and state.

36.3 BRACE

Use a brace to show that information placed vertically on the page is related.

Farley Hawkins,
Plaintiff,
vs.
Vera Hawkins
et al.
Defendants

7

36.4 BRACKETS

Use brackets to enclose insertions and to set off parenthetical expressions

INSERTIONS

A word (or words) from another source inserted within a quotation is enclosed in brackets.

> Helms said, "Under no circumstances will he [Herman Browne] be eligible for parole until 2019."

SIC

The Latin word *sic,* means that the writer has quoted the material exactly as stated or originally shown, including any errors.

> The production manager stated in his memo that "the Personal [sic] Department has not supplied an adequate training program for first-line supervisors."

PARENTHETICAL EXPRESSIONS

A parenthetical expression within parentheses is set off by brackets.

> (See Appendix B [Charts Showing the Rate of Return on Stocks X and Y for the Past Five Years].)

36.5 COLON

Use the colon after a complete statement that introduces a list, explanation, or example.

LIST

A colon is used after a complete statement indicating or implying that a list follows.

> The following items were requisitioned: paper clips, letterhead, and bond paper.
> The class meets four nights each week: Monday, Tuesday, Wednesday, and Friday.

Do not separate the preposition from its object(s) with a colon.

> The class meets on Monday, Tuesday, Wednesday, and Friday. (not—on: Monday)

LEAD-IN

A colon is used after a complete or incomplete lead-in statement preceding a tabulated list.

> Please use this format for your proceedings:
> 1. Underscore all headings.
> 2. Enumerate the points under each heading.
> 3. Use letters to designate subheadings.
>
> The sale items include:
> 3 sofas
> 11 occasional chairs
> 21 end tables
> 30 vanity lamps

INDEPENDENT CLAUSES

A colon is used between two independent clauses without a connective when the first clause introduces the second. It is also used after a complete clause that introduces a formal statement of a rule, policy, directive, and so on.

> The employee was confused for this reason: he was required to report to three supervisors.
>
> Our Board of Directors has established this policy regarding the attendance of employees: A maximum of 30 days' annual leave each year will be granted to employees who have been with the firm twenty years. Under no circumstances can leave time be carried over to the succeeding year.

Capitalize the first word of the material following a colon when it consists of:

1. A formal rule, policy, or directive.

2. Two or more statements.

3. A tabulated list.

4. A statement preceded by an introductory word, such as *Caution* or *Note*.

IN PLACE OF COMMA

A colon is used in place of a comma (1) after an independent clause that introduces a quotation or (2) if the quotation is long.

> Mr. Jacks made this comment at the meeting: "The criteria upon which the petroleum study was based are no longer applicable."
>
> The speaker said: "The trend in interior decorating is toward the eclectic look. Various woods, finishes, textures, and styles are being combined to develop an informal arrangement."

36.6 COMMAS

Use a comma to set off unnecessary words, phrases, and clauses.

DIRECT ADDRESS

A noun in direct address is set off by commas. The noun may be (1) a person's surname preceded by a courtesy title, (2) a person's first name, (3) a substitute for the names of persons receiving the communication, or (4) a substitute for a person's name (courtesy, position, or job title).

> Yes, Mr. Austin, your order will be shipped before May 1.
>
> We are happy that you decided to join our staff, Ms. Harris.
>
> Yes, sir, this complete package is only $10.95.
>
> Gentlemen, our lawyer advises us not to comply with your request.

COORDINATE ADJECTIVES

Two consecutive coordinate adjectives are separated by a comma. The adjectives are coordinate if they meet these tests:

1. They can be reversed and the sentence is logical.

2. The word *and* can be inserted between them and the sentence is logical. (Notice that a comma is not used between the last adjective and the noun it modifies.)

> He is a diligent, enthusiastic employee.
>
> The old brick building will become an office complex.

Elements within a series are separated by commas. A series consists of three or more words, phrases, or clauses of equal rank; for example, three nouns, prepositional phrases, or dependent clauses. Do not use a comma to separate the elements of a series if they are joined by coordinate conjunctions: *and, but, or, for, nor.* Also use a comma before and after *etc.* when it ends a series.

(Words in series) The president, vice president, and corporate secretary were present at the last meeting.

(Infinitive phrases in a series) To type reports, to file correspondence, and to answer the phone are the receptionist's duties.

(Dependent clauses in a series) Employees who have worked for the company for one year, who have a satisfactory performance rating, and who are recommended by their supervisors may apply for training under this program.

Mr. Young reported to me that he had not looked on the desk or in the folder or under the cabinet for the missing document.

Books, periodicals, cassettes, videotapes, etc., are available in the company library.

INTRODUCTORY ELEMENTS

Introductory elements—words, phrases, and clauses—are set off under certain circumstances, not all of which are applicable to each element.

1. Set off an introductory word that is not necessary to the thought of the sentence. Do not set off an introductory word that is necessary to the thought of the sentence.

Furthermore, no brokers shall be permitted to assist new clients without the approval of the vice president.

However important these test results may be, they must be substantiated by additional screening procedures.

2. A phrase is a group of grammatically related words without a subject or verb. Gerund, infinitive, participial, and prepositional phrases frequently occur at the beginning of a sentence. An introductory phrase is set off unless (a) it is required to complete the meaning of a sentence or (b) it contains the subject of a sentence.

7

a. Prepositional phrases.

1. Set off a long introductory prepositional phrase (or consecutive prepositional phrases).

In the plan for the new building, the cafeteria is located on the tenth floor.

2. Set off a short prepositional phrase if it is not necessary to the thought of the sentence.

By the way, your payment has been received.

3. Do not set off a short phrase that is necessary to the thought of the sentence.

On March 1 the regulation will become effective.

b. Infinitive phrases. Set off an introductory infinitive phrase unless it is the subject of the sentence. An infinitive begins with "to" followed by a verb and its modifiers.

To explain the organization of this company is a difficult task. (The infinitive phrase is the subject and cannot be separated from the verb with a comma.)

c. Participial phrase. Set off an introductory participial phrase. A participle is a verb form used as an adjective. A participial phrase begins with a participle which may include the word *have* or *having*.

Walking into the office, James saw the opened safe.

d. Gerund phrase. Do not set off an introductory gerund phrase. A gerund is a verb form, ending in *ing*, and used in a noun position. An introductory gerund phrase is the subject of a sentence.

Having modern word processing equipment contributes to the efficiency of an office.

3. An independent clause is a group of grammatically related words that contain a subject and verb and express a complete thought. A dependent clause is a group of grammatically related words that contain a subject and verb but do not express a complete thought.

7

a.   Set off an introductory dependent clause.

> When you come to Boston next week, the sales figures will
> be ready for analysis.

Do not set off an introductory clause that is used as the subject.

> Whomever you name as your guest will be invited to attend
> the showing of the new models.

b.   Set off an elliptical clause (one in which the subject and verb are implied).

> If so, please let me know immediately.

COMPOUND SENTENCE

A compound sentence consists of two or more independent clauses connected with a coordinate conjunction: *and, but, for, or, nor.*

1.   Use a comma before the coordinate conjunction that connects two independent clauses of a compound sentence.

> We are pleased with all aspects of the construction in our
> new building, and we shall call you when we are ready to
> begin planning our Omaha factory.

2.   Use a comma before the coordinate conjunction that connects the independent clauses in a compound-complex sentence. This type of sentence has two or more independent clauses and one or more dependent clauses. A semicolon rather than a comma may be used before the coordinate conjunction if (1) the sentence would be confusing or (2) the writer desires to emphasize the ideas.

> If Ms. Simmons responds before the end of the month, please
> approve her account, but if she does not respond by that
> time, write to her and encourage her further consideration of
> our offer.

PARENTHETICAL EXPRESSIONS

A parenthetical expression consists of a word, phrase, or clause that is unnecessary to complete the structure or the meaning of a sentence. Such an expression is an interrupting thought when it ap-

7

pears in the middle of a sentence or an afterthought when it appears at the end of a sentence. A parenthetical expression that occurs at the beginning of a sentence may be a transitional word, phrase, or clause. To indicate that a parenthetical expression is not necessary, set it off with commas. When *too* is used as *also* at the end of the sentence, the comma is usually omitted. If *too* is used as an interrupter, it is set off.

> I do think, however, that production should be increased before next year.
>
> He was, in my opinion, a very hard worker.
>
> The new product line is expected to bring considerable profit, so they say.
>
> The price of a loaf of bread has increased 5.2 percent, but on the other hand, the price of wheat cereal has increased only 2.3 percent.
>
> She, too, will attend the meeting.

APPOSITION

A word, phrase, or clause is in apposition when it renames or explains the word (usually a noun) next to which it stands. If the word, phrase, or clause is necessary to the meaning of a sentence, it is considered restrictive, meaning that it restricts the meaning of the sentence. Restrictive appositions are not set off by commas.

To make the punctuation decision, read the sentence with and without the element in apposition. If the element is not necessary to the construction or meaning (nonrestrictive), set it off.

An appositive is nonrestrictive and is set off when it is specifically identified: (1) by title or proper noun; (2) by one of these words: this, that, these, those; (3) by a personal pronoun, such as my, your, his; or when it renames or explains a noun. Do not set off a restrictive word in apposition:

> The word *check* has many meanings.

1. Set off a nonrestrictive word in apposition.

> The sales manager, Mr. Planer, said that sales increased this quarter. (identified by title)

2. Set off a nonrestrictive phrase in apposition. Do not set off restrictive phrases.

Eleanour Latrec, having been graduated from a university in France, worked as an interpreter at the United Nations. (participial phrase: identified by a proper noun)

A young woman *having been graduated from a university in France* can become an interpreter at the United Nations.

3. Set off a nonrestrictive clause. Do not set off restrictive clauses.

Mr. Ellenberg, who operates a travel agency in this city, is the new president of the association. (clause is identified by a proper noun)

The concept *that management is getting work done through people* is well established in the business world.

a. Certain words identify clauses that are always nonrestrictive; for example: *all of which, although, no matter what (why, or how), none of which, some of whom, whereas.*

We have three candidates for the position, all of whom are well qualified.

b. Set off an adverbial clause at the end of the sentence only if it is not necessary to the construction or meaning of the sentence.

The headquarters will be moved to Phoenix, as you know.

You will not receive your certification until you pass Part VI of the examination. (clause is necessary to the meaning)

MISCELLANEOUS COMMA USAGES

These comma usages are not covered by any of the previous rules.

1. Set off items in dates, locations, and sources. Commas are not used when the date is reversed.

I was graduated on August 20, 1967.

James Dunn lives at 2100 Oak Street, Madison, Wisconsin.

This quotation is from Chapter II, Section 281.4, page 42 of the handbook.

10 January 1888

2. Set off identical or repeated words.

Many taxpayers who pay, pay because they are frightened to do otherwise.

3. Set off contrasting expressions.

> The more I get paid, the less I save.

4. Use commas to show the omission of words within a sentence.

> District 3 exceeded last year's sales by 21 percent; District 4, by 24 percent; and District 1, by 26 percent.

5. Use commas to clarify the meaning.

> On the whole, office procedures have changed drastically over the last ten years.

6. Use a comma to separate a short question from a preceding statement.

> You are working during the convention, aren't you?

36.7 DASH

Use a dash to set off important or unimportant information. It is an emphatic, but informal, mark of punctuation and should be used in moderation; otherwise, the set-off information loses its impact. The dash consists of two hyphens typed without a space preceding, between, or following. Its primary usages are (1) as an alternative mark of punctuation and (2) in miscellaneous positions.

The dash is most frequently used in direct-mail letters. Here it serves to call attention to selling points and to words, phrases, or clauses that tend to be persuasive in nature. Because direct-mail letters are usually somewhat unorthodox in structure, the punctuation may also be slightly different in presentation; for example, in such a letter the dash may be shown with a space before and after.

ALTERNATIVE MARK

The dash may be used as an alternative punctuation mark to a comma, semicolon, colon, and parentheses.

1. Use a dash in place of a comma to set off an element that already contains commas.

7

288

Each of the six largest cities in the survey—New York, Philadelphia, Houston, Los Angeles, Detroit, and Chicago—employs over 450,000 workers in administrative, uniformed, and institutional services.

2. Use a dash in place of a semicolon to achieve a more emphatic but less formal break between two closely related independent clauses.

> Barry was appointed as chairman—moreover, the committee was overwhelmingly in favor of his appointment.

3. Use a dash in place of a colon to achieve a more emphatic but less formal break before explanatory words, phrases, or clauses.

> He has one weakness—procrastination.
>
> The study group meets three times a week—Monday at 7:30; Tuesday at 8:15; and Thursday at 6:30.

4. Use dashes in place of parentheses if the parenthetical element requires emphasis rather than deemphasis.

> Cates Associates—the largest auction company in the country—is handling the sale of this ranch.

MISCELLANEOUS USAGES

The dash is used frequently to set off (1) an afterthought, (2) an abrupt break in thought, and (3) summarizing words that follow a list.

1. Use a dash to set off an afterthought.

> Ed spent some time in the service—the Navy, I believe.

2. Use a dash to set off an abrupt break in thought.

> This car will outperform any other—at a more economical cost to you, too!

3. Use a dash to set off words that summarize and follow a list.

> Lettuce, beans, carrots, and onions—these are cold-weather crops.

7

36.8 ELLIPSIS

Use ellipsis marks to indicate the omission of a word, phrase, clause, sentence, or paragraph in quoted material that is presented in either line or block form. The ellipsis consists of three or four periods with a space between each period. An ellipsis must not destroy grammatical structure or meaning of the quoted material.

THREE PERIODS

An ellipsis consisting of three periods with a space before, between, and after is used to show an omission within a sentence.

Original:

> As well as offering the conventional banking services (savings accounts, bank-box rentals, loans, identification cards, and special accounts—Christmas Club and line-of-credit accounts), the bank provides financial management services, such as investment advice and trust supervision.

Omission within a sentence:

> As well as offering the conventional banking services . . . the bank provides financial management services, such as investment advice and trust supervision.

Internal punctuation that precedes or follows the omission in the original version may be retained if it helps to clarify or explain the omission.

> As well as offering the conventional banking services . . . , the bank provides financial management services, such as investment advice and trust supervision.
> (The comma after "services . . ." is optional)

FOUR PERIODS

An ellipsis consisting of four periods is used to show an omission (1) at the end of a sentence, (2) at the end of one sentence and the beginning of the next sentence, (3) of one or more sentences, and (4) of one or more paragraphs. The first period immediately follows the last letter of the last word preceding the omission; each remaining period is preceded by a space. The first word following the ellipsis is not capitalized unless it begins a sentence or it is a proper

7

noun. Any end-of-sentence punctuation mark used in lieu of a sentence period is followed by three spaced periods. Ending quotation marks are always placed outside the last period of the ellipsis.

Original:

> The Potomac National Bank is a financial institution that provides many and various services to its commercial and noncommerical customers. In addition to the bank located in downtown Washington, Potomac National has branches throughout the area and 24-hour automated banking service at convenient locations. As well as offering the conventional banking service (savings and checking accounts, bank-box rentals, loans, identification cards, and special accounts— Christmas Club and line-of-credit accounts), Potomac provides financial management services, such as investment advice and trust supervision.

Omission at end of sentence and end of paragraph:

> The Potomac National Bank is a financial institution that provides many and various services. . . . In addition to the bank located in downtown Washington, Potomac National has branches throughout the area. . . .

Omission at the end of one sentence and the beginning of the next:

> The Potomac National Bank is a financial institution that provides many and various services to its commercial and noncommercial customers. In addition to the bank located in downtown Washington, Potomac National has branches throughout the area. . . . Potomac provides financial management services, such as investment advice and trust supervision.

36.9   EXCLAMATION POINT

Use an exclamation point to show the emphasis or emotion necessary to convey a thought in the proper perspective. It may follow a word or sentence that shows strong emotion or requires emphasis. The most common usages are in written reports having verbatim remarks from employees (for example, critical incident reports and

7

interviews) and in direct-mail letters. This punctuation mark should be used sparingly; otherwise, its impact is reduced.

An exclamation point is used after a word or sentence that shows strong emotion (anger, shock, surprise, exhilaration, and so on) or requires emphasis.

> (Direct mail) With all these outstanding features, the WHIZ is only $49.95!
>
> (Report) I did not make that statement!

Only one ending mark of punctuation should be used; choose the stronger of two possibilities. The strongest marks in order are (1) exclamation point, (2) question mark, and (3) period.

> Did you say this recorder is only $9.95! (exclamation point replaces question mark to show surprise)
>
> SKYADE was used as refreshment by the astronauts! (exclamation point replaces period to emphasize the remark)

36.10 HYPHEN

Use a hyphen to join (1) compound numbers from 21 to 99, (2) compound adjectives preceding a noun, and (3) compound fractions.

> Thirty-four respondents did not answer this question.
> The up-to-date report is in the library.
> self-esteem   Governor-elect Brown
> anti-American   post-World War II
> Three-fourths of the respondents did not answer this question.

36.11 PARENTHESES

Use parentheses to set off explanatory items, such as words, phrases, clauses, dates, directions, and enumerations. In many instances either a dash or a parenthesis may be used; however, dashes emphasize and parentheses deemphasize the material that is set off. The writer makes the distinction based on the importance of the material and the emphasis to be placed upon it. If a parenthesis mark occurs with another punctuation mark, the writer must choose the appropriate mark or combination according to its position in the sentence.

COMMON USAGES

1. Parentheses are used to enclose an explanatory word, phrase, or clause; dates that are used as reference points; and reference sources and directions, particularly in reports.

> A few employees (eleven) chose not to take the health insurance provided by the company.
>
> Mrs. James (nee Mable Ashton of Los Angeles) took over the presidency of the company upon her husband's death.
>
> Mr. Parton (he is a partner in the firm of Parton and Welsh) believes that we have a good chance to win the suit.
>
> Frederick W. Taylor (1856–1915) is well known for his theories of scientific management.
>
> Adams' theory (pp. 125–131) will be included in the examination.
>
> Responses were received from 89 personnel directors (see Appendix A).
>
> Responses were received from 89 personnel directors. (See Appendix A.)

The direction may be placed within or after the sentence to which it pertains. Use directions in parentheses to direct the report reader to a table, another page or section, the appendix, and so on.

2. Parentheses are used in lieu of commas if the parenthetical element already contains commas and if a dash would emphasize the material more than is necessary.

> The water-damaged appliances in your kitchen (stove, dishwasher, and refrigerator) are insured under this policy and can be replaced immediately.

WITH OTHER PUNCTUATION

No mark of punctuation precedes a left (opening) parenthesis. However, the order of punctuation used with the right (closing) parenthesis has an influence on the meaning of the sentence.

1. Parenthetical element within a sentence

a.   Any sentence punctuation required in conjunction with the right parenthesis follows this parenthesis.

> If you leave early (before 4:30 p.m.), obtain permission from your immediate supervisor.
>
> Riley was absent one day (Monday); however, he said that he was ill.
>
> We appear to lack a vital ingredient for expansion (perhaps the most important one): money!
>
> Harvey's request for a transfer was turned down by the vice president of finance (see the attached memo)—and he has worked here for 16 years.

b.   Do not use a period before the right parenthesis except for that following an abbreviation.

> The Seattle Plant (it has been operating at capacity) cannot accommodate any more orders this month.
>
> Robert Evans (he arrived at 3:30 a.m.) will meet with the analysts this afternoon.

The first word within the parenthetical element is not capitalized unless it is a proper noun or adjective.

2. Parenthetical element at the end of a sentence

a.   Place the end-of-sentence punctuation outside the right parenthesis.

> He will arrive on September 3 (Tuesday).
>
> Do you know Fred Conners (he spoke at the sales meeting in Boise)?

b.   Use a question mark or exclamation point before the right parenthesis only when it applies to the material within parentheses and the end-of-sentence punctuation is different.

> I completed the report last month (haven't you seen it yet?).
>
> Are you going to the meeting (did you attend the last one)?

3. Parenthetical element in a separate sentence. Observe these rules:

a.   Begin the parenthetical element with a capital letter.

b. Place end-of-sentence punctuation before the right parenthesis.

c. Do not place any punctuation after the closing parenthesis.

Richard is a capable administrator. (He received awards from two professional organizations.) The company is fortunate to have hired him.

36.12 PERIOD

A period is used after a statement, abbreviation, and a number or letter that identifies a list.

SENTENCES

Use a period:

1. After a declarative sentence (one that states a fact).

    The accountant prepared the financial report.

2. After an imperative sentence.

    Please return the contract by September 1.

3. After a courteous request.

    Will you please complete and return the application blank.

A courteous request is a statement that is phrased as a courteous question. Suggestions, commands, or requests may be phrased as courteous questions. If the reader is expected to respond by *action* rather than with an oral or written reply, a courteous request has been made.

4. After a meaningful fragment.

    No.
    Of course.

5. After an indirect question.

    The manager asked when you will return from the sales meeting.

7

ABBREVIATIONS

Abbreviations are shortened forms of words, groups of words, or names. (See Abbreviated Forms, Chapter 33.) Use only one period at the end of a statement. The period following an abbreviation becomes end-of-sentence punctuation for a statement. At the end of a question or exclamation, the period following an abbreviation precedes the question mark and the exclamation point.

ENUMERATIONS

Periods are used after numerals or letters that designate items in an outline or tabulated list unless the letters or numbers are enclosed within parentheses.

1.   Use a period after each number in a list, but do not use a period at the end of a line in a tabulation if that line does not complete the sentence.

> The company promoted three employees:
> 1.   Tom Jones
> 2.   Mary Brown
> 3.   Joe Yates

2.   Use a period after each letter in a list and at the end of a line in a tabulation if that line completes the sentence.

> Use a period after a(n):
> a.   Declarative sentence.
> b.   Imperative sentence.
> c.   Courteous request.

36.13   QUESTION MARK

Use a question mark:

1.   After a direct question (one that requires an answer).

> When will the meeting be held?

After a rhetorical question. This question does not require an oral or written response, but the reader is required to think about the answer. This type of question is often used to begin a persuasive request letter that transmits a questionnaire.

> What will be your take-home pay in the year 2000?

2. After a question at the end of a statement.

> My records indicate that you agreed to become a member of the Speakers' Bureau; is that correct, Mr. Smith?

3. After a brief question within a sentence.

> Ask what? or whom? after the verb; the noun or pronoun that answers this question is the direct object.

4. Within parentheses to show that the preceding fact is questionable.

> Sam is the oldest (?) of three children.

5. Do not use a question mark after a statement that shows interest. Such statements often begin with words such as "I wonder . . ." or "I would like to know . . ."

> I would like to know the dimensions of the modular desk.

Such statements reflect poor usage because they are not concise; a direct question is more to the point.

> What are the dimensions of the modular desk?

36.14 QUOTATION MARKS

Quotation marks are always used in pairs.

DIRECT QUOTATIONS

Quotation marks are used to enclose the exact words of a speaker or writer. One set of the pair of quotation marks precedes the quoted material and the other follows it.

> Mr. Hanson, the manager, said in his recent memo, "I shall expect all employees to attend the film shown at noon on March 26."

"We need the program immediately," wrote Ed Gray, who is systems manager at the Brady Company.

Do not use quotation marks to enclose an indirect quotation.

Mr. Hanson, the manager, said in his recent memo that he expected all employees to attend the film shown at noon on March 26.

The clerk asked how the paychecks were to be distributed.

Many people said that they enjoyed the performance held from noon until nine in the bank lobby.

WITH OTHER PUNCTUATION

Convention and the sentence relationship determine the position of punctuation marks in relation to quotation marks.

1. Place a period inside the quotation mark.

Mr. Hall remarked, "Rewrite the letter so that it gives the impression that we are making the refund gladly."

2. Place a comma inside the quotation mark.

"I collected the balance from Mr. Bane on October 20," the credit manager said.

"If we can agree on a date," the sales manager said, "we will hold the meeting in Houston."

3. Place a semicolon outside the last quotation mark.

Page 2 of the contract reads as follows: "In case of negligence, the party of the first part agrees to pay the party of the second part the sum of $4,500"; however, our oral agreement was on a $4,000 reparation settlement.

Use a colon after a complete introductory statement and before a long quotation.

The company president made this comment: "New industry will come to a city only if that city provides an adequate labor force. It must also have sufficient transportation facilities and establish an equitable tax base."

7

4. Place a colon outside the closing quotation mark.

> File these items in the drawer marked "Territories": sales reports, accounting reports, and discrepancy reports.

Isolated words may be emphasized by quotation marks.

5. Question mark.

a.   Place a question mark inside the closing quotation mark if only the quoted material is a question.

> Mrs. Pate said, "When will I receive my free copy of this magazine?"

b.   Place a question mark outside the closing quotation mark if the entire sentence is a question.

> Did Mrs. Pate say in her letter, "I expect to receive my free copy this month"?

6. Exclamation point

a.   Place an exclamation point inside the closing quotation mark if only the quoted material is an exclamation.

> She said, "The temperature in this room must be 95 degrees!" (exclamation at the end of a statement)

b.   Place an exclamation point outside the closing quotation mark when it applies to the entire sentence.

> Mary announced to the group, "Mr. Jones said my new job will bring a 15 percent salary increase."!

TITLES

Enclose within quotation marks the parts of complete published works: chapters, articles, and features. Also include in quotation marks lectures, sermons, songs, essays, and short poems.

> We have a copy of your last article, "The Future of Real Estate Investment Trusts."
> In addition to the assignment, please read Chapter VII, "Cash Flow Analysis."

7

SPECIAL USAGES

Two sets of quotation marks are used to set off emphasized words; single quotation marks are used to designate a quotation within a quotation.

1. Use quotation marks to enclose a word(s) which is emphasized.

> The refrigerator crates were clearly stenciled, "This side up."

2. Use a pair of single quotation marks to set off a quotation within a quotation.

> Mrs. Clark said, "Please send the file marked, 'Rejects.'"
> The workshop instructor asked, "Have you read the article, 'The Young Entrepreneurs'?"

Like double quotation marks, the single quotation marks are placed outside periods and commas and inside semicolons and colons. Their relationship to question marks and exclamation points is dependent upon whether they belong to the material within the single quotation or to that within the double quotation.

QUOTED MATERIAL

In the body of a report, the presentation of quoted material depends upon the length of the quotation. All quotations regardless of length are introduced with qualifying or explanatory information.

1. *Run-in Quotations.* A quotation requiring three or fewer typewritten lines is usually treated as part of the sentence and set off with double quotation marks.

> Gates said, "I investigate the credit of potential customers, establish lines of credit, and handle collections."[1]

The superior number indicating a footnote follows the punctuation.

2. *Block Quotations.* Quotations of four or more lines are presented in block format and without quotation marks. The first line of the quotation begins a double space below the last line of the body. If the quotation begins a paragraph, it is indented. All quoted paragraphs are indented four spaces from the left margin, and the first line of a complete paragraph is indented an additional four spaces.

The prospectus description of Pinetree Products, Inc., reads as follows:

> This company manufactures wood office furniture that it sells directly to retailers. By processing the wood pulp and other byproducts of the operation, it also manufactures three types of paper products: for general use—bond, reproduction, and notebook paper; for computer installations—printout paper; for newspapers—newsprint. . . .
>
> The furniture and paper products are manufactured at different sites to achieve maximum efficiency in production with minimum cost. All paper products are sold to wholesalers who, in turn, sell them to retailers for future resale to customers.
>
> Pinetree Products, Inc., sells its furniture and paper products primarily on the West Coast and throughout the Pacific Northwest; however, it also markets to wholesalers in Hawaii and Alaska.[2]

The ellipsis marks at the end of the first paragraph indicate that one or more paragraphs have been omitted (see Ellipsis, pp. 290–291).

A double space between paragraphs facilitates the reading. If the second paragraph does not begin with the first sentence of the paragraph, it may be set flush with the margin (as shown), or it may be preceded by a four-space indentation and three spaced periods to represent the omission.

36.15 SEMICOLON

Use a semicolon:

1. Before a conjunctive adverb or a transitional expression that joins two independent clauses.

> We did not receive the sales figures on time; consequently, we could not bid on the contract.
>
> This policy will provide the funds for your child's education; that is, it will mature in 1998, when your child is ready to enter college.

A comma is used after the conjunctive adverb unless it is a one-syllable word.

> We waited until 10 o'clock; yet the mail had not come.

2. Between two closely related clauses that are not joined by a conjunction.

> Mr. Davis is a diligent employee; we are quite pleased with his work.

3. Before a coordinate conjunction (*and, but, for, or, nor*) that connects two independent clauses if (1) the clauses would be confusing with only a comma before the conjunction or (2) each clause is to be emphasized.

> When you come to the conference, please bring the Ried, Goff, and Randle files; and the Wray, Fenton, and Smith files will be mailed.

4. To separate the items in a series that already contains commas.

> Appearing in the picture will be Shirley Gale, buyer of women's coats; Joseph Blund, assistant manager of the Tulsa stores; and Maria Duvall, manager of a Paris fashion house.

5. To separate a series of dependent clauses that contain internal punctuation or are exceptionally long.

> Ms. Ivy said that she would perform a product analysis on Products A, B, and C; that she would perform a market analysis on Products B, C, and D; and that she would prepare a sales compaign for radio, television, and professional journals.

6. Before a transitional expression that introduces a list, example, or illustration at the end of a sentence. Such an expression is followed by a comma.

> The program has many flaws; for example, hours worked by part-time student employees were omitted.

36.16   UNDERSCORE

Use the underscore to underline the titles of complete works: books, magazines, newspapers, brochures, manuals, pamphlets, and so on.

> The company had sold 2,000 copies of <u>Machine Transcription for Business</u> by September. (book)

7

Business Week is required reading in some classes.

The stock quotations are published in The Wall Street Journal.

Underscore the spaces within a title, but do not underscore the punctuation at the end unless it is part of the title.

EMPHASIS

Use the underscore to underline a word when attention is called to its usage.

The word check has many meanings.

The word accommodate is frequently misspelled.

7

Sources Consulted

Acronyms and Initialisms Dictionary. 2d ed. Detroit: Gale Research Company, 1965.

Berenson, Conrad, and Colton, Raymond. *Research and Report Writing for Business and Economics*. New York: Random House, 1971.

Brusaw, Charles T.; Alred, Gerald J.; and Oliu, Walter E. *The Business Writer's Handbook*. New York: St. Martin's Press, 1976.

Clark, James L., and Clark, Lyn R. *HOW: A Handbook for Office Workers*. Belmont, Calif.: Wadsworth Publishing Company, Inc., 1975.

Lesikar, Raymond V. *Basic Business Communications*. Homewood, Ill.: Richard D. Irwin, Inc., 1979.

————. *Report Writing for Business*. Homewood, Ill.: Richard D. Irwin, Inc., 1977.

A Manual of Style. 12th ed., rev. Chicago: Univ. of Chicago Press, 1969.

Menning, J. H., and Wilkinson, C. W. *Communicating through Letters and Reports*. 5th ed. Homewood, Ill.: Richard D. Irwin, Inc., 1972.

Menning, J. H.; Wilkinson, C. W.; and Clarke, Peter B. *Communicating through Letters and Reports*. 6th ed. Homewood, Ill.: Richard D. Irwin, Inc., 1976.

7

Meyer, Lois, and Moyer, Ruth. *Machine Transcription for Modern Business*. New York: John Wiley & Sons, Publishers, 1978.

MLA Handbook. New York: Modern Language Association, 1977.

Modern Language Association Style Sheet. New York: Modern Language Association, 1970.

Moyer, Ruth. *Business English Basics*. New York: John Wiley & Sons, Publishers, 1980.

Nanassy, Louis C.; Selden, William; and Lee, Jo Ann. *Reference Manual for Office Workers*, Beverly Hills: Benziger Bruce & Glencoe, Inc., Glencoe Press, 1977.

Pinney, Thomas. *A Short Handbook and Style Sheet*. New York: Harcourt Brace Jovanovich, Inc., 1977.

Publication Manual of the American Psychological Association. 2d ed. Washington, D.C.: American Psychological Association, 1974.

Sabin, William A. *(The) Gregg Reference Manual*. 5th ed. New York: Gregg Division, McGraw-Hill Book Co., 1977.

Turabian, Kate L. *A Manual for Writers of Term Papers, Theses, and Dissertations*. 4th ed. Chicago: Univ. of Chicago Press, 1973.

———. *Student's Guide for Writing College Papers*. 3d ed., rev. & exp. Chicago: Univ. of Chicago Press, 1976.

A Uniform System of Citation. 12th ed. Cambridge, Mass.: Harvard Law Review Assn., 1976.

Vardman, George T., and Vardman, Patricia Black. *Communications in Modern Organizations*. New York: John Wiley & Sons, Inc., 1973.

Whalen, Doris H. *Handbook for Business Writers*. New York: Harcourt Brace Jovanovich, Inc., 1978.

Wolf, Morris Phillip; Keyser, Dale F.; and Aurner, Robert R. *Effective Communications in Business*. 7th ed. Cincinnati: South-Western Publishing Co., 1979.

7

Index

Index to
Reference Sources

INDEX OF REFERENCE SOURCES